FUNNY SHAPED BALLS

FUNNY SHAPED BALLS

Jonathan Swan

EBURY
PRESS

5 7 9 10 8 6 4

Published in 2009 by Ebury Press, an imprint of Ebury Publishing
A Random House Group company

Copyright © Jonathan Swan 2009

Jonathan Swan has asserted his right to be identified as the author of this Work
in accordance with the Copyright, Designs and Patents Act 1988

The Random House Group Limited Reg. No. 954009

Addresses for companies within the Random House Group can be found at
www.randomhouse.co.uk

A CIP catalogue record for this book is available from the British Library

Printed and bound in Great Britain by CPI Group (UK) Ltd, Croydon, CR0 4YY

ISBN 9780091930608

The Random House Group Limited supports the Forest Stewardship
Council (FSC®), the leading international forest certification organisation.
Our books carrying the FSC label are printed on FSC® certified
paper. FSC is the only forest certification scheme endorsed by the
leading environmental organisations, including Greenpeace.
Our paper procurement policy can be found at
www.randomhouse.co.uk/environment

To buy books by your favourite authors and register for offers visit
www.randomhouse.co.uk

Contents

All aboard

A gynaecologist was getting sick of his job and decided that he needed a career change. He'd always enjoyed tinkering with engines so thought he'd become a marine diesel mechanic.

So he went along to marine mechanics school and the final test was to strip the diesel engine completely and reassemble it – obviously back into perfect working order. So our gynaecologist friend did the test and anxiously awaited the result. The day he received the results he got quite a surprise, he got 150%! He quickly phoned the instructor and queried the mark.

The instructor said, 'No, no, that's right. Half the marks were for stripping down the engine – I gave you full marks for a very thorough job. Then I gave you the full 50% for reassembling it – a fantastic job really. Then I gave you a 50% bonus for doing it all through the exhaust port.'

☺ Sailing for Beginners – by Abel C. Man

A sailor meets a pirate in a bar, and they take turns recounting their adventures at sea. Noting the pirate's peg-leg, hook and eye patch, the sailor asks, 'So, how did you end up with the peg-leg?'

The pirate replies, 'We was caught in a monster storm off the cape and a giant wave swept me overboard. Just as they were pullin' me out, a school of sharks appeared and one of 'em bit me leg off'.

'Blimey!' said the sailor. 'What about the hook?'

'Ahhhh ...' mused the pirate, 'We were boardin' a trader ship, pistols blastin' and swords swingin' this way and that. In the fracas me hand got chopped off.'

'Zounds!' remarked the sailor. 'And how came ye by the eye patch?'

'A seagull droppin' fell into me eye,' answered the pirate.

'You lost your eye to a seagull dropping?' the sailor asked, incredulously.

'Well ... ' said the pirate, ' ... it was me first day with the hook.'

⊙ Why do opera singers make good sailors?
Because they can handle high Cs.

Keith died. So Mary went to the local paper to put a notice in the obituaries. The gentleman at the counter, after offering his condolences, asked Mary what she would like to say about Keith. Mary replied, 'You just put, 'Keith died."

The gentleman, somewhat perplexed, said, 'That's it? Just "Keith died"?' Surely, there must be something more you'd like to say about Keith. If it's money you're concerned about, the first five words are free. We really should say something more.'

So Mary pondered for a few minutes and finally said, 'OK, then. You can put "Keith died. Boat for sale."'

An old salt sailor, a tugboat crewman and a recreational sailor went into a bar to get a drink. They each found a fly floating around in their beer. The recreational sailor looked in his glass and said, 'Hey, barman, I have a fly in my beer. Give me another.' The tugboat crewman looked in his beer, found the fly, picked it out and continued drinking. The old salt sailor looked in his beer, saw the fly, grabbed it by the wings, shook it over the glass and yelled, 'Spit it out, Spit it out!'

Sherlock Holmes and Dr Watson were on a sailing trip. They had gone night sailing and were lying on the deck looking up at the sky. Holmes said, 'Watson, look up. What do you see?' 'Well, I see thousands of stars,' said Watson. 'And what does that mean to you?' 'Well, I suppose it means we will have another nice day tomorrow. What does it mean to you, Holmes?' 'Well, to me, it means someone has stolen our sail!'

Two blondes were driving along a road by a wheat field when they saw a blonde in the middle of the field rowing a row boat. The driver blonde turned to her friend and said, 'You know – it's blondes like that that give us a bad name!' To this, the other blonde replies, 'I know it, and if I knew how to swim, I'd go out there and drown her.'

Hull University decides to field a rowing team. But they lose race after race. Even though they practice and practice for hours every day, they never manage to come in any better than dead last. Finally the team decides to send their captain to spy on Oxford, the boat race winners. So he sets off to Oxford and hides in the bushes by the river, from where he carefully watches the Oxford team at their daily practice. After two weeks, he finally returns to Hull. 'Well, I figured out their secret,' he announces. 'What? Tell us! Tell us!' his team-mates all want to know. 'We should have only one guy yelling. The other eight should row.'

⊙ Two people are out sailing when suddenly a hand appears in the sea. 'What's this?' asks the skipper. 'It looks as if someone is drowning!' 'No,' explained his crew, 'it's just a little wave.'

A depressed young woman was so desperate that she decided to end her life by throwing herself into the ocean. When she went down to the docks, a handsome young sailor noticed her tears, took pity on her, and said, 'Look, you've got a lot to live for. I'm off to Europe in the morning, and if you like, I can stow you away on my ship. I'll take good care of you and bring you food every day.' Moving closer, he slipped his arm around her shoulder and added, 'I'll keep you happy, and you'll keep me happy.'

The girl nodded, 'Yes.' After all, what did she have to lose? That night, the sailor brought her aboard and hid her in a lifeboat. From then on, every night he brought her three sandwiches and a piece of fruit, and they made passionate love until dawn.

Three weeks later, during a routine inspection, she was discovered by the captain. 'What are you doing here?' the captain asked. 'I have an arrangement with one of the sailors,' she explained. 'We're going to Europe, and he's taking me for the ride.' 'He sure is, lady,' said the captain. 'This is the Isle of Wight Ferry.'

A gust of wind blew a woman's hat into the water while sailing on a tall ship. A body hurled over the rail and saved the hat. Coming back on board, the man was cheered by the other passengers. The captain said to the man, 'Brilliant job, mate. Is there anything I can do for you?' The man said, 'You can tell me who pushed me!'

An old sea captain was sitting on a bench near the wharf when a young man walked up and sat down. The young man had spiked hair and each spike was a different colour – green, red, orange, blue and yellow.

> After a while the young man noticed that the captain was staring at him.

> 'What's the matter, old timer, never done anything wild in your life?'

> The old captain replied, 'Got drunk once and married a parrot. I was just wondering if you were my son!'

'My wife went on a sailing course in Poole.'

'In Dorset?'

'Yes, she'd recommend it to anyone.'

Common Sailing Terms

Amidships – condition of being surrounded by boats.

Anchor – a device designed to bring up mud samples from the bottom at inopportune or unexpected times.

Anchor light – a small light used to discharge the battery before daylight.

Beam aea – a situation in which waves strike a boat from the side, causing it to roll unpleasantly. This is one of the four directions from which wave action tends to produce extreme physical discomfort. The other three are 'bow sea' (waves striking from the front), 'following sea' (waves striking from the rear), and 'quarter sea' (waves striking from any other direction).

Berth – a little addition to the crew.

Boat ownership – standing fully clothed under a cold shower, tearing up £50 notes.

Boom – sometimes the result of a surprise jibe. Called boom for the sound that's made when it hits crew in the head on its way across the boat.

Calm – sea condition characterised by the simultaneous disappearance of the wind and the last cold beverage.

Chart – a type of map which tells you exactly where you are aground.

Clew – an indication from the skipper as to what he might do next.

Course – the direction in which a skipper wishes to steer his boat and from which the wind is blowing. Also, the language that results by not being able to.

Crew – heavy, stationary objects used on board ship to hold down charts, anchor cushions in place and dampen sudden movements of the boom.

Dead reckoning – a course leading directly to a reef.

Dinghy – the sound of the ship's bell.

Displacement – when you dock your boat and can't find it later.

Estimated position – a place you have marked on the chart where you are sure you are not.

Flashlight – tubular metal container used on board ship for storing dead batteries prior to their disposal.

Gybe – a common way to get unruly guests off your boat.

Headway – what you are making if you can't get the toilet to work.

Landlubber – anyone on board who wishes he were not.

Latitude – the number of degrees off course allowed a guest.

Mast – religious ritual used before setting sail.

Mizzen – an object you can't find.

Ram – an intricate docking manoeuvre sometimes used by experienced skippers.

Sailing – the fine art of getting wet and becoming ill, while going nowhere slowly at great expense.

Shroud – equipment used in connection with a wake.

Starboard – special board used by skippers for navigation (usually with 'Port' on the opposite side.)

Tack – a manoeuvre the skipper uses when telling the crew what they did wrong without getting them mad.

Yawl – a sailboat from Texas, with some good bourbon stored down yonder in the cabin.

Zephyr – warm, pleasant breeze. Named after the mythical Greek god of wishful thinking, false hopes and unreliable forecasts.

A burglar broke into a boat one night. He shone his torch around, looking for valuables, and when he picked up a CD player to place in his sack, a strange, disembodied voice echoed from the dark, saying, 'Jesus is watching you.'

He nearly jumped out of his skin, clicked his torch out, and froze. When he heard nothing more after a while, he shook his head, promised himself a holiday after the next big score, then clicked the light on and began searching for more valuables.

Just as he pulled the stereo out so he could disconnect the wires, clear as a bell he heard, 'Jesus is watching you.'

Freaked out, he shone his light around frantically, looking for the source of the voice. Finally, in the corner of the room, his torch beam came to rest on a parrot. 'Did you say that?' he hissed at the parrot. 'Yep,' the parrot confessed, then squawked, 'I'm just trying to warn you!'

The burglar relaxed. 'Warn me, eh? Who in the world are you?' 'Moses,' replied the bird.

'Moses?' the burglar laughed. 'What kind of people would name their bird Moses?'

'The same kind of people that would name their Rottweiler Jesus.'

After one particularly difficult passage, a yachting couple find themselves at the Pearly Gates, where their lines are taken by St Peter himself.

'There doesn't seem to be much record of you, good or bad,' he says, 'so I'm going to let you decide for yourselves whether you go to heaven or hell.

'First let me describe them for you. On the one hand, you could spend eternity in cramped quarters, your beds a few inches shorter than you are tall, your food and water always rationed, and a shower something you could only dream of.'

'And what about hell?' the couple asked.

The shipwrecked mariner had spent several years on a deserted island. Then one morning he was thrilled to see a ship offshore and a smaller vessel pulling out towards him. When the boat grounded on the beach, the officer in charge handed the marooned sailor a bundle of newspapers and told him, 'With the captain's compliments. He said to read through these and let us know if you still want to be rescued.'

One morning John noticed something floating towards the deserted island that had become his home since the ship sank six months ago.

As the object came closer, he realised that it was a large barrel. He very soon thereafter realized that hanging on to the barrel was a very scantily clad woman. In fact she was the most beautiful woman he had ever seen.

Arriving on shore the woman left the barrel and slowly and suggestively walked towards John. She whispered into John's ear, ' I have something you want!'

John broke into a run towards to breaking waves, yelling, 'Don't tell me you've got beer in that barrel!'

⊙ Blackbeard sailed to Jamaica for some arrr and arrr. He turned back a week later as it was farrr too farrr.

A woman was having a medical problem – her husband was snoring very loudly and every night! So she called the doctor one morning, and asked him if there was anything he could do to relieve her 'suffering'.

'Well, there is one operation I can perform that will cure your husband,' said the doctor, 'but it is really rather expensive. It will cost you £10,000 down and payments of £1,000 for thirty-six months, plus payments for extras, of course.'

'My goodness!' the woman exclaimed, 'that sounds like I'm buying a yacht!'

'Hmm,' the doctor murmured, 'too obvious, huh?'

The headmistress of a girls' school asks the local vicar to give her pupils a talk on Christianity and sex. The vicar is happy to do so but doesn't want to upset his prudish wife so he tells her he'll be giving the girls a talk about sailing. A week later the headmistress meets the vicar's wife in the street and tells her what a good talk her husband gave. 'I can't imagine it was that good,' says the wife. 'He's only ever done it twice. The first time he was sick, and the second time his hat blew off.'

⊙ Why did the captain lose the yacht race?
He found himself in a no-wind situation.

☺ Wife to husband: 'When I married you, you said you had an ocean-going yacht!' Husband: 'Shut up and row.'

Once upon a time there was a famous sea captain. This captain was very successful at guiding merchant ships all over the world. Never did stormy seas or pirates get the best of him. He was admired by his crew and fellow captains.

However, there was one thing different about this captain. Every morning he went through a strange ritual. He would lock himself in his captain's quarters and open a small safe.

In the safe was an envelope with a piece of paper inside. He would stare at the paper for a minute then lock it back up. After, he would go about his daily duties.

For years this went on, and his crew became very curious. Was it a treasure map? Was it a letter from a long-lost love? Everyone speculated about the contents of the strange envelope.

One day the captain died at sea. After laying his body to rest, the first mate led the entire crew into the captain's quarters. He opened the safe, got the envelope, opened it and ... the first mate turned pale and showed the paper to the others. Four words were on the paper, two on each line: Port Left, Starboard Right.

☺ Why couldn't the sailors play cards?
Because the captain was on the deck!

Two businessmen are fishing in a rowing boat when a storm blows up and capsizes them. One of the men can swim but the other can't. 'Can you float alone?' shouts the swimmer to his sinking partner. The partner shouts back, 'This is no time to talk shop!'

☺ Old yachtsmen never die, they simply keel over.

American football

Why did the coach go to the bank? To get his quarter back!

What's the best-smelling position on the football team? Right guard!

☺ Our offensive line was so good that even our backs couldn't get through it.

As John Madden says, 'If you see a defensive line with a lot of dirt on their backs, they've had a bad day.'

We play in a dome stadium. We always prefer to kick with the air-conditioning at our backs.

The coach was marching on the field alongside the band. A majorette threw her baton in the air and then dropped it. A fan yelled, 'Hey, I see you coach the band, too.'

☺ I say let's make football more entertaining and give the quarterback something else to think about. Let's arm each middle linebacker with a coconut custard pie.

The coach was always a step ahead of all opposing coaches. When they started the two-platoon system, he had a three-platoon system – one on offence, one on defence, and one to go to classes.

They call it their nickel defence, because that's what it's worth.

This year I can assure you that we are going to move the ball. I just hope that it's forward.

⊙ You know that your coaching job is in trouble when the marching band forms a noose at half-time.

During the Super Bowl, there was another football game of note between the big animals and the little animals. The big animals were crushing the little animals and at half-time, the coach made a passionate speech to rally the little animals. At the start of the second half the big animals had the ball. The first play, the elephant got stopped for no gain. The second play, the rhino was stopped for no gain. On third down, the hippo was thrown for a 5-yard loss. The defence huddled around the coach and he asked excitedly, 'Who stopped the elephant?' 'I did,' said the centipede. 'Who stopped the rhino?' 'Uh, that was me too,' said the centipede. 'And how about the hippo? Who hit him for a 5-yard loss?' 'Well, that was me as well,' said the centipede. 'So where were you during the first half?' demanded the coach. 'Well,' said the centipede, 'I was having my ankles taped.'

⊙ How many Vikings does it take to win a Superbowl? No one knows, and we may never find out!

A Tucson Arizona cable television provider has apologized to area customers after thirty seconds of porn was mistakenly shown during the Super Bowl. Customers angrily called when programming returned to the Super Bowl.

⊙ Old quarterbacks never die. They just pass away.

It was reported today that the artificial turf in Texas Stadium is being replaced because the Cowboys play much better on grass.

⊙ There are four Dallas Cowboys in a car. Who's driving? The police.

The huge college freshman figured he'd try out for the football team. 'Can you tackle?' asked the coach. 'Watch this,' said the freshman, who proceeded to run smack into a telephone pole, shattering it to splinters. 'Wow,' said the coach. 'I'm impressed. Can you run?' 'Of course I can run,' said the freshman. He was off like a shot, and in just over nine seconds, he had run a hundred-yard dash. 'Great!' enthused the coach. 'But can you pass a football?' The freshman rolled his eyes, hesitated for a few seconds. 'Well, sir,' he said, 'if I can swallow it, I can probably pass it.'

⊙ What do they call a drug ring in Dallas? A huddle.

⊙ The Dallas Cowboys have adopted a new 'Honour System'. 'Yes, your Honour', 'No, your Honour'.

Two elderly sisters donated five dollars to a charity and, to their surprise, won tickets to a football game. Since they had never seen a live football game before, Madge thought the free tickets would provide an excellent opportunity for doing so. 'I think so, too,' said Mabel. 'Let's go!'

They soon found themselves high in a noisy stadium overlooking a large, grassy expanse. They watched the kick-off and the seemingly endless back-and-forth struggles that comprised the scoreless first half.

They enjoyed the band music and cheerleader performance that followed. Then came the second half. When the teams lined up for the second-half kick-off, Madge nudged her sister.

'I guess we can go home now, Mabel,' she said. 'This is where we came in.'

⊙ What do you call a Mexican quarterback? El Paso.

Athletics

Shot putters do it on one leg.

😃 How do you start a jelly race? Get set!

How do you start a tapioca race? Sago!

How do you start a Teddy Bear race? Ready, Teddy, go!

😃 How do you start a firefly race? Ready, set, glow!

Who's the English shot putt champion? Eva Brick.

Who was the fastest runner? Adam. He was first in the human race.

😃 Did you hear about the Irish athlete? He ran a bath and came in second.

A javelin thrower called Vicky
Found the grip of her javelin sticky.
When it came to the throw
She couldn't let go
Making judging the distance quite tricky.

😃 What runs but never moves? A fence.

What do runners do when they forget something? Jog their memory.

If athletes get athlete's foot, what do astronauts get? Missiletoe.

☺ My grandmother started marathon training at sixty. She's ninety-seven now and we don't know where the hell she is.

The only reason a pervert would take up athletics is so that he could hear heavy breathing again.

☺ I joined a running club last year, spent about four hundred quid. Haven't lost a pound. Apparently you have to show up.

I have to exercise in the morning before my brain figures out what I'm doing.

☺ Gymnastics! If God meant us to touch our toes, he would have put them further up our body.

☺ Did you hear about the runner who had flabby thighs? Fortunately her stomach covered them.

The advantage of doing athletics every day is that you die healthier.

☺ If you are going to try cross-country running, start with a small country.

☺ I don't jog. It makes the ice jump right out of my glass.

Newspaper headlines before, during and after Jamaican-born Canadian sprinter Ben Johnson was found to have used illegal steroids:

First Headline 'Canadian Sprinter Wins Gold in 100 Metres!'
Second Headline 'Jamaican-Canadian Athlete Tests Positive for Steroids!'
Third Headline 'Jamaican Athlete Stripped of Gold medal!'

☺ What are the most athletic rodents?
Track and field mice.

Michael Johnson, the Olympic gold medal runner, was on his way to a club with some friends. At the door, the bouncer turned to him and said: 'Sorry, mate, you can't come in here – no denim.' Michael was quite annoyed at this and retorted: 'Don't you know who I am? I'm Michael Johnson.' 'Then it won't take you long to run home and change, will it?' replied the bouncer.

Two men entered the London Marathon. The race started and immediately one fell to the back and was the last of the runners. It was embarrassing. The man who was in front, second to last, was making fun of him. He said, 'Hey, how does it feel to be last?' The other man replied: 'Do you want to know?' and dropped out.

☺ A runner asked his wife: 'What do you love most about me? My tremendous athletic ability, or my superior intellect?' 'What I love most about you,' responded the man's wife, 'is your enormous sense of humour.'

Deciding to take up jogging, the man was astounded by the wide selection of jogging shoes available at the local sports shoe store. While trying on a basic pair of jogging shoes, he noticed a minor feature and asked the assistant: 'What is this little pocket thing here on the side for?' The assistant replied: 'Oh, that's to carry spare change so you can call your wife to come and pick you up when you've jogged too far.'

⚆ The trouble with jogging is that by the time you realize you are not in shape for it, it's too far to walk back.

One man's hobby was running. He spent all his weekends on the park trails, paying no attention to weather. One Sunday, early in the morning, he went to the park as usual. It was still dark, cold and raining, so he decided to return to his house. He came in, went to his bedroom, undressed and laid near his wife. 'What terrible weather today, darling,' he said to her. 'Yes,' she replied 'but my idiot husband still went running!'

⚆ How do crazy runners go through the forest?
They take the psycho path.

A man had been driving all night and by morning was still far from his desti-nation. He decided to stop at the next city he came to and park somewhere quiet so he could get an hour or two of sleep. As luck would have it, the quiet place he chose happened to be on one of the city's major jogging routes. No sooner had he settled back to snooze when there came a knocking on his window. He looked out and saw a jogger running on the spot. 'Yes?' 'Excuse me, sir,' the jogger said, 'do you have the time?' The man looked at the car clock and answered, '8.15.' The jogger said thanks and left. The man settled back again, and was just dozing off when there was another knock on the window and another jogger. 'Excuse me, sir, do you have the time?' '8.25!' The jogger said thanks and left. Now the man could see other joggers passing by and he knew it was only a matter of time before another one disturbed him. To avoid the prob-lem, he got out a pen and paper and put a sign in his window saying, 'I do not know the time!' Once again he settled back to sleep. He was just dozing off when there was another knock on the window. 'Sir, sir? It's 8.45!'

⚆ What's worse than track? Field!

☺ A transvestite friend of mine has just decided to give up triathlon. He wasn't experiencing enough drag on the bike!

Running shoes these days are more and more technologically advanced. A man went in this store and they told him that a new model of running shoes could even predict the weather! He asked how and the salesperson told him: 'Leave your shoes outside the window for a little while: if they are wet, it's raining, if they are dry, it's sunny, if you can't see them, it's foggy.'

Two gas company servicemen, a senior training supervisor and a young trainee were out checking meters. They parked their truck at the end of the road and worked their way to the other end. At the last house a woman looking out of her kitchen window watched the two men as they checked her gas meter. Finishing the meter check, the senior supervisor challenged his younger co-worker to a race down the road back to the van to prove that an older man could outrun a younger one. As they came running up to the van, they realized the lady from that last house was huffing and puffing right behind them. They stopped and asked her what was wrong. Gasping for breath, she replied, 'When I see two gas men running as hard as you two were, I figured I'd better run too!'

A triathlete was walking around in town one day when his friend, another triathlete, rode up on an incredible shiny new bike.

The first chap was stunned and asked, 'Where did you get such a fantastic bike?'

The friend replied, 'Well, yesterday I was out running in the forest just minding my own business, when this beautiful woman rode up to me on this bike. She threw the bike to the ground, took off all her clothes and said, "Take what you want!"'

The first chap nodded approvingly. 'Good choice. The clothes probably wouldn't have fitted you anyway.'

⊙ If a jogger runs at the speed of sound, can he still hear his iPod?

A man was out jogging in the forest one day when a frog called out to him and said, 'If you kiss me I'll turn into a beautiful princess.'

He bent over, picked up the frog, and put it in his pocket.

The frog spoke up again and said, 'If you kiss me and turn me back into a beautiful princess, I will tell everyone how smart and brave you are and how you are my hero.'

The man took the frog out of his pocket, smiled at it, and returned it to his pocket.

The frog spoke up again and said, 'If you kiss me and turn me back into a beautiful princess, I'll stay with you for a year and do ANYTHING you want.'

Again the man took the frog out of his pocket, smiled at it, and put it back into his pocket.

Finally the frog asked, 'What's the matter? I've told you I'm a beautiful princess, that I'll stay with you for a year and do anything you want. Why won't you kiss me?'

The man replied, 'Look, I'm a triathlete. I don't have time for a girlfriend, but a talking frog is cool.'

⊙ My first job was in a running shoe company; I tried but I just didn't fit in. So then I got a job in a gym, but they said I wasn't fit for the job.

It is well documented that for every mile that you jog, you add one minute to your life. This enables you, at age eighty-five, to spend an additional five months in a nursing home at £5,000 per month.

⊙ If you jog backwards, will you gain weight?

⊙ Running is never fun. Running is something you do when there's a man chasing you with a knife.

I'm on a strict running programme. I started yesterday. I've only missed one day so far.

⊙ I belong to a gym now. Well, let me rephrase that: I don't belong there at all, but I go.

Three men were trying to sneak into the Olympic Village to scoop souvenirs and autographs. The first says, 'Let's watch the registration table to see if there's a crack in the security system that we can utilize to scam our way in.'

Immediately a burly athlete walks up to the table and states, 'Angus MacPherson. Scotland. Shot putt.' He opens his gym bag to display a shot putt to the registration attendant.

The attendant says, 'Very good, Mr MacPherson. Here is your packet of registration materials, complete with hotel keys, passes to all Olympic events, meal tickets and other information.'

The first man gets inspired and grabs a small tree sapling, strips off the limbs and roots, walks up the registration table and states: 'Mick Davis. England. Javelin.'

The attendant says, 'Very good, Mr Davis. Here is your packet of registration materials, hotel keys, passes, meal tickets and so forth. Good luck!'

The second man grabs a manhole cover, walks up to the registration table and states: 'Owen Evans. Wales. Discus.'

The attendant says, 'Terrific, Mr Evans. Here is your packet of registration materials, hotel keys, a full set of passes and meal tickets. Enjoy yourself.'

They scamper in, but suddenly realize the third man is missing. They groan, because he's a simpleton from Donegal. They forgot to make sure he doesn't do something stupid and blow their cover stories.

Just then he walks proudly up to the table with a roll of barbed wire under his arm and states: 'Pat O'Conner. Donegal, Ireland. Fencing.'

☺ What did the two strings do in the race? They tied!

Why does someone who runs marathons make a good student? Because education pays off in the long run!

☺ What is a runner's favourite subject in school?

Jog-raphy!

Baseball

(!) A conceited new rookie was pitching his first game. He walked the first five men he faced and the manager took him out of the game. The rookie slammed his glove on the ground as he yelled, 'Damn it, the jerk took me out when I had a no-hitter going!'

A doctor at an insane asylum decided to take his patients to a baseball game. For weeks in advance, he coached his patients to respond to his commands.

When the day of the game arrived, everything seemed to be going well. As the National Anthem started, the doctor yelled, 'Up Nuts!' And the patients complied by standing up.

After the anthem he yelled, 'Down Nuts!' And they all sat back down in their seats. After a home run was hit, the doctor yelled, 'Cheer Nuts!' They all broke out into applause and cheered. When the umpire made a particularly bad call against the star of the home team, the doctor yelled, 'Booooo Nuts!!!' and they all started booing and cat-calling.

Thinking things were going very well, the doctor decided to go and get a beer and a hot dog, leaving his assistant in charge.

When he returned, there was a riot in progress. Finding his assistant, the doctor asked, 'What in the world happened?' The assistant replied, 'Well, everything was going just fine till a vendor passed by and yelled PEANUTS!'

(!) What does baseball have in common with pancakes? They both rely on the batter.

Did you hear about the Yankee stadium falling apart? A huge beam fell through the deteriorating roof. In fact, this was the first time the Yankees have had a problem with crack without it resulting in the suspension of a player.

How do baseball players stay cool?
They sit next to their fans.

A man walks into a bar with a dog. The bartender says, 'You can't bring that dog in here.' 'You don't understand,' says the man. 'This is no regular dog, he can talk.' 'Listen, pal,' says the bartender. 'If that dog can talk, I'll give you a hundred bucks.' The man puts the dog on a stool, and asks him, 'What's on top of a house?' 'Roof!' 'Right. And what's on the outside of a tree?' 'Bark!' 'And who's the greatest baseball player of all time?' 'Ruth!'

'I guess you've heard enough,' says the man. 'I'll take the hundred in twenties.' The bartender is furious. 'Listen, pal,' he says, 'get out of here before I belt you.' As soon as they're on the street, the dog turns to the man and says, 'Do you think I should have said "DiMaggio?"'

Confucius say: Baseball very funny game – man with four balls, no can walk!

A recent Scottish immigrant attends his first baseball game in his new country and after a base hit he hears the fans roaring, 'run... run!' The next batter connects heavily with the ball and the Scotsman stands up and roars with the crowd in his thick accent: 'R-r-run, ya bahstard, r-run, will ya!' A third batter slams a hit and again the Scotsman, obviously pleased with his knowledge of the game, screams, 'R-r-run, ya bahstard, r-run, will ya!' The next batter held his swing at three and two and as the umpire calls a walk the Scotsman stands up yelling, 'R-r-run, ya bahstard, r-r-run!' All the surrounding fans giggle quietly and he sits down confused.

A friendly fan, sensing his embarrassment whispers, 'He doesn't have to run, he's got four balls.' After this explanation the Scotsman stands up in disbelief and screams, 'Walk with pr-r-ride, man! Walk with pr-r-ride!!!!'

What is the difference between Yankee fans and dentists? One roots for the yanks, and the other yanks for the roots.

☺ What are O. J.'s favourite baseball teams? The Red Sox and the Dodgers.

A Spaniard named Jose came to Miami and wanted to attend a big league game. To his dismay he found that all the seats were sold out. However, the management gave him a high seat by the flagpole. When he returned to his home country his friends asked him, 'What kind of people are those Americans?' He said, 'Fine people, they gave me a special seat at the ball game and just before the game started they all stood up and sang, "Jose can you see ..."'

Bill Clinton was at a baseball game. Before the game began a secret service man came up to him and whispered in his ear. President Clinton suddenly picked up Hillary and threw her out on the field. The secret service man came running up to him and said, 'Mr President, sir, I think you misunderstood me; I said throw out the first pitch.'

☺ Why did the coach kick Cinderella off the baseball team? Because she ran away from the ball.

Two old men had been best friends for years, and they both live to their early nineties, when one of them suddenly falls deathly ill. His friend comes to visit him on his deathbed, and they're reminiscing about their long friendship, when the dying man's friend asks, 'Listen, when you die, do me a favour. I want to know if there's baseball in heaven.' The dying man said, 'We've been friends for years, this I'll do for you.' And then he dies.

A couple of days later, his surviving friend is sleeping when he hears his friend's voice. The voice says, 'I've got some good news and some bad news. The good news is that there's baseball in heaven.' 'What's the bad news?' 'You're pitching on Wednesday.'

This couple just recently got a divorce and they decided to move away from each other and go their separate ways. So, the father sat down and talked with his son and he said, 'Son, I think that it is best that you go and live with your mother.' The kid said, 'No, I won't because she beats me.' Then, the mother came in and talked to the son, 'I think it is best that you go and live with your father.' 'NO, NO,' he replied. 'He beats me.' So then, both the parents sat down and said to their son, 'Well, if we both beat you, then who do you want to live with?' The son said, 'The Red Sox. They can't beat anyone.'

⚐ Who's the most famous Los Angeles Dodger?

O. J. Simpson.

You heard about the big oil spill off the coast here? Well, they've hired the Dodgers to help clean it up. Yeah, they just go out there and throw in the towel.

⚐ What did the baseball glove say to the ball?

Catch you later!

When does a baseball player wear armour? At the knight game.

A little boy put on his baseball uniform and went outside to play, chanting, 'I'm the best baseball hitter in the world!'

He throws the ball in the air, swings and misses. Strike one!

He adjusts his hat and says, 'I'm the best baseball hitter in the world!'

He throws the ball in the air, swings and misses. Strike two!

He adjusts his hat a little more, takes a couple of practice swings and says, 'I'm the best baseball hitter in the world!'

Once more, he throws the ball in the air, swings and misses again. Strike three!

He thinks about what just took place for a few moments then says, 'I'm the best pitcher in the world!!'

⊕ Why did the surfer wear a baseball mitt?

To catch a wave.

Why are baseball players so rich? Because they play on diamonds!

⊕ Why are most baseball games at night?

Because the bats sleep in the day!

What animal is best at hitting baseballs? A bat.

⊕ What baseball player lives under a tree?

Babe Root!

Why did the cop go to the baseball game? He heard someone had stolen second base!

What's a wombat for? A womball.

⊕ Why don't grasshoppers go to baseball games?

They prefer cricket.

The wrong pitcher is the one who's in there now.

⊕ Baseball players do it at home.

Why did the player take a dummy to the game? He wanted to play like the Babe!

⊕ Where does the baseball catcher sit for dinner?

Behind the plate.

At one point during a baseball game, the coach called one of his young players over to have a talk with him.

'Do you understand what co-operation is? What a team is?' asked the coach.

The little boy nodded yes.

'Do you understand that what matters is whether we win together as a team?' the coach asked.

Again, the little boy nodded in the affirmative.

'So,' the coach continued, 'when a strike is called, or you're out at first, you do not argue or curse or attack the umpire. Do you understand all of that?'

Once more the little boy nodded yes.

'Excellent,' the coach said. 'Now go on over there and explain it to your mother!'

Little Billy rushed home after his Little League game, threw open the door and was jumping up and down with excitement.

'How was the game, son? How did you do?' asked his father, who was unable to attend the game.

'You aren't going to believe it, Dad,' Billy exclaimed, 'I was responsible for the winning run!'

'That's wonderful,' his dad said. 'How did you do that?'

'I dropped the bat!'

Basketball

When basketball players win the championship do they feel ten feet tall?

We have so many injuries we're considering hiring nurses for cheerleaders.

☺ He was known for his famous hook shot. Every time he'd fire one up, the coach gave him the hook.

Two basketball players are talking about Michael Jordan. 'Is he hard to play against?' asks the first man. 'Put it like this,' replies his friend, 'I've guarded guys that could leap before, but all the others came down.'

☺ Have you heard about the forward who was so slow he could only play indoors? If he ever got caught in the rain he'd rust.

Life is much like basketball: some score points, while others just dribble.

☺ One centre entered professional boxing after retiring from basketball. He's since developed a cauliflower navel.

He looks like a flagpole with hair. In the off-season, he models for silos.

We have so many injuries the team picture is an X-ray.

Most basketball players aren't very bright. They've banged their heads on too many doorways.

He's such a versatile basketball player. He can do anything wrong.

⊙ The point guard is a yoga master. He learned yoga trying to fit into airline seats.

His seats are so good that occasionally Jack Nicholson has to tell him to sit down.

He's the oldest player in the NBA. He leads the league in career sweat.

College basketball exists out of necessity. If there was no basketball, it would be necessary for the players to attend class.

⊙ I can remember the old days of basketball – when they shot the ball up at the basket, not down into it.

I play in the over-forty basketball league. We don't have jump balls. The ref just puts the ball on the floor and whoever can bend over and pick it up gets possession.

What do you call two Mexicans playing basketball? Juan on Juan.

You might be a redneck if you think the last words to the 'Star Spangled Banner' are: 'Play Ball.'

Why do basketball players like biscuits? Because they can dunk them!

⊙ What's a personal foul? Your very own chicken.

Why did the basketball player go to jail? Because he shot the ball!

Why did the basketball player go to the doctor's? He needed a shot!

! How did the basketball court get wet?
The players dribbled all over it!

Why did the chicken get sent off? For persistent fowl play!

What stories are told by basketball players? Tall stories!

! The NBA season is so long the players seldom get time to spend at home with their butlers and chauffeurs.

The coach has a run and shoot offence. If an opponent outruns you, the coach shoots you.

We were the surprise team of last season. We did worse than anybody expected.

The coach is preparing the team for the crowd noise they'll hear during the season. He runs practices with a laugh track.

! What do you call a pig who plays basketball?
A ball hog!

Bodybuilding

How do Colombians develop muscle? By pushing drugs!

Gold's Gym was robbed last week. That's the last time they recommend free weights.

☺ Why did the stupid bodybuilder train at the zoo?
He wanted to get ripped to shreds.

Newspaper Headline:
ZOMBIE BODYBUILDER DOES THE DEADLIFT.

Randy bodybuilders do reps in the morning and company reps in the evening.

Who invented the lat pulldown? An unknown Latvian.

Two bodybuilders were having a fight in the street after one stole the other's hormones. One of them tore off a car exhaust pipe and tried to ram it down the throat of the other builder. 'This is what I call the pre-exhaust principle.'

Why wasn't the bodybuilder evicted? Because he was squatting.

☺ A bodybuilder said to a reporter, 'Would you like to see my traps?' And the reporter said, 'Yes'. So he took him down to his cellar and pushed him down a trapdoor.

At a bodybuilding contest a moron put oil all over his body and started sliding around all over the stage. He won the contest because the top three competitors slipped and broke their necks.

⊙ Interviewer: 'What's the best protein source a body-builder can eat?' Pro: 'Another bodybuilder.'

A bodybuilder picks up a blonde at a bar and takes her home with him.

He takes off his shirt and the blonde says, 'What a great chest you have.'

The bodybuilder tells her, 'That's one hundred pounds of dynamite, baby.'

He takes off his trousers and the blonde says, 'What massive calves you have.'

The bodybuilder tells her, 'That's one hundred pounds of dynamite, baby.'

He then removes his underwear and the blonde goes running out of the apartment, screaming in fear.

The bodybuilder puts his clothes back on and chases after her. He catches up to her and asks why she ran out of the apartment like that.

The blonde replies, 'I was afraid to be around all that dynamite after I saw how short the fuse was.'

Bowling

Ten-pin bowlers do it with something to spare.

Bowling is a sport that should be right down your alley.

⚠ If you can't hear a pin drop, then something is definitely wrong with your bowling.

Why were the bowling pins lying down? They were on strike!

Our small town used to have a bowling alley, but somebody stole the pin.

'Something is wrong with my bowling delivery,' Tom said, gutturally.

I'll never bowl with him again. After he got a strike, he spiked the ball.

If our town didn't have bowling, there'd be no culture at all.

I go bowling once every four years to make sure I still hate it.

Why should bowling alleys be quiet? So you can hear a pin drop!

Where do old bowling balls end up? In the gutter!

Old bowls players never die, they simply jack it in.

⚠ What kind of cats like to go bowling? Alley cats!

Boxing

After the success of the George Forman grill, Audley Harrison is launching his own toaster. The problem is it can only do four rounds!

He's an ambidextrous fighter. He can get knocked out with either hand.

☺ This trainer came up to this boxer. He said, 'Are you ready for another fight?' The boxer said, 'Just a bout.'

Don't ever go down the pub with Audley Harrison. He can't even get a round in.

He was a crossword-puzzle boxer. He entered the ring vertical and left horizontal.

I quit because I had a problem with my hands. The refs kept stepping on them.

☺ Did you hear about the Irishman who thought sugar diabetes was the South African flyweight champion?

Ex-boxer: 'I'm in great shape. Every artery in my body is hard.'

Manager: 'How would you like to fight for the crown?'
Boxer: 'Great. I think I can take the queen in about three rounds.'

What do Michael Jackson and Audley Harrison have in common? They both wear gloves for no reason.

⊕ When I was a fighter I kept my head. I lost my teeth, but I kept my head.

What do you call a boxer crossed with a vacuum cleaner? Mike Dyson!

I know that there will never be women's boxing. A woman wouldn't think of putting on gloves without a bag and shoes to match.

⊕ Boxer, after battering opponent unmercifully: 'There'll be no rematch for that chump. My hands couldn't stand the punishment.'

What's Audley Harrison's favourite film? *Gone in Sixty Seconds.*

He boxed as Kid Candle. One blow and he was out.

The boxer had written on his tombstone: 'You can stop counting. I'm not getting up.'

⊕ His trainer told him to stay down till eight. He looked up from the canvas and said, 'What time is it now?'

He only learned to count up to ten. He thought that after ten came, 'You're out!'

He boxed under the name of Kid Cousteau because he took so many dives.

The boxer was so far behind in points he had to knock out his opponent just to get a draw.

He's the only boxer in the history of the sport to be knocked out while shadow boxing.

☺ A fighter was taking a terrific beating. When the bell rang, he staggered to his corner. His manager looked at him: 'Let him hit you with his left for a bit. Your face is crooked.'

'Just think of it,' said the boastful boxer to the manager. 'Tonight I'll be fighting on TV before millions of people.' 'Yes,' replied the manager, 'and they'll all know the results of the fight at least ten seconds before you do.'

☺ Mike Tyson has agreed to fight Prince Charles for his next boxing match. It seems that no one else has big enough ears to go twelve rounds.

A young boxer was in his first fight. It was soon apparent that the boy was no match for the other, more experienced fighter. When the battered boxer reeled into his corner at the end of the first round, his trainer tried to keep up the fighter's confidence. 'You're doing great; he hasn't laid a hand on you,' he said. The next round was even worse than the first, but the boy was game and lasted it out. As he returned to his corner, his trainer assured him, 'You're beating him bad; he still hasn't laid a glove on you.'

The process continued through several rounds, each time the trainer assuring the boxer he was doing well. Finally, after the seventh round the bruised and bleeding young man barely managed to stagger back to his corner. When the trainer assured him the other guy still hadn't laid a hand on him, the young man looked up through the eye that was still open and pleaded, 'Then you better keep your eye on the referee this next round because somebody is beating the hell out a me!'

⊕ What did Mike Tyson say to Van Gogh?
                              You gonna eat that?

Tyson already has his next fight lined up, with Lorena Bobbitt. Winner eats all.

What is Mike Tyson's favourite food? Macearoni cheese.

⊕ What did Louis Farrakahn say to Mike Tyson after the fight? No, stupid. An eye for an eye!

What do they call a boxer who gets beat up in a fight? A sore loser.

Did you hear about the boxing referee who used to work at a space rocket launching site?

⊕ If a fighter was knocked down he'd count, 'Ten, nine, eight, seven ...'

'My dad is a boxer.' 'What is your mother?' 'Extremely cautious!'

Cheerleaders

What do cheerleaders drink before they go to a game? Root beer!

⊙ Why did the ghost become a cheerleader?
She liked to show off her school spirit!

What is a cheerleader's favourite colour? Yeller!

⊙ How does a cheerleader answer the phone?
H-E-L-L-O!

A cheerleader sees a sign reading, 'Press bell for night watchman.' She does so, and after a few seconds she hears the watchman clomping down the stairs. He then proceeds to unlock first one gate, then another, then shut down the alarm system, and finally makes his way through the revolving door. 'Well,' he says. 'What do you want?' The blonde replies, 'I just wanted to know why you can't ring the bell yourself?'

What can save a dying cheerleader? Hair transplants.

⊙ What did the cheerleader say when someone blew in her bra? 'Thanks for the refill.'

Did you hear about the cheerleader who went to a library and checked out a book called *How to Hug*? She got it home and found it was volume seven of the encyclopaedia.

CHEERLEADERS

How do cheerleaders pierce their ears? They put tacks in their shoulder pads.

How do you change a cheerleader's mind? Blow in her ear.

⚠ How do you make a cheerleader's eyes sparkle?
Shine a torch into her ear.

What are the six worst years in a cheerleader's life? Third grade.

What's five miles long and has an IQ of forty? A cheerleader parade.

⚠ Why did the cheerleader have square boobs?
She forgot to take the tissues out of the box.

Why can't cheerleaders pass their driving test first time? Whenever the car stops, they hop in the back seat.

How do you determine a cheerleader's IQ ? With a tyre gauge.

⚠ How do you drown a cheerleader?
Put a scratch 'n' sniff sticker at the bottom of a pool.

How do you get a one-armed cheerleader out of a tree? Wave to her.

⚠ How does a cheerleader commit suicide?
She gathers her clothes into a pile and jumps off.

What is a cheerleader's favourite food? Cheerios!

Chess

A group of chess grandmasters checked into a hotel and were standing in the lobby discussing their recent tournament triumphs. After about an hour, the manager came out of the office and asked them to disperse. 'But why?' they asked, as they moved off. 'Because,' said the manager, 'I can't stand chess nuts boasting in an open foyer.'

⊙ What's the difference between a chess player and a highway construction worker? A chess player moves every now and then.

A chess player is walking from the lake carrying two fish in a bucket. He is approached by the game warden who asks him for his fishing licence. The chess player says to the warden, 'I did not catch these fish, they are my pets. Every day I come down to the water and whistle and these fish jump out and I take them around to see the sights only to return them at the end of the day.' The warden does not have any idea what he's talking about. Not believing him he reminds him that it is illegal to fish without a licence. The chess player turns to the warden and says, 'If you don't believe me then watch,' as he throws the fish back into the water. The warden says, 'Now whistle to your fish and show me that they will come out of the water.' The chess player turns to the warden and says, 'What fish?'

⊙ In a park some people come across a man playing chess against a dog. They are astonished and say, 'What a clever dog!' But the man protests, 'No, no, he isn't that clever. I'm leading by three games to one!'

A man is talking with his friend, 'I can see why my wife like chess,' he says, 'the king is stationary and the queen has all the power!'

☺ 'So I was having dinner with Garry Kasporov – problem was, we had a chequered tablecloth and it took him two hours to pass the salt!'

Which chess piece is the most powerful? The knight – it goes over the top.

Two friends meet in the street and one of them says, 'My wife says that if I go to the chess match tomorrow she will take my children and leave me.' Shocked, the friend asks him what he will do. 'E4, same as always!' he replied.

☺ Which group of women is the best chess players? Feminists. Their opponents begin with king and queen, but they always start with two queens.

Three retired international chess grandmasters were playing chess in the park. The first grandmaster said, 'It's windy today.' The second grandmaster said, 'No, it's Thursday today.' The third said, 'Me too, let's go back inside for a drink!'

☺ 'I've created a chess programme that mimics human play,' said the computer science major. 'So it plays at GM level then?' asks the advising professor. 'No, but it does blame its loss on outside conditions!'

Why can't episcopalians play chess? They don't know the difference between a bishop and a queen!

Two men were sitting outside a café playing a game of five-minute chess against the clock. Suddenly, a funeral procession moved past the café. One of the men stood up and watched the procession go by with his clock running. His opponent could not believe it but the man just stood there while the funeral procession passed by and his flag fell and he lost the game. When he sat down his opponent asked him why he did not play the mate in 3. 'Well,' he replied 'it was the least I could do – I was married to her for thirty years!'

He's one of the finest chess officials money can buy.

① What is the difference between a large cheese pizza and a chess grandmaster? A pizza can feed a family of four.

Old chess players never die, they simply go to pieces.

Travelling on a train on a quite cold and blustery day the traveller is surprised when the man opposite stands up, goes to the window and opens it wide. Politeness lasts a minute or two of icy blast until the traveller stands up and angrily closes the window, looking pointedly at the man opposite. The man responds a few minutes later by opening the window again. After shutting, opening, shutting, opening again the traveller is worked up enough to speak. 'Just what is your game?'

'Draughts,' the man replies.

Climbing

Some signs you might have chosen the wrong guide up Everest:

- The last three days, all you've had to eat is bagels.
- Every morning greets the group with, 'Wonder who'll die today?'
- Doesn't worry about provisions, as there's bound to be a Starbucks or McDonald's every half-mile or so.
- Gets lost in the 'Sherpa Shack' gift shop.
- Makes everyone do upside-down shots off the St Bernard's collar.
- First day's preparation devoted entirely to making snow angels.
- Every ten minutes, stops and yells, 'RICOLA.'
- Throws a fit when her stiletto heel gets stuck in the ice.
- Has everyone stick their tongues to an orange lolly, 'for practice'.
- Keeps repeating, 'Is it me, or is it cold up here?'
- 'Map, schmap – you see the top from here!!'
- Two words: golf clubs.
- Forgets to wear socks with his sandals.
- Keeps using the oxygen tanks to make balloon animals.
- Every so often, turns and screams, 'Stop following me!'
- Squeezes your bum then yells, 'Hey, if we get stranded we can live off Tubby here for a week!'

⊙ How do you get a blonde to climb on the roof?
        Tell her that the drinks are on the house!

A party of economists was climbing in the Alps. After several hours they became hopelessly lost. One of them studied the map for some time, turning it up and down, sighting on distant landmarks, consulting his compass, and finally the sun. Then he said, 'OK, see that big mountain over there?'
    'Yes,' answered the others eagerly.
    'Well, according to the map, we're standing on top of it.'

⊙ A little old lady, who lived on the third floor of a boarding house, broke her leg. As the doctor put a cast on it, he warned her not to climb any stairs. Several months later, the doctor took off the cast. 'Can I climb stairs now?' asked the little old lady. 'Yes,' he replied. 'Thank goodness!' she said. 'I'm sick and tired of shinning up and down that drainpipe!'

A guide is leading a client up a challenging first ascent. Every time the guide gets to a particularly dangerous section, he stops and puts on the same red shirt. The guide climbs pitch after difficult pitch, beautifully. As they near the top, the client finally asks about the red shirt. 'If I had fallen,' says the wise and courageous guide, 'this shirt would disguise the blood, and you would not be frightened and lose heart.' 'Amazing,' thought the client, marvelling at this forethought. The next day, as they neared the summit, a section more difficult than any before loomed above them. The guide started up, then climbed down and started rummaging in his pack. 'What are you looking for?,' asked the client. 'My brown trousers,' came the reply.

⚠ Yo momma's so fat ... when she went rock climbing the whole mountain collapsed.

What's the difference between a climber and a golfer? A golfer goes: whack, ooops! A climber goes: ooops, WHACK!

Two climbers are lost and alone on the side of Mont Blanc as night falls. Freezing, they stagger on but hope is fading fast. Suddenly, a St Bernard dog with a huge flask of brandy round its neck bounds up to them. 'Look, man's best friend!' cries the first climber. 'Yes,' his companion replies, 'and a dog, too.'

⚠ Old mountaineers never die.

They simply lose their grip.

Cricket

A couple of fans were watching a county championship match on a particularly dark and dismal afternoon. Neither team was on top form and the match had rapidly become boring and lifeless. Suddenly the stadium lights flickered and then went out, leaving the pitch in semi-darkness. It was impossible to continue and the match was quickly abandoned.

'Well!' said one fan to his neighbour. 'That's the first time I've ever known bad play stop light!'

Which insect loves sport? A cricket.

What animal is the best cricket player? The bat.

⊙ When Ian Bell went to get a Chinese takeaway was he out for a Peking duck?

When Ian Bell goes to the off-licence is he out for a six-pack?

Cricketer: 'Doctor, I'm having a terrible time. I'm not getting any runs, my ground fielding is dreadful and I can't hold my catches. What should I do?'
Doctor: 'Try a different sport.'
Cricketer: 'I can't. I'm captain of England!'

⊙ Last night at the annual cricket club dance the music was so bad that when someone sounded the fire alarm everyone got up to dance.

(!) 'Boy. That bowler is good,' said the American, 'he hits that bat right in the middle every time.'

The public school was at home to a cricket eleven from the coal mines. A miner approached the school captain. 'Here, where are your bowlers?'
    'Bowlers, old boy? We don't have bowlers – we have caps.'

A man took his Greek brother-in-law to a Test match. After watching for a while, the visitor turned to his companion and said: 'I don't know what you think of this cricket, but it's all English to me.'

The reason so many cricketers look weather-beaten is that rain stops play so often.

(!) A young Irish cricketer on tour in Canada was delighted when he was given a room with running water, as he had always wanted to meet a Red Indian.

A bowler came home disconsolate. 'I had three catches dropped today,' he moaned to his wife. 'That's not your fault,' she exclaimed. 'Yes,' he replied, 'but they were all dropped by spectators in the stand!'

Wife: 'Cricket! Cricket! Cricket! That's all you think about. If you mention cricket once again I'll die, that's what I'll do, just die!'
Husband (bowling an off spinner with an orange): 'Promises! Promises! Promises!'

(!) Did you hear about the streaker who ran on to the playing area at the Oval during a Test match? He was caught by the short leg and led off.

First MCC member: 'My wife's in bed with shingles.'
Second MCC member: 'Nice chap, Shingles. Used to open the innings with him at Oxford.'

The batsman was out first ball. On the long walk back to the pavilion he had to pass the incoming batsman. 'Hard luck,' sneered the new batsman. 'Yes. It's a shame that I had to be in the middle of a hat trick!'

⚠ During the second day of the Test match at Lords the Queen paid a visit to the ground and play was halted while the teams were presented to her. It was a case of reign stopped play.

Announcement at a village cricket match: 'For the benefit of the players, here are the names of the spectators.'

'I can't understand it,' said the dismissed batsman. 'The ball hit my head and first slip caught it and the umpire gave me out.' 'I know,' said his friend. 'Sometimes they go by the sound.'

Silas t'Yorkshireman was asked if he thought W. C. Grace would have played Twenty20 well. After pondering it for a while he replied. 'I doubt it, lad. He would be over one hundred and fifty years old!'

'Can I have your autograph, mister?' the boy asked the cricketer. The cricketer tried to brush him off. 'I really don't play cricket,' he said. 'I know that,' replied the boy, 'but I'd like to have it anyway!'

Owing to a clerical error, castor oil instead of salad oil was delivered to the Melbourne Cricket Club where the third Test match is being played. The Australians are batting and are expected to make a lot of runs this afternoon.

A word of advice was given by the old captain to his replacement: 'If I can be of any help just ask. You know two heads are better than one – especially if they are on a coin.'

☺ Two rappers are discussing cricket: 'Can he bowl a Chinaman?' 'Naw. He couldn't bowl his Sugar Puffs, Dogg.'

Captain: (to dismissed batsman): 'What happened?'
Batsman: 'The ball came back very quickly.'
Captain: 'And so did you.'

The Devil proposed a cricket match between Heaven and Hell. St Peter smiled, 'It wouldn't be fair, for we have all the cricketers.' 'Ah,' pointed out the Devil, 'we have all the umpires!'

'Cricket, cricket, cricket,' the wife nagged. 'That's all you ever think of. Why, I bet you don't even remember the day we were married!' 'Of course I do,' replied the husband. 'It was the day Denis Compton scored one hundred and seven against Yorkshire!'

The captain was giving the young batsman some advice. 'Now, when you go in, watch that slow left-hand bowler very carefully. Keep your eye on the ball from when it leaves the bowler's hand and watch it all the way.'
  'Never mind the bowler,' shouted a spectator. 'Watch the umpire; that's his dad!'

☺ The batsman stormed into the pavilion: 'That umpire who gave me out lbw should be carrying a white stick.' 'Did you get his name?' 'No, but I'd know his laugh anywhere!'

At the Lords Taverners' Annual Ball held at Lords Cricket Ground last night Jordan and Jodie Marsh were refused admittance as the President had ruled out bouncers.

It was a return match and the batsman was out first ball.

'Not like last week,' grinned the happy bowler. 'Not likely,' said the batsman. 'Last week I made one hundred and fifty, and when I went in all the beer was gone!'

The office boy had asked for the afternoon off to attend his uncle's funeral. Instead, he went to a cricket match where the score was two hundred and twenty for nought. Suddenly, he felt a tap on his shoulder and there was his boss. 'So this is your uncle's funeral?' scowled the boss. 'Looks like it,' replied the boy, 'he's the bowler!'

☺ 'My wife's going to leave me if I don't stop playing cricket.' 'Oh dear! That's too bad.' 'Yes, I'll miss her.'

Cricketer: 'How do I stand for a test trial?' Selector: 'You don't stand, you grovel.'

The visitor was having lunch at Lords with a member. 'Do we say grace?' he asked. The member looked appalled. 'Good heavens, sir, this is Lords,' he thundered. 'We always say "Compton".'

'I can't understand it,' said the captain. 'It was such an important match that I bribed the umpire and we still lost.' 'Terrible, isn't it,' the wicketkeeper said. 'It's getting so that you can't trust anyone.'

☺ A spectator called out to a batsman making his way back up the pavilion steps: 'I see you were using old polo today.'

'Why do you call my bat polo? Because it has a sweet sound?'
'No, because it seems to have a hole in the middle.'

A fielder had dropped five catches during the innings. As he left the field he asked, 'Has anyone got ten pence? I want to telephone a friend.' 'Here's twenty pence,' said the bowler, 'telephone them all!'

⊙ Why do grasshoppers not go to many football matches? They prefer cricket matches!

The young batsman returned to the pavilion after a short knock. 'That was a lovely stroke,' remarked the incoming batsman. 'Which one?' 'The one when you hit the ball!'

A lady approached a member of the village team: 'Excuse me, but I'm making a quilt and I would be so grateful if you could supply me with the down.'
　　Cricketer: 'I'm sorry ma'am, I can't help you as I haven't any down. Why ask me?'
　　Lady: 'Well, your friends told me you had more ducks than anyone else this season.'

A sheik and a cricketer were watching a match: 'It is said he has eighty maidens,' said the sheik, gesticulating at a player. 'Another five and he can get a new ball,' replied his companion.

The farmer swung at the ball, missed it and it thudded into his box. As he lay doubled up on the ground the friendly wicketkeeper patted him on the shoulder and said, 'Look on the bright side, that's increased the size of your farm – you've got a couple more acres.'

⊙ Mountbatten, Stan Bowls and W. C. Fields.

Slowly, the batsman dragged his bat into the pavilion and slumped down on the bench. 'I've never played so badly before.' 'Oh?' said the interested captain. 'You've played before, have you?'

⚠ He was a loyal supporter: 'All Middlesex have to do to win the County Championship is to win eleven of their last four matches.'

A man and his girlfriend were at the cricket: 'Why is that man running?' asked the girl. 'He hit the ball,' the man patiently explained. 'Oh I see,' she replied, 'isn't it his?'

Middlesex and Yorkshire were playing at Lords. A man sporting a large white rose appeared at the ticket office and asked the price of admission. 'Two pounds, sir,' was the reply. 'Then here's a pound, lad. There's only one team worth watching.'

Man on telephone: ' ... and after I pour the drinks I'm going to lead you into the bedroom, put you on the bed, strip you naked and make mad passionate love to you – and would you stop telling me the Test match score!'

'Doctor, come quickly. The scorer has swallowed his pen!'
'I'll be there immediately. What have you done?'
'Borrowed another one!'

⚠ How long were you in the first eleven?' 'Oh, about five feet eight inches.'

The bowler was having terrible luck; another coat of varnish and he would have had a wicket. The batsman missed every ball. At the end of the over, the batsman turned to the wicketkeeper and sneered: 'He must be the worst bowler in the country!'
      'That would be too much of a coincidence!' replied the wicketkeeper.

'Doctor, I feel like a small cricket stump.'
'A little off, eh?'

'Doctor, I feel like a cricket ball.'
'You'll soon be over that.'

'Doctor, I keep seeing ducks before my eyes.'
'Have you seen an optician?'
'No, just ducks.'

'Doctor, every time I lift my bat I feel like crying.'
'Perhaps it's a weeping willow.'

'Doctor, I feel just like an umpire.'
'Don't be silly. There must be someone somewhere who likes you a little.'

☺ 'Who's the batsman dressed like a sailor?'
'Oh, he's the anchor.'

Two old men were talking about their cricketing days. 'What was your highest score?'
  'One hundred and fifty.'
  'Mine was two hundred not out. And what was your best spell of bowling?'
  'Oh no! You first this time.'

A cricketer was sitting on the bench suffering the effects of a night out as the captain approached him.
  Captain: 'Glad to see you at practice last night.'
  Cricketer: 'Oh, was that where I was?'

A young batsman had collected three ducks in a row and naturally was rather depressed. The club bore patted him on the shoulder and said, 'Don't worry, old boy. Two seasons ago I went through a very bad patch and I'll tell you what brought on the change.' Overhearing this, the captain laughed: 'What change?'

A batsman played forward and pushed the ball slightly wide to mid-off. 'No, no, no!' he yelled to the non-striker who was backing up.

'You know,' said the other batsman as he grounded his bat, 'you sound just like my girlfriend.'

A batsman is in the pub, slowly sinking a pint. Another drinker asks him how the match went: 'If it wasn't for Steve Black we would have lost the match today.'

'Is he a batsman or bowler?'

'Neither. He's the umpire.'

A spectator had to be removed from a cricket match as she had kept shouting, 'Kill the umpire, kill the umpire!'

She has since been identified as the umpire's wife.

☺ Jimmy studied the examination question thoughtfully. 'What was the main cause of the Wars of the Roses?' After much consideration he wrote: 'The County Championship.'

A match was very dull and not a run was scored for an hour. Suddenly, there was a loud bang as a car backfired. A voice shouted: 'Tell that man to be quiet, or he'll wake up the scorer!'

A batsman kept playing the ball back to the bowler for over after over. A visitor turned to a home supporter next to him.

'Does that batsman ever score runs?'

'Impossible to say,' was the reply. 'I've only been coming here for three years.'

A match was very dull and one spectator turned to his friend: 'I'm surprised the spectators don't barrack.'

'Difficult to shout and yawn at the same time,' replied his friend.

⚠ 'What did Boycott say when he was run out?'
'Shall I leave out the swear words?'
'Yes.'
'He never spoke.'

Two wives were talking in the pavilion. 'What do you think about Mandy, she's gone off with the cricket coach.'
'I didn't know she could drive.'

'Jones had a terrible row with his wife last week.'
'What happened?'
'Well, he told her he had to act as night watchman, so she expected a little extra in her allowance.'

Two cricketers were having a drink in their local.
'What do you mean, you had a hard time explaining the cricket match to your wife?' said one. 'She found out I wasn't there,' replied his companion.

⚠ Sir Don Bradman, Sir Len Hutton, Sir Jack Hobbs and Sir Frank Worrell – all batsman; seems the last bowler to be knighted was Sir Francis Drake!

A jilted bride drove to the cricket ground and confronted her fiancé who was buckling on his pads.
'How could you do it? Everyone at the church except you. Why didn't you come?'
'Don't you ever listen,' he answered as he pulled on his gloves. 'I distinctly said only if it rained!'

Cricketer: 'I've been to my doctor and he says I can't play cricket.'
Coach: 'Oh? When did he see you play?'

'Doctor, every night I have the same dream. I'm opening for England against Australia and I'm always bowled first ball. It's just driving me mad.'

Doctor: 'Well, try dreaming of Scarlett Johansson instead.'

Cricketer: 'What? And miss my turn to bat?'

A captain looked at his middle-aged batting partner who had just had him run out. 'It's a great pity you hadn't taken the game up sooner.'

'You mean I'd be playing Test cricket by this time?'

'No, you'd have already retired!'

A Test player stalked into the pavilion and growled, 'That new Irish doctor doesn't know what he's talking about.'

'What did he say?'

'He told me I had tennis elbow!'

☺ A Yorkshire man on a world cruise received the following radio message from his father: 'Regret your mother died this morning. We're one hundred and eighty-four for two. Boycott ninety-two not out.'

A batsman mistimed the ball and it just touched his off stump, and one bail gently fell to the ground. Ignoring convention, the batsman replaced the bail and remarked cheerfully, 'Rather a strong wind today.'

'Indeed there is, so be careful it doesn't blow your cap off on your way back to the pavilion,' replied the umpire.

'I really had him in two minds that time,' said the bowler, returning to his mark.

'Sure you did. He didn't know whether to hit you for a six or four,' replied the captain.

A young batsman was apologizing to his captain for getting yet another duck.

'Perhaps I should have another net.'

'Make it a fishing one!'

A wicketkeeper had had a bad day in the field, dropping six catches, and now as he sat huddled in the dressing room he could feel a cold coming on. 'I think I've caught a cold,' he muttered.

'Thank goodness you're able to catch something,' grunted the captain.

☉ Did you hear about the cricket-loving shop steward? He liked to get them all out before lunch.

Husband (watching TV): 'Joel Garner has come back to bowl with a new ball.'
Wife (knitting): 'Wonderful what doctors can do these days.'

The handsome and dashing batsman had been struck several times in the ribs by the fast bowler and had been taken to the local hospital for a check-up. The pretty nurse told him to go behind the screen and take his clothes off.

Having done so he called, 'I've taken my clothes off, nurse. Where shall I put them?' 'On top of mine,' came the reply.

A batsman was going well against the fast bowlers and was approaching his first ever century, when the twelfth man ran out and whispered to him. The batsman walked over to the fielding captain and said, 'I say, my wife's expecting twins any minute and she wants me at the hospital. Any chance of putting on your spinners?'

☉ Did you hear about the hit-and-run driver? He's top of the batting averages in the prison team.

Ashes to ashes.
Dust to dust.
If the batsmen can't score,
The bowlers must.

Cricketer: 'Captain, I've an idea which may help team win a few matches.'
Captain: 'So sorry to hear you're leaving!'

'Now remember,' said the coach, 'You must always get behind the ball.'
'Now, how do I do that?' demanded the Irishman.
'Sure, it's the same all the way round?'

'Mummy, why do fairy tales always start with "Once upon a time?"'
'They don't always, dear. The ones your father tells usually start, "I never touched the ball … "'

☺ 'That was my best innings ever,' said the young batsman. 'Well,' grunted the old pro, 'don't let that discourage you.'

When an expectant father telephoned the hospital to see how his wife was getting on, he was connected to the local cricket club instead. 'What's the news?' he asked.
'Great,' came the reply. 'We've got four out already and hope to have the rest out before lunch. And by the way, the last one was a duck.'

A wicketkeeper applied for a trial with a local team. After the trial he was advised that he would not be invited to join the club. However, he asked the captain for a letter of introduction to another club. The captain, not wishing to dampen the young man's enthusiasm, gave him a letter which stated, 'As the wicketkeeper, the bearer is passable.'

Cricketer: 'What's my temperature, nurse?'
Nurse: 'A hundred and one.'
Cricketer: 'That's the first time I've reached a hundred before lunch.'

☺ Bowler (looking at the incoming batsman): 'Is he a good hooker?'
'No, you're thinking of his sister.'

🙂 How do you bowl an Irishman? Hand him two glasses of Guinness when he's batting.

A member of the MCC was asked to state the difference between an Australian Test cricketer and an English Test cricketer.

He straightened his brightly coloured club tie and said, 'An Australian cricketer walks out to bat as if the ground belongs to him, an English cricketer walks out as if he doesn't give a damn to whom it belongs.'

Doctor: 'What your husband needs is complete rest, so he'll be fit for the Test match on Thursday. Here are some sleeping tablets.'
Mrs Boycott: 'Very good doctor. How many should I give him?'
Doctor: 'Don't give him any, take them yourself!'

🙂 The batsman played back to the fast bowler. The ball came sharply off the shoulder of the bat and struck him in the face. He fell back on his wicket and sprawled on the ground. As he lay there spitting out blood and broken teeth, the wicketkeeper looked down at him: 'Lucky for you it was a no-ball!'

Old pro: 'When you're bowling, you must bowl with the head.'
Young debutant: 'Is it not hard on the ears?'

The nervous young batsman was having a terrible time and was lucky to still be at the crease. During a lull, he stammered to the wicketkeeper, 'Well, I expect you've seen worse players.'

Silence ...

First slip added, 'He said I expect you've seen worse players.'

'I heard him the first time. I was just trying to think.'

Jack decided to learn a trade to keep him going in the winter months when he wasn't earning money playing county cricket. He signed up to train as an electrician. A few weeks later he bumped into a team mate in the pub, who enquired how the training was going. 'Oh, I passed the practical exam easily,' said Jack, 'but I failed the written exam.' 'What went wrong?' asked his friend. 'Well, it was all going well until they asked me what DC was,' replied Jack. 'And what did you put?' 'Denis Compton.'

⊙ Patient: 'Doctor, doctor, I've got a cricket bat stuck in my ear. Doctor: 'How's that?' Patient: 'Don't you start!'

There's a man in Finchley who claims to have invented a game that in certain respects is a bit like cricket.

What he doesn't know is that the England team has been playing it for years.

The standard of batting in the local side was very low. Even at the net practice, they couldn't hit a thing. Finally, the captain rushed forward and grabbed the bat.

'Now bowl me some fast ones!' he yelled. Six fast balls came down in quick succession and the captain missed them all. Not to be put off he glared at the team and shouted, 'Now that's what you're all doing. Get in there and hit them!'

⊙ 'I've been invited to join Yorkshire, they want me to play for them very badly.' 'Well, in that case you're just the man.'

The eager young batsman had just scored yet another duck and was apologizing to the captain.

'I think I could do with some advice. What sort of coach would you recommend?'
'A long-distance one.'

The batsman had a high opinion of his prowess.

He was approached by a club member who couldn't resist saying to him, 'You know, whenever I watch you bat, I always wonder ...'

'I know, I know. How I do it.'

'No. Why you do it.'

The captain called the batsman into his room. 'We've got some very tough matches coming up,' he said, 'and I wanted to talk to you because we need someone with an iron nerve, a strong constitution and great skill in the side. That's why I'm asking you to resign.'

The captain insisted that Joe opened the innings against the other side's demon bowler. After the match, his mate Bill came up.

'How did you get on against the fast bowler?'

'No problems. I was having my teeth out tomorrow anyway.'

☺ What happens to a cricketer when his eyesight starts to fail? He becomes an umpire!

The fast bowler hit the batsman on the head and the batsman danced around in agony, clutching his foot. The opposing captain ran up to help and then said, 'Wait a minute. You were hit on the head. Why are you holding your foot?'

'My corn's giving me hell!' moaned the batsman.

The game had been a bitter affair, with neither side giving anything away and an unusual amount of hostile bowling. Several injuries were sustained, and after the game one of the batsmen was seen pacing up and down the pitch.

'Ah, I see you're reliving the battle,' said the groundsman.

'No,' said the player. 'I'm looking for my teeth.'

☺ Did you hear about the man arrested for trying to set fire to Lords? He had a burning interest in cricket.

The batsman said to the bowler, 'Give me an easy one, will you? I bet a fellow in the crowd five pounds that I'd score four runs.' The bowler did so and the batsman hit it to the boundary. Straight away, he walked for the pavilion.

'You're not out,' said the bowler. 'Where are you going?'

The batsman yelled back: 'I'm going to find the chap who bet me!'

The batsman was having a bad time. He played and missed at every ball and was becoming more hot and flustered every minute. As the bowler was walking back; the batsman turned to the wicketkeeper.

'Phew,' he said, 'what couldn't I do with a bottle of beer.'

The wicketkeeper thought for a moment. 'Hit it with the bat?'

During the game, the batsman noticed that the splice was coming out of his bat. In his small village, he was at a loss where to take it to be repaired. Finally, he decided that the blacksmith might do the job and went along to ask. 'Splice coming loose, eh?' said the blacksmith. 'I get a lot of you chaps in here. I'll have it fixed in a minute.' He put the bat on the anvil, took an enormous hammer and gave it a mighty smash. The bat was as good as new.

'Marvellous!' enthused the batsman. 'How much do I owe you?'

'Let's say a fiver, eh?' said the blacksmith.

'A fiver? All you did was hit it with a hammer.'

'I'll make you out a bill,' said the blacksmith.

He scribbled on a piece of paper and handed it over. The batsman read: hitting bat with hammer: ten pence. For knowing where to hit: four pounds ninety pence.

☺ Two onlookers were talking during the village match. 'The batsman was late for the first delivery,' observed one. 'He always is,' said the other. 'That's our postman.'

The batsman was new to the side, and in his first innings he did so badly that the crowd began to slow hand-clap and barrack him. Things got worse. The language got more and more abusive, his play more inept, and finally he was out. As he dashed for the pavilion, rotten fruit and eggs were thrown at him, but he managed to gain the safety of the dressing room, where the captain was waiting for him.

'Blimey!' panted the batsman. 'They don't like that umpire, do they?'

☺ Why don't spiders play cricket? Because the only way to get them out is lllllllbw.

The despairing umpire was trying to control a ladies' cricket match. Preparing to give a guard to the opening bat, he asked, 'What would you like?'

'I'll have middle and leg ... by the way, that sight screen is filthy and is my hair OK?'

A dedicated batsman was up against the fast bowler and he was doing well. As he was getting into his stride, a note was brought out to him and the game was interrupted.

He frowned as he read it, and called over the umpire.

'I say,' he said, 'I've just heard that my wife's dangerously ill and she's calling for me. Do you think you could ask the bowler to shorten his run-up?'

The batsman strolled up to the crease and carefully took guard. He looked round the field, noting the position of each player.

With great elegance, he patted down several invisible bumps on the pitch and at last signalled that he was ready to accept the first delivery.

The ball came and uprooted the middle stump.

'What a shame,' said the wicketkeeper. 'Just as you were getting set!'

It was the last county match of the year, and they were at the bottom of the table. A customer came to the ticket window.

'May I have two, please,' he asked, putting down a five-pound note.

'Certainly, sir,' said the cashier. 'Batsmen or bowlers?'

The small village ground was crowded – all were there to see the two Australian fast bowlers who were guests on the visiting team.

The village captain won the toss and decided to bat, which was a poor decision on his part. In the first over one fast bowler took all six wickets. The second over produced one run and the fall of the remaining four wickets.

'It must be disappointing for the crowd,' said one of the village players.

'Yes,' agreed the captain, 'but at least they got a run for their money.'

☺ Which insect didn't play well at slip?
The fumble bee!

The batsman mistimed the fast bowler and was struck on the pad. The bowler appealed for lbw, but the batsman paid no attention as he stood leaning on his bat, swinging his damaged leg. Slowly the umpire approached him.

'Can you walk?' he asked kindly.

'I think so.'

'Then walk back to the pavilion, son. You're out!'

The village match was short of an umpire so an announcement went out asking if there was an umpire present.

One man stepped forward: 'I'm an umpire.'

'Have you stood before?' asked one captain.

'Of course I have, and my three friends here will vouch for that,' was the reply.

The two captains consulted briefly together.

'Thank you for offering, but we don't think we'll accept.'

'You don't think I'm an umpire!'

'Quite frankly we don't, because we've never heard of an umpire having three friends.'

Two bitter cricket widows are talking: First Wife: 'How's your husband today?'

Second Wife: 'His cricket bat is giving him a lot of pain.'

First Wife: 'How can his cricket bat give him pain?'

Second Wife: 'I hit him over the head with it.'

It was the cricket club's annual dinner and the members settled back for a long boring talk by the president of the club who had a reputation for drivelling on and on.

He had been speaking for about five minutes and was still talking of his schoolboy cricketing days, when the captain passed him a note. The speaker glanced at the note, closed his speech quickly and sat down. The members could hardly believe their good luck and asked the captain what he had written on the note. The captain grinned: 'Only four words: "Your flies are open."'

Umpire: 'Doctor, I can't sleep at night.'
Doctor: 'How long has this been going on?'
Umpire: 'Oh, about three months.'
Doctor: 'That's terrible. You haven't slept for three months!'
Umpire: 'Oh, I sleep during the matches; it's just at night I can't sleep!'

The incoming batsman took guard, did a spot of gardening, tugged at his cap, looked at the scoreboard which showed 5 for 5, scanned the field positions and faced up to the first ball.

It was a fast rising ball which struck him on the left elbow. He dropped his bat and rubbed his injured arm. The second ball was even faster and rapped him on the left hand, he waved it around in agony. He checked his mark and faced his third ball which thudded into his ribs. Slowly he hobbled from the wicket towards the pavilion.

'I say,' shouted the umpire, 'you're not out.' 'No', replied the batsman ruefully, 'but I'm going.'

⚠ Why is it called a hat trick?
Because it's performed by a bowler.

The ball had hit the batsman on the arm and yet he was still given out. As he passed the umpire, he asked, 'How was that out?'

'Why don't you look in the paper tomorrow?' replied the umpire, smugly.

'Why don't you look?' said the batsman. 'I'm the editor!'

The club captain was showing a new member around and explaining the procedure. 'We have nets four evenings a week. Tuesday, Wednesday, Thursday and Friday.'

'Four evenings? Isn't that a lot? Must you attend all four nets?'

'Oh, not at all, but most of the boys do attend all four as after a net we usually have a little entertainment. For instance, after practice on Tuesday we usually have a poker school.'

'I don't play poker.'

'Oh! Well, after practice on Wednesday night we have a right old booze-up.'

'I don't drink.'

'Well, not to worry. After practice on Thursday night we have a few girls in.'

'I'm not interested in girls.'

'Are you gay?'

'Certainly not!'

'Well, there goes Friday night as well!'

☉ Did you hear about the batsman who held up one end all day and got a hernia?

It was the after-lunch session, and the next batsman in hadn't left the bar. When it was his turn to bat he confessed to the captain that he could see three of everything.

'Well,' said the captain, 'when you get out to the wicket just hit the middle ball.'

The batsman made his way to the middle and was bowled first ball.

'What happened?' asked the captain. 'Did you play the wrong ball?'

'No, the wrong bowler!'

There was a cricketing vicar who never waited for an appeal but always walked. One day his captain approached him and suggested he should wait for the umpire's decision.

'I know when I'm out,' replied the vicar. 'I'd rather commit adultery than cheat at cricket.'

'Who wouldn't!' replied the captain.

It hadn't rained for months and the Indians were worried about the drought. 'Let us do the English Rain Ritual,' said one Indian.

'What is that?'

'When I was in England I saw two men in white coats hammer six sticks into the ground, then two men carrying clubs came out and stood in front of the sticks and then eleven more men came out blowing on their hands. Then one of the white coats shouted, "Play," and that's when the rain came pouring down!'

! 'I've never umpired a cricket match before. Do I have to run after the ball?' 'No, after the match.'

The president of a cricket club was also the local undertaker, and a dinner was given in his honour on his retirement. In replying to the toast to his health he said he had very happy memories of the club, he appreciated their kindness and although he wished them all long life and happiness if one of the members should die he would bury him free of charge.

There was a loud report at the end of the table and it was found a Scotsman had shot himself.

The annual match between two rival police forces was taking place and an opening policeman had been at the wicket for over an hour and had only scored a single.

Every ball he played the same – a sound defensive shot. Suddenly the umpire raised his finger and said, 'Out.'

'What for?' asked the batsman.

'Loitering with intent,' came the reply.

A cricketer died and went to heaven. One day he looked down to hell, and there to his amazement saw a cricket ground with fielders out and batsmen at the crease.

'I say,' he said to St Peter, 'look at that. A cricket match about to start. And you call that hell? Why, I'd love to be playing.'

'So would they,' smiled St Peter, 'but they haven't got a ball!'

An Irish cricketer arrived at the gates of heaven and was greeted by a cheerful saint. 'Well, well, well! A cricketer from Ireland. You know you're the first one we've got.'

'Well, I hope there'll be many more,' replied the cricketer.

'I'm sure there will be,' smiled the saint. 'You have reached heaven, but just before you pass through the gates is there any little thing you want to tell me? It can't be much or you wouldn't be here. But perhaps some small incident which is on your conscience?'

'Well,' exclaimed the cricketer, 'there is one thing.'

'What is it, my son?'

'A couple of years ago I was playing for Ireland against the MCC at Lords and the bowler appealed for a catch behind the wicket, but the umpire said "not out", so although I knew I had touched the ball I stayed and scored two hundred runs.'

'Who won?'

'We did. We beat the MCC by fifty runs, but ever since then I've always thought I should have walked.'

'Not at all, my son,' boomed the saint, 'you did the right thing. Don't give it another thought. You may enter.'

'I'm very relieved,' replied the cricketer. 'Thank you very much, St Peter!'

'Oh, by the way,' grinned the saint, 'I'm not Peter, I'm St Patrick!'

☺ Did you hear about the Irish umpire who would never give lbw? He couldn't say if the ball would have hit the stumps as there was always a leg in the way!

He was in a reflective mood as he sat staring into the flickering fire. His wife looked at him with a romantic smile. 'Do you remember when you proposed to me?'

'Of course I do. It was behind the pavilion when we were playing Yorkshire seconds.'

'You were bold.'

'No I wasn't. I was caught!'

! A woman was taken to her first cricket game. She watched the players come out, the captains toss up, the fielders fan out across the pitch and the bowler run in. After six balls the umpire called, 'Over.' 'Well,' she said, getting her coat on, 'it seems a nice enough game but it's very short, isn't it?'

The team captain was rather surprised when a horse arrived and asked for a trial. The captain suggested that the horse play in a trial match which was about to begin. 'What number do you bat?' he asked the horse.

'I usually open,' came the reply.

So the horse opened the innings, clad in whites and wearing a brightly coloured cap at a rakish angle over one ear. Every ball he played in the first over was a boundary, four fours and two sixes.

The bowling changed and the batsman pushed the first ball he received gently to the covers and shouted 'One' as he ran. The horse didn't move and the batsman was run out. As he stalked by the horse he growled, 'It was my call. Why didn't you run?'

'Run?' replied the horse. 'Don't be daft, I can't run. If I could run I'd be at Ascot and not playing this bloody stupid game!'

A cricketer was sat gloomily on the pavilion steps. His friend nudged him gently. 'I say, you're looking very sad.'

'My wife ran away with my best friend this morning.'

'Oh, that's terrible!'

'Yes, it means we've got no wicketkeeper this afternoon.'

The two Royal Navy chaplains sat in the members' stand watching a hard-fought match between an Army XI and a Royal Navy XI. One chaplain nudged his colleague, 'You know, cricket really is a wonderful game, the perfect expression of sportsmanship and fair play. Here we are watching a battle between two great services and the important thing is not who wins but how the game is played.' He paused, 'Providing, of course, we beat those Army bastards!'

George always played cricket on Sunday. This troubled his wife, who asked the vicar, 'Is it a sin for him to play on Sunday?'

'It's not a sin,' replied the vicar. 'The way he plays, it's a crime!'

☺ Why couldn't the West Indian player called Robin play cricket? He'd lost his bat, man.

In a Test match in Headingley the umpires were taking a lot of verbal abuse from the Western Terrace regarding their decisions on lbw. At the end of an over the two umpires walked to the terrace and seated themselves with the spectators.

'What do you think you're doing, lad?' one was asked.

'Well,' replied the umpire, 'it appears you get a better view from here.'

A cricketer was going through a very lean period. He had been dropped from the first eleven and he had not even been selected for the seconds. His wife had insisted he visit the doctor and on his return home asked the outcome.

'He says I'm suffering from syncopation – whatever that is.'

As his wife didn't know either she consulted the dictionary and read: 'Syncopation – an uneven movement from bar to bar.'

The bowler had just gone in to bat when the telephone rang in the pavilion. A player answered it to be told it was the bowler's wife and she wanted to speak to her husband.

'I'm sorry, but he's just gone in to bat.'

'Oh, that's all right,' replied the wife. 'I'll hold on!'

The bowlers were getting a lot of stick from the opposing opening pair. The captain decided a new player should have a bowl. He handed the ball to the young man with the advice, 'Keep the ball well up.'

'Don't worry,' was the chirpy reply. 'I know his weakness.'

He bowled four balls and every one cleared the boundary.

'I see what you mean,' said the captain. 'He's got a weakness for sixes.'

A cricketer was planning his wedding with his fianceé: 'Oh darling, I'm looking forward to our wedding and all your cricketing friends making an arch for us by holding up their bats, just like they did for Mike,' she said.

'I don't think we'll have an arch, dear.'

'Why not, darling?'

'They held up their bats because he was a batsman.'

'So?'

'I'm a bowler!'

During the match, the fieldsman positioned just behind the umpire kept trying to distract the batsman as the ball was bowled to him. Several appeals for lbw were turned down, and finally the umpire turned to the fieldsman and said sternly:

'I've been watching you for the last twenty minutes.'

'I thought so,' came the reply, 'I could tell you weren't watching the game!'

The club's leading player had just received the award for the best batting average of the season. In his speech of thanks he said it was mainly due to his wife that he received the award. 'At the beginning of the season my wife and I agreed that whenever we had an argument the one who was wrong would pay a little forfeit. Mine was to have an extra two hours at the nets and my wife was to work for two hours in the garden. That is why I have the best betting average and the worst garden in the country.'

⊙ Which team plays cricket while half undressed?
The Vest Indies.

In a small country game, the bishop was taking part and was at the crease. The bowler was the local vicar who sent down a wide ball. 'I say,' called the bishop, 'keep it in the parish, would you?'

The vicar ran up, bowled, and knocked the middle stump out of the ground.

'I think that's about in the diocese, my lord,' he said.

A visitor booked into a hotel and was delighted as he looked around his room. It was full of cricket paraphernalia. A couple of bats, caps, a box with a dent, trophies and scores of photographs and newspaper cuttings.

As he examined some of the trophies, he noticed a small tarnished and uncared for urn on the top shelf of a bookcase.

'What's this?' he asked, lifting the urn.

'The ashes,' grunted the host.

'The ashes!' exclaimed the visitor. 'Why are they not in pride of place?'

'Don't see why they should be,' replied his host, 'the wife never cared for cricket!'

The village teams were ready to begin their match but discovered that they were without an umpire. They decided that they would use a member of the crowd even though he knew nothing of the rules. When he was dressed in his white coat and hat, he went up to the captain of the home side.

'What do I do?' he asked

'It's very simple,' said the home captain. 'When I shout "HOWZAT!" you simply put up your finger and say "OUT".

'When it's our turn to bat, I'll tell you a little bit more!'

⊙ How does an umpire check that the bails are the correct weight? He takes them to the bail-weigh station.

A lord was entertaining some guests at his country estate and they were playing cricket. The lord was batting and his chief footman was the umpire. A guest bowled and caught the lord plum lbw.

They appealed to the footman. 'Lord Ponsonby is not at home,' he intoned gravely.

'What the devil?' said the lord.

'Well, your Lordship,' said the footman, 'to speak plainly, you're out!'

On the day of the local match, the captain was talking to one of his men.

'Look, here's a fiver,' he said. 'Go out and buy a new ball or something. Anything that'll help us win.'

The match began and the captain noticed that the same old ball was being used.

He called his man over. 'What did you do with the fiver?' he asked.

'Well, you said anything to help us win.'

'Yes.'

'I gave it to the umpire.'

⊙ 'You need glasses,' shouted the dismissed batsman as he passed the man in the white coat. 'So do you, mate,' answered the man. 'I'm selling ice cream.'

A lot of wides were being bowled, but it was obvious that the umpire didn't know that anything was wrong.

After a particularly wide delivery, the exasperated batsman said, 'Surely that was a wide!'

The umpire nodded vigorously. 'Oh yes,' he said. 'Appalling. I don't think I ever saw one wider!'

The local barber was umpiring in the village match, and when one of the batsmen was apparently run out he said: 'Not out.'

The batsman looked at him thankfully. 'That was a close shave,' he said.

'Aye,' said the umpire, 'and if you 'adn't been a regular customer it would 'ave been "Next gentleman, please"!'

Mrs Jones: 'I'd like my son to be excused playing cricket. I don't think he should mix with that sort of person.'

Teacher: 'How d'you mean?'

Mrs Jones: 'Well, I distinctly heard him say that the man in the white coat was a vampire!'

The captain was talking to the umpire. 'Now when you're out there, I expect you to be perfectly fair and stick to the rules. But I'd like to point out that this ground is right next to the hospital, the canal runs down the other side and we haven't lost a game all season!'

The umpire had been hard on the bowler, no-balling him and turning down his every appeal. 'By the way,' asked the bowler, 'how do you spell your name?'

'Timms,' said the umpire, 'T-i-m-m-s.'

'Just as I thought,' murmured the bowler, 'only one "i!"'

⊙ Did you hear about the Irish cricketer?
He had his pads strapped onto his wellies.

The batsman was caught on the pads.

'Owwzat!' shouted the bowler

'Out,' said the umpire, raising his finger.

'I'll have you know, my good man,' blustered the batsman, 'that I am Sir Cecil Fortesque-Thomas.'

'In that case,' said the umpire, 'I'm afraid you're both out.'

⊙ It was the convict's cricket match. The fast bowler whizzed down a screamer which just missed, but a bail gently toppled off. 'Not out,' protested the batsman, 'it was the wind.' 'Wind or not,' said the umpire, 'you're out on bail!'

Two dedicated Yorkshiremen at the Roses match. One discovers that he's left his wallet at home. His friend offers to go back for it. He returns pale and shaken. 'I've got bad news for thee, Bob. Your wife's run off and left thee, and your house 'as burned to the ground!'

'I've got worse news for thee, lad. Boycott's out.'

The visiting team was surprised to find that there were no scoring facilities at the village ground. The captain approached the opposing leader.

'How do you keep the score?' he asked.

'Oh, we keep it in our heads, ' replied the captain, a burly blacksmith, 'and if there's any argument we settle it behind the pavilion after the game.'

⊙ What do you call an Englishman with one hundred runs against his name? A bowler.

A small village side clubbed together and sent a request to a famous cricketer to appear with their team for charity, but they could only afford a small fee.

The cricketer sent back a telegram: 'Will accept double your offer or count me out.'

Later that day the famous player received a telegram: '1, 2, 3, 4, 5, 6, 7, 8, 9, 10 ...'

An American who knew nothing of the game had been taken to a few cricket matches by a friend and was now studying the end-of-season averages. Every now and then he came across an asterisk and the words: 'Signifies not out.' Finally, he turned to his friend and said: 'Why don't you get this guy Signifies to play for your side? He's never out!'

An office worker was talking to his friend on the train home after a hard day.

'What a day I've had,' he said.

'One of the office juniors asked for the afternoon off to go to his grand-mother's funeral. I thought I was on to him, and went along, too.'

'Good idea,' said his friend. 'How was the match?'

'That's where I lost out. It *was* his grandmother's funeral!'

The phrenologist was carefully feeling the head of the man.

'Ah yes,' he said. 'Now that bump indicates a love of children.'

'Love of children?' snorted the man. 'That's where my son hit me with a cricket bat!'

The ball had been knocked out of the ground into the lane and everybody was out looking for it. One of the players came across an old tramp, lying in the shade.

'Excuse me,' said the cricketer, 'but have you seen a cricket ball?'

'No, I haven't,' replied the tramp. 'But I've brought one from home I could sell you!'

The boys were playing cricket in the garden and were using a shiny new ball.

'Where did you get the ball?' asked their father.

'We found it.'

'Are you sure it was lost?'

'Of course it was lost. We saw them looking for it.'

⊕ Why did an outfielder take a piece of rope onto the field? He was the skipper!

During the local match, a spectator was surprised to see a dog walk onto the pitch and start bowling off breaks, eventually taking five wickets for twenty runs.

'That's incredible!' he exclaimed to the man next to him.

'Yes,' he said, 'but he's a terrible disappointment to his parents. They wanted him to be a lawyer.'

Two boys were playing cricket in the street. This always annoyed the man outside whose house they were playing and he ran out and accosted the one who was bowling.

'How many times do I have to tell you? I don't want you playing cricket outside my house! D'you understand?'

The boy said nothing.

'I said, do you understand?'

The boy remained silent and walked away.

The irate householder turned to the other boy. 'He's not much of a talker, is he?'

'He's not much of a bowler either. He just put the ball through your window!'

Two men were discussing the importance of fitness in the game of cricket. Said the fat one, 'When I'm at the crease, my body is highly tuned and as taut as a bowstring. The bowler comes up, bowls and my brain snaps out a command to my body to get quickly behind the line, raise the bat and execute a perfect stroke.'

'Then what happens?'

'My body says: "Who, me?"'

☺ I wanted to take the family to a Test match game, but the bank wouldn't approve my loan.

Two Yorkshiremen were talking:

'If your wife and Geoff Boycott were in a house that was falling over a cliff, who would you save?'

'Are you kidding?' was the reply. 'My wife's a rubbish bat.'

Cricket: You have two sides, one out in the field and one in. Each man that's in the side that's in goes out, and when he's out he comes in and the next man goes in until he's out. When they are all out, the side that's out comes in and the side that's been in goes out and tries to get those coming in, out.

Sometimes you get men still in and not out. When a man goes out to go in, the men who are out try to get him out, and when he is out he goes in and the next man in goes out and goes in.

There are two men called umpires who stay out all the time and they decide when the men who are in are out. When both sides have been in and all the men have out, and both sides have been out twice after all the men have been in, including those who are not out, that is the end of the game!

It was match day at the local ground. The groundsman was in the car park when a car drew up and a man looked out. 'Excuse me,' he said. 'Did I accidentally leave a cigarette alight and burn your pavilion to the ground the last time I was here?'

The groundsman recognized him. 'Yes, you certainly did!'

'Oh good, we're at the right ground!'

A priest visits a man who is grieving over the death of his aged father. 'I'm so sorry to hear of your loss,' says the priest. 'Did you try taking him to Lourdes as I suggested?' 'Yes, we did,' replies the man. 'But we'd only been there a few minutes when he passed away.' 'Was it his heart?' asks the priest. 'No father,' replies the man. 'He got hit on the head by a cricket ball.'

⊙ What does Steve Harmison put in his hands to make sure the next ball almost always takes a wicket? A bat.

In school, the sports master and English teacher asked one of his brighter pupils to spell 'bowling'.

Back came the answer : 'B-o-e-l-i-n.' 'That,' said he, 'is the worst spell of bowling I've ever seen.'

The quick bowler sent his thunderbolts whizzing past batsman and wicket-keeper for boundary byes from every ball of his opening over. The captain said, 'I think I'll rest you for a while.'

'You can't do that,' said the bowler. 'I've just bowled a maiden over.'

'Women like that are a luxury I can't afford at the moment,' replied the captain.

Cycling

'I don't remember *you* ever beating Lance Armstrong,' said the journalist to a cyclist. 'When was that?' 'In the seventh stage of the Tour de France in 2002,' replied the cyclist. 'I beat him over the head with my water bottle – but he still won!'

☺ 'The hardest thing about learning to ride a bicycle is the road!'

Jack and Jill have just climbed Alpe d'Huez on a tandem: 'Phew, that was a tough climb,' said Jack. 'Yeah,' replied Jill, 'good job I kept the brakes on or we'd have slid all the way back down!'

What is the cheapest type of bicycle you can buy? A penny farthing!

'I've really had it with my dog,' said his owner, 'he'll chase anyone on a bicycle.'
   'So what are you going to do, leave him at the dog's home? Give him away? Sell him?' asked his friend. 'No, nothing that drastic,' replied the owner, 'I think I'll just confiscate his bike.'

☺ Did you hear about the cyclist who used Viagra eye drops? They made him look hard!

Mary had a bicycle
She rode it on the grass
Every time the wheel went round
A spoke went up her ...

I was speeding down a narrow, twisting, mountain road. The woman was driving very slowly uphill, honking her horn and shouting at me: 'PIG! PIG!!' I flipped her the finger and shouted back, 'Silly cow!!' Then I collided with the pig!

☺ I like cycling because it keeps me off the street.

'Where's your bicycle, vicar,' I said, (because it was the first time I had seen him walking in ten years!). 'Don't know, I think it might have been stolen, but I will get it back on Sunday,' he replied. 'At my next sermon I will go through the ten commandments. When I get to "Thou shalt not steal," God will sort it out, I've got faith.' The following week, sure enough he was riding the bike again. So I asked him if the ten commandments thing had worked as planned: 'Yes!' he said. 'I got as far as thou shall not commit adultery ...then I suddenly remembered where I left the bike!'

A piece of motorway and piece of dual carriageway are enjoying a drink in the pub. In walks a piece of red tarmac. The bit of motorway whispers to the bit of carriageway, 'Come on, let's drink up and go before the trouble starts. He's a bit of a cyclepath!'

☺ Did you hear the one about the cyclist who didn't know he had diarrhoea until he removed his bike clips!

Three cyclists went for a meal. When the waiter appeared with the bill, the first cyclist said, 'The meal's on me, lads, I'll pay.' The headlines the following day read: 'Cycling ventriloquist found dead in a ditch.'

An over-zealous traffic policeman stopped a vicar on his bicycle. After checking the bike thoroughly and finding nothing wrong he had to let the vicar go. 'You will never arrest me because God is with me wherever I go,' said the vicar. 'Right then,' said the cop, 'I'm nicking you for carrying a passenger on a single-seater vehicle!'

① A cyclist's prayer: 'Dear God. If there is such a thing as reincarnation then please may I return as a ladies' bicycle seat!'

A cyclist was stopped by customs. 'What's in the bags?' asked the officer, pointing to his panniers. 'Sand,' said the cyclist. 'Let me take a look,' said the cop. The cyclist did as he was told, emptied the bags, and proving they contained nothing but sand, refilled the bags, and continued across the border.

A week later, the same thing happened, and continued every week for a year, until one day the cyclist with the sand bags failed to appear.

A few months later, the cop saw the cyclist living it up downtown. 'You sure had us foxed,' said the cop. 'We knew you were smuggling something across the border. I won't say a word – but what was it you were smuggling?

'Bicycles!' the cyclist replied.

① Why can't a bicycle stand up on its own?
Because it's too tyred!

A tired cyclist stuck his thumb out for a lift. After three hours, he hadn't got anyone to stop. Finally, a guy in a sports car pulled over and offered him a ride. But the bike wouldn't fit in the car. The driver got some rope out of the boot and tied it to his bumper. He tied the other end to the bike and told the rider: 'If I go too fast, ring your bell and I'll slow down.'

Everything went well until another sports car blew past them. The driver forgot all about the cyclist and put his foot down. A short distance down the road, they hammered through a speed trap. The cop with the radar gun radioed ahead that he had two sports cars heading his way at over 150 mph. He then relayed, 'And you're not going to believe this, but there's a cyclist behind them ringing his bell to pass!'

① Encyclopaedia is a fetish for very small bicycles.

A pedestrian steps off the kerb into the road without looking and gets knocked down by a passing cyclist.

'You were lucky,' said the cyclist.

'What are you on about! That really hurt!' said the pedestrian.

'Usually I drive a bus!' the cyclist replied.

⊙ What do you call a bicycle built by a chemist?
Bike-carbonate of soda!

A very devout cyclist dies and goes to heaven. St Peter meets him at the gate. First thing the cyclist asks is if there are bicycles in heaven. 'Sure,' says St Peter, 'let me show you,' and he leads the guy into the finest velodrome you can imagine. 'This is great,' the cyclist says. 'It certainly is,' says St Peter. 'You will have a custom bike and the best cycling clothes you've ever seen, and your personal masseuse will always be available.' As they speak a blur streaks by them on the boards riding a gold-plated Cinelli. 'Wow!' the cyclist exclaims. 'That guy was so fast that can only be Eddy Merckx!' 'No,' says St Peter, 'that was God on the bike, he only *thinks* he's Eddy.'

⊙ 'Do you realize you have left your shorts at home?' I said as I rode alongside a rather exposed-looking cyclist. 'Yeah, it was the wife's idea,' he replied. 'Last week I went out without my jersey and finished up with a stiff neck!'

Two cyclists are riding along on a tandem. Suddenly, the one on the front slams on the brakes, gets off and lets the tyres down. The one on the back says: 'Why did you do that?' The one on the front replies: 'My saddle's too high.' The one on the back gets off, loosens his saddle with a spanner and turns it round. The one on the front says: 'What are you doing?' The one on the back replies: 'Look, mate, if you're going to muck about, I'm going home!'

A man stands on top of a building, obviously ready to commit suicide. A negotiator is sent in to talk him down.

'Mate, don't do it, think of your family!' says the negotiator.

'They're all dead,' replies the man.

'Oh. Well, your friends then.'

'Don't have any.'

'Pets? Work colleagues? Associations?'

'Run over, sacked, asked to leave.'

'Well, think of all the great sporting events to look forward too, the World Cup, the Superbowl, the Tour de France!'

'Tour de France, what's that?'

'Jump, ya idiot!'

☉ When I was young I used to pray for a bike. Then I realized that God didn't work that way, so I stole a bike and prayed for forgiveness instead.

A motorist was pottering around the Essex lanes when he was overtaken by a cyclist in a dinner suit apparently going to a function. He sped up and eventually overtook the cyclist. Moments later the cyclist overtook him again. 'Blimey!' exclaimed the motorist, 'he's fast.'

Coming to the open road the driver again overtook the cyclist, but again, moments later, the cyclist overtook him.

'Phew!' said the motorist, 'I wonder how fast he can go?' So he sped up even more, well beyond a reasonable speed for a cyclist. But, again, he was overtaken. Perplexed, the motorist put his boot to the floor and accelerated away from the cyclist at break-neck speed. But incredibly the cyclist passed by even faster than before. Confused and bewildered the motorist slowed to a crawl and strangely so did the cyclist. As they approached each other the cyclist turned around and the motorist wound down his window.

'Thanks for stopping,' said the cyclist, 'I've got me braces caught up in your wing mirror!'

You know you're addicted to cycling if:

- You hear someone had a crash and your first question is: 'How's the bike?'
- You have stopped even trying to explain to your other half why you need more than one bike – you just go and buy another one and figure it will all work out in the divorce settlement.
- You buy your crutches instead of renting.
- You see nothing wrong with discussing the connection between hydration and urine colour.
- You find your Shimano touring shoes to be more comfortable and stylish than your new trainers.
- You refuse to buy a settee because that patch of wall space is taken up by the bike.
- You have more money invested in your bike clothes than in the rest of your combined wardrobe.
- Biker chic means black Lycra, not leather, and a Bianchi, not a Harley.
- 'Four cheeseburgers and four large French fries' is for you.
- You see a fit, tanned, Lycra-clad young thing ride by, and the first thing you check out is her bicycle.
- You empathize with roadkill.
- Despite all that winter weight you put on, you'll take off weight by buying titanium components.
- You use wax on your chain, but not on your legs (girls).
- You use wax on your chain, AND on your legs (boys)
- Your current bike is older than your grown-up children.
- You yell 'Car!' when passing another car, and 'Bump!' when you see a pothole – while driving your car.

- Your bike has more miles on its computer than your car has done.

- You wear your bike shorts swimming.

- Your bikes are worth more than your car.

- You buy a people carrier and immediately remove the rear seats to allow your bike to fit.

- When you move to a new area the first thing you look for is a bike shop.

- You have more bike jerseys than low-cut tops.

- You take your bike along when you shop for a car – just to make sure the bike will fit inside.

- You view crashes as an opportunity to upgrade components.

- You clean your bike more often than your house.

- You spend weeks during the summer spraying arrows on the sides of roads.

- You and your significant other wear identical riding clothes.

- You put your bike in your car and the value of the total package increases by a factor of four.

- You can't seem to get to work by 8.30 a.m., even for important meetings, but you don't have any problems at all meeting your mates at 5.30 a.m. for a hundred-miler.

- You regard inter-gender discussion of your genital pain/size/shape/utility as normal.

- Your New Year's resolution is to put more miles on your bike than your car, and you do.

- You can tell your other half, with a straight face, that it's too hot to mow the lawn and then bike off for a few hours.

- You know your cadence, but you have no idea what your speed is.

- When driving your car you lean over the steering wheel.

- Your kids bring a rear derailleur to 'Show and Tell'.

- Your car sits outside your garage because your garage is full of bikes and cycling gear.

- Your surgeon says you need a heart valve replacement and you ask if you have a choice between Presta and Schrader.

- A measurement of 44–36–40 doesn't refer to the latest *Playboy* centrefold, but that new gear ratio you were considering.

- You wear your heart monitor to bed to make sure you stay within your target zone during any extracurricular activities.

- You experience an unreasonable envy over someone who has bar end extenders longer than yours.

- You're too tired for hanky-panky on a Friday night but pump out a five-hour ride on Saturday.

- There is no time like the present for postponing what you ought to be doing and going bicycling instead.

- You no longer require a hankie to blow your nose.

- You smile at your evening date, and she politely points out that you seem to have bugs in your teeth.

Knock, knock.
Who's there?
Isabel ...
Isabel who?
Is a bell necessary on a bike?

Why couldn't the flower ride her bicycle?
She had no pedals!

CNN is reporting that Lance Armstrong may be stripped of his sixth Tour de France title. In a random check for banned substances, three were found in Armstrong's hotel room. The three substances banned by the French that were found in his hotel room were as follows:

Toothpaste • Deodorant • Soap

The French officials also found several other items which they had never seen before, including a backbone ....

⊙ What do you get if you tie two bikes together?
Siamese Schwinns.

Two Kerrymen were sitting in a pub when the Tour de France came onto the television. The two lads watched the cyclists for a while when one asked, 'Why do they do that?' 'Do what?' said the other. 'Go on them bikes for miles and miles, up and down the hills, round the bends. Day after day, week after week. No matter if it's icy, raining, snowing, hailing ... why would they torture themselves like that?' 'It's all for the money,' says the other. 'The winner gets half a million pounds.' 'I see,' says the first. 'But why do the others do it?'

A young man asks his friend, 'What is the definition of engaged?' His friend replies, 'Well, let me explain by giving you an example. Being engaged is like getting a bicycle for Christmas but not being allowed to ride it until the summer.' 'Oh,' the young man replies, 'Yes, I see. But am I allowed at least to ring the bell while I wait?'

Mother Superior is sitting quietly in the convent garden when her prayers are interrupted by a heated argument between two nuns. She listens for a few minutes, but when it becomes apparent that they won't come to their own solution she closes her book and walks over to them.

'I've heard enough!' she snaps. 'Sister Mary, you may have the bicycle Tuesday and Thursday mornings from nine to noon. Sister Catherine, you may have the bicycle Monday and Wednesday afternoons from one to four. Now not another word or I'll put the seat back on!'

Darts

A man who has never played darts before decides to enter a competition. His first dart hits the double twenty. He throws another and hits double twenty again, but the third dart bounces out and hits a nun who is watching the game. The dart hits her smack between the eyes and kills her stone dead. After a terrible silence the referee calls out, 'One nun dead and eighty!'

A guy teaches his dog to play darts. When the dog is really good he takes him to the pub and bets that his dog can beat anyone there. A player takes on the challenge and gets 140 on his first throw. The dog remains motionless. The guy tells him to throw the darts but the dog just sits there. The guy gives the dog a nudge but no amount of encouragement makes any difference. After he's been laughed out of the pub and lost a tenner on the bet, the guy and the dog are walking home. The guy says, 'Why the hell didn't you throw the darts tonight? We've been practising for months, you could have easily won.' The dog says, 'Yeah, I could have, but think of the odds you'll get next week!'

⚠ A research programme has just been completed into the contents of a pint of beer and it has been discovered that all beer contains female hormones. This of course explains why after ten pints of beer you talk a load of nonsense and can't throw a dart straight!

A man says to his mate, 'You up for a game of darts?' The mate replies, 'OK then.' The man says, 'Nearest to bull starts.' So his mate says, 'Baa!' 'Moo,' the man replies.
He said, 'You're closest!'

A drunk goes into a bar. He is very, very drunk – can hardly stand up. He slurs his way up to the bar and says: 'Hey! Gimme a Martini!' 'No, no,' says the barman. 'You've had too much already.' The drunk spies a dartboard behind the bar. 'Tell you what,' he says. 'If I can throw three bullseyes with that dart set would you let me have the drink?' 'Sure,' says the barman, thinking the man would leave after the little game. He hands the drunk three darts. 'Look out, everybody!' Thud, thud, thud. The drunk throws three quick bullseyes. The barman had never seen anything like that before, but he has to make good on the wager, so he makes a Martini and sets it before the drunk. He then puts a napkin next to the drink and sets a turtle on it. 'What's this?' says the drunk. 'That's a prize for such fine dart throwing,' says the barman. The drunk drinks his Martini, picks up the turtle, puts it in his coat pocket, and leaves.

Well, the next night, the same drunk goes into the same bar. Again, he is hopelessly inebriated; totally drunk. 'Barman,' he says. 'Gimme a Martini!' 'No, no,' says the barman. 'You're too drunk already. Go home.' Again the drunk notices the darts. 'If I can throw three bullseyes would you gimme the Martini?' he asks. The barman thinks, 'He can't be that lucky again. I'll get rid of him.' 'Sure, sure,' he says, handing the darts over. Thud, thud, thud. Three bullseyes.

'Holy cow,' says the barman, and he gives the drunk guy a Martini. Again, he sets a turtle next to it.

'What's this?' asks the drunk. 'That's a prize for being such a good shot.' 'Oh,' says the drunk, and he quaffs his Martini, puts the turtle in his coat pocket, and leaves.

Believe it or not, the very next night the same drunk enters the same bar. 'Gimme a Martini!' he demands. 'No, no,' says the barman. 'You've had enough. Get on home.' Spying the dartboard once more, the drunk says: 'Would throwing three bullseyes prove that I'm not too drunk?'

The barman can't believe that anybody this drunk could possibly hit the dartboard, let alone get three bullseyes. 'OK,' he says, handing over the three darts. The drunk deftly grabs all three darts and tosses them simultaneously. Thump! All three darts land solidly in the bullseye! 'Unbelievable!' says the incredulous barman. True to his word, he prepares a Martini and sets it before the drunk. He then lays a beautiful long-stem rose on the bar next to the cocktail. 'What's this?' asks the drunk. 'That's a special prize for being so good at darts,' says the barman. 'Oh,' says the drunk. 'All out of roast beef on a hard roll, huh?'

☺ I've got nothing against watching a darts match. I just wish my IQ were low enough to enjoy it.

Doris and Fred had started their retirement years and decided to raise some extra cash by advertising for a tenant for their terrace house. After a few days, a young attractive woman applied for the room and explained that she was a model working in a nearby city centre studio for a few weeks and that she would like the room from Mondays to Thursdays, but would pay for the whole week.

Doris showed her the house and they agreed to start straight away. 'There's just one problem,' explained the model. 'Because of my job, I have to take a bath every night, and I notice you don't have a bath.' 'That's not a problem,' replied Doris. 'We have a tin bath out in the yard and we bring it in to the living room in front of the fire and fill it with hot water.' 'What about your husband?' asked the model. 'Oh, he plays darts most weekdays, so he will be out in the evenings,' replied Doris. 'Good,' said the model. 'Now that that's settled, I'll go to the studio and see you tonight.'

That evening, Fred dutifully went to his darts match while Doris prepared the bath for the model. After stripping off, the model stepped into the bath. Doris was amazed to see that she had no pubic hair. The model noticed Doris's staring eyes, so she smiled and explained that it is part of her job to shave herself, especially when modelling swimwear or underclothes. Later when Fred returned, Doris related this oddity and he did not believe her. 'It's true, I tell you!' said Doris. 'Look, if you don't believe me, tomorrow night I'll leave the curtains slightly open and you can peek in and see for yourself.' The next night, Fred left as usual and Doris prepared the bath for the model. As the model stepped naked into the bath, Doris stood behind her. Doris looked towards the curtains and pointed towards the model's naked pubic area. Then she lifted up her skirt and, wearing no panties, pointed to her own. Later Fred returned and they retired to bed. 'Well, do you believe me now?' she asked Fred. 'Yes,' he replied. 'I've never seen anything like it in my life. But why did you lift up your skirt and show yourself?' 'Just to show you the difference,' answered Doris. 'But I guess you've seen me millions of times.'

'Yes,' said Fred, 'I have – but the rest of the dart team hadn't.'

⊙ I used to play darts with the wife until her head got blunt.

A man goes into a strange pub and starts chatting to some of the local darts players when they ask him if he wants a game. He says, 'I have never played a game of darts before but I will give it a go if you tell me what to do.' After playing for about an hour he has not lost a single game and has hit some fantastic shots. One of the players says to him, 'I thought you had never played before?' The man replies, 'No I haven't, but there are a lot of flies in my flat and I have got some old darts which I throw at them and pin them to the wall.' 'No wonder you are so good then if you can do that. But doesn't it make a mess on the wall?' 'Not really,' replies the man, 'because I only pin them by their back legs.'

⊙ I got 501 in one throw the other day ...I chucked a hedgehog!

Extreme sports

Two Irishmen walk into a pet shop in Dingle. They walk over to the bird section and Gerry says to Paddy, 'Dat's dem.' The owner comes over and asks if he can help them.

'Yeah, we'll take four of dem dere little budgies in dat cage up dere,' says Gerry.

The owner puts the budgies in a cardboard box. Paddy and Gerry pay for the birds, leave the shop and get into Gerry's truck to drive to the top of the Connor Pass.

At the Connor Pass , Gerry looks down at the 1,000-foot drop and says, 'Dis looks like a grand place.' He takes two birds out of the box, puts one on each shoulder and jumps off the cliff. Paddy watches as the budgies fly off and Gerry falls all the way to the bottom, killing himself stone dead. Looking down at the remains of his best pal, Paddy shakes his head and says, 'Feck dat. Dis budgie jumping is too dangerous for me!'

Moments later, Seamus arrives up at Connor Pass. He's been to the pet shop too and walks up to the edge of the cliff carrying another cardboard box in one hand and a shotgun in the other. 'Hi, Paddy, watch dis,' Seamus says. He takes a parrot from the box and lets him fly free. He then throws himself over the edge of the cliff with the gun. Paddy watches as halfway down Seamus takes the gun and shoots the parrot. Seamus continues to plummet down and down until he hits the bottom and breaks every bone in his body. Paddy shakes his head and says, 'And I'm never trying dat parrotshooting either!'

Paddy is just getting over the shock of losing two friends when Sean appears. He's also been to the pet shop and is carrying a cardboard box out of which he pulls a chicken. Sean then takes the chicken by its legs and hurls himself off the cliff and disappears down and down until he hits a rock and breaks his spine. Once more Paddy shakes his head. 'Feck dat, lads. First dere was Gerry with his budgie jumping, den Seamus parrotshooting ... And now Sean and his hengliding!'

There are two guys who don't speak Spanish but really loved bungee jumping, so they go down to Sonora and they open a bungee-jumping business on a cliff over the town of Guaymas. Well, the first time one took a practice jump, he went over fine, but when he sprang back up he was all covered in scratches. His friend obviously freaked out, but the man went back down before he could help him. When he flew back up, the scratches had progressed to bruises, but his friend on top again couldn't catch him. Finally, on the third spring back, his friend nabbed him. He was covered in open, bleeding wounds.

'What happened?' his friend asks him. 'Was the cord too long?'

'No, the cord was fine,' the leaper said. 'It was terrible. There were these gangs down there and they were screaming and yelling and every time I'd get to the end of the cord, they'd hit me with sticks!'

'What were they screaming?' his friend asked.

'I don't know, I could only make out one word. What's a *piñata*, anyway?'

(!) Yo mama's so fat when she bungee-jumps she brings down the bridge as well.

A blonde, a redhead and a brunette are all skateboarding and bragging about their best tricks. The brunette says, 'I can do a double impossible and a misty.' The redhead says, 'That's nothing. I can do a 1080 flip off a quarter pipe, then do a double double and land it without falling.' Then the blonde says, 'I don't know what the big deal is with all of you guys, I can do all those with no hands!'

(!) Gliders do it and can keep it up all day.

(!) Hang-gliders do it on their own.

Fencing

⊙ Fencing jokes? What's the point?

A pair of fencing coaches, a man and his wife, are talking, and she asks that dreaded question, 'Darling, if I die, will you date?' 'Well, maybe,' he replied, 'I don't know.' 'You should,' she said, 'I'd want you to be happy.'

'Well, if you say so, I guess I will,' he agreed. 'Would she be a fencer?' she then asked. 'Well, she would have to be, to keep up with me,' he said.

'Will she use my gear?' she asked finally. 'No dear, she'll be left-handed!'

⊙ How many epeeists does it take to change a light bulb? Two, but they have difficulty getting both bulbs in at the same time.

How many sabreurs does it take to change a light bulb? Eight: Two to charge at each other screaming, one to call the halt and four to abstain from making any claims. The eighth guy runs and gets someone to change the light bulb.

⊙ How many sabreurs does it take to change a light bulb? None. Sabreurs aren't afraid of the dark.

How many foilists does it take to change a light bulb? Trick question; changing light bulbs is too practical for foilists.

⊙ Fencers always do it with protection.

☺ How many classical fencers does it take to change a light bulb? Five, one to change the bulb and the other four to complain because it's electric.

Three male fencers (one of each weapon) participated in a group wedding to save money, but they all had different approaches once they retired to their respective honeymoon suites. The foilist turned on two lights (one of them red, one of them white) for the mood and slowly approached his wife in bed, and accelerated at the last moment. The saber fencer only left on a red light, threw his wife down on the bed and jumped on top screaming. The epeeist left the lights off, donned his protective gear, waited for his wife to initiate contact, and at the last second touched her first. Then, he wondered why the light didn't come on and demanded a third party check his equipment.

Fishing

A fisherman was sat by the riverbank when a snake wriggled by with a frog in its mouth. Desperate for a catch, the fisherman thought he could try the frog as bait, so he pinned the snake down with a stick and tried to get the frog out if its mouth, but the snake wouldn't let go. Realizing that he needed to distract the snake into opening its mouth, the fisherman reached into his pack and took out the small bottle of whisky he kept there for those cold days, and poured a bit on the snake's head. Immediately the snake opened its mouth to lick the whisky off, and the fisherman promptly took the frog out. The snake wriggled off, and the fisherman stuck the frog on his hook and cast out his line, only to feel a nudge on his leg. Looking down he saw the snake was back, with another frog in its mouth!

☺ The vicar was taking Sunday school: 'Well, Billy, which Bible story do you like best?'
'The one about the man who just loafs and fishes.'

Aware that the fishing industry was in decline, Jethro and Barnaby decided to diversify into tourism. They gave their trawler a lick of paint, and advertised scenic tours of the coast. Their first booking was a party from the Women's Institute. On the morning of their maiden voyage, a panic-stricken Jethro approached Barnaby. 'What are we going to do?' he asked. 'We've all these women comin' aboard and we ain't got no toilet.'

'Well,' relied Barnaby, 'there's polite ways of saying these things. Like you can use the expression "relieve yourself".'

'OK, got it,' replied Jethro. Later that day the ladies arrived and Barnaby asked them if there were any questions. One lady raised her hand. 'Where is the bathroom?' she enquired. Jethro stepped confidently forward: 'Ladies, please be aware that if you wish to relieve yourself, you'll have to piss over the side.'

Dave gets a new boat and decides to invite Steve and Dan out for a day's fishing. They put out to sea and drop anchor to start fishing, when Dan asks: 'Do you mind if I fish off the left side of the boat?' The others agree to this, and start to fish off the right side. All day they catch nothing, while Dan on his side pulls out fish after fish.

A few weeks later they go out in the boat again, and when they drop anchor Dave asks Dan if he wants to fish off the left side again. 'No thanks,' he replies, 'I'll fish off the right today if you don't mind.' Once again, the others fish on the opposite side of the boat to Dan, and, once again they catch nothing while it's like the sea of Galilee on his side of the boat. Eventually Dave and Steve can take it no more, and ask Dan his secret of knowing which side of the boat to fish off.

'Well, boys,' says Dan, 'it's like this. When I wake up in the morning I look over at the wife. If she's sleeping on her left side, then I fish off the left side of the boat. And if she's sleeping on her right, then I know that the right side is the one to go for that day. Simple.'

'And what if she's on her back?' asks Dave.

'If she's on her back,' replies Dan, 'then I don't go fishing.'

(!) A fly fisherman was on the bank, despondently flicking his line over the water when a passer-by came up. 'Having any luck?' he enquired. 'It looks like a good river for trout.' 'It is,' replied the fisherman. 'It's so good that they won't leave it.'

Two men were having a pint when another bloke walked in carrying a big sack. One of the men nudged his friend: 'That's the bloke who caught the monster cod. Oi, mate, how big was that cod you landed?' The man with the sack came over, 'Well it was too big to fit on my lorry, so I hacked its head off as proof of its size.'

'You mean that big lump in the sack is its head?'

'Nah. I couldn't carry the whole head. This is one of its eyes.'

A fisherman was boasting in his pub about an enormous fish he'd caught. 'It was massive,' he bragged, 'every fisherman for miles around had tried to get him, but he'd always broken free.'

'Did you eat it?' asked one of the crowd.

'Nah. He was so full of hooks I sold it for scrap.'

A kind stranger passed a miserable-looking old man fishing on a canal side in the hot sun. 'How many have you got today, mate?' he asked. 'None,' the old man replied sadly. Taking pity on him, the stranger invited him to a nearby pub for a pint to raise his spirits. Seated at the table, the stranger asked, 'Tell me really, how many have you caught today?'

'You're the fifth,' replied the old man slyly.

① Scientists have discovered that physical factors can determine the capability for truthfulness in anglers. They found that long-armed fishermen were much more likely to lie than short-armed ones.

A man was fishing in a puddle of rainwater when a passer-by approached. 'You'll never catch anything in there,' he scoffed. 'What are you hoping to catch, anyway?'

'Trout,' replied the angler.

'You're mad,' laughed the passer-by, 'and anyway, the season's closed for trout.'

'Is it? I'm glad you told me! I'll put a bigger hook on and go for bream.'

A fisherman, fed up with being accused of always exaggerating, bought a pair of scales to weigh his fish. For months he insisted on weighing everything he caught in front of witnesses. Some months later his wife gave birth to their baby at home. The doctor wanted to weigh the new infant, so he borrowed the fisherman's scales. He placed the baby on them, and read the numbers with a puzzled look. 'Are these scales accurate?' he asked the proud father. 'One hundred per cent,' he replied. 'Well,' said the doctor, 'then I'm pleased to tell you that you have a healthy son weighing just a shade under seventy-five pounds.'

☺ I was glad when one fish got away. There wouldn't have been room in the boat for both of us.

A man went on a fishing holiday to Scotland. Every day the menu was the same – salmon for breakfast, salmon for lunch, salmon for dinner. After a week he'd had enough and decided to leave. As he went to check out the clerk noticed he still had another week booked. 'Why are you leaving so soon?' he asked.

'With the food I've been getting,' replied the man, 'I've got to hurry upriver to spawn!'

A man was invited by his new neighbours for dinner. Above the mantelpiece he noticed a large stuffed shark. 'I see you've noticed my display,' said the host, 'it's quite a story. I was out fishing on my own when this beast took my bait. I played it for hours, and it dragged my boat right out to sea. In the end I landed him, but he thrashed around so much I thought he'd capsize us. I can't swim a stroke, so I had to kill him with my bare hands. It was either him or me.'

'Well,' replied the guest, 'I must say the fish makes the better decoration.'

Len was boring everyone in the bar with his fishing stories: 'Did I tell you about the giant mackerel I once caught? I fought it for seven hours, and it topped the scales at two hundred pounds.'

'That's nothing,' replied Fred. 'I once caught a ship's lantern that was over two hundred years old. When I hauled it out, I couldn't believe it. The candle was still alight after all that time under water!'

'That's ridiculous,' exclaimed Len. 'You can't expect us to believe that.'

'I'll tell you what,' replied Fred. 'You take one hundred and ninety-five pounds off your mackerel and I'll blow out my candle.'

A tourist was fishing in the outback of Australia. Conditions were terrible – hot and dry, the river barely a trickle. The man despaired of catching anything. Suddenly, a man sitting further down the bank called out: 'Fish on their way!'

'How do you know?" asked the tourist.

'You can see their dust cloud!' replied the man.

An angler got a licence to fish on a coveted piece of prime riverbank. The only condition was that he was allowed to catch just one fish per day. But when the day came the fish were biting and he just couldn't help himself and he shot past his limit. On the way home he was stopped by the inspector, who quickly found out that he had taken twenty more fish than he was allowed. A court hearing was duly arranged, and when the fisherman came before the magistrate he pleaded guilty. He was fined five hundred pounds and the magistrate asked him if he had anything to say.

'Yes, your honour. Can I have a copy of the court order to show my friends?'

☉ What's the definition of a fishing rod? A stick with a worm at one end and an idiot at the other.

A man was fishing on a quiet riverbank when another chap came and stood close behind him. He tried to ignore him, but after a while he became annoyed. Turning round he asked: 'Would you mind moving on? You've been stood there for two hours. Why don't you get your own rod if you're so interested, instead of watching me?'

'Oh no,' said the man. 'I haven't got the patience for fishing!'

A fisherman was telling his friend about a recent trip: 'It was great. I got one that was about ten inches.'

'Ten inches? That's nothing. I've caught loads which measured more than that.'

'What, between the eyes?'

Two men were preparing to go sea fishing. While one got the boat ready, the other popped back to his friend's house to pick up some extra tackle. When he got there, he saw through a window his friend's wife in bed with another man. He returned to the boat and told his friend he had bad news. He took the news calmly. 'I thought you'd be more upset,' said his friend.

'Upset? When you said you had bad news, I thought you were going to say the cod weren't biting!'

The parable of the fisherman

Behold the fisherman; mighty are his preparations.

He riseth up before the sun, and setteth all his household in commotion.

He goeth forth filled with hope, with companions like unto himself.

His labours are great; small indeed are his rewards.

Long after the sun has gone down he returneth home smelling of strong drink;
the truth is not in him.

What profiteth a man if he possesses the charity of St Peter and the patience
of Job

If, in the end, the fish are smarter than he?

Frank was telling Stan about a top spot he'd found to go fishing.

'First, you go up the old lane. Do you know it?'

'Oh yeah.'

'Right, so you carry on until you come to a sign that says "Strictly no Trespassers". Go straight past that until you come to a sign saying "Danger – keep out!" Ignore that until you come to a river where there's a sign saying "Absolutely NO Fishing".'

'What about it?'

'That's the place.'

Paul had returned from a fishing trip, and was telling his friends:

'The fish were so big, every time I pulled one out the lake level fell by three inches. In the end I caught so many that the boat was high and dry. I had to throw a few back just to get afloat again.'

Pat and Mick hired a boat and went fishing. They found a great spot, pulling in fish all afternoon. When it was time to go home, they decided to mark the spot so they could return the next day. When they had given the boat back Mick asked Pat: 'Sure, did you make a mark on that spot of ours?'

'I did,' said Pat. 'I put a chalk mark on the side of our boat.'

'You eejit,' said Mick. 'That's no use at all. What if we don't get the same boat tomorrow?'

A young boy came home in floods of tears after a day out fishing with his father. 'What's the matter?' asked his mum.

'Dad caught a great big fish,' sobbed the boy, 'but just as he was about to catch it in his net it broke the line and swam off.'

'That's no reason to cry,' said his mum, 'you should have laughed instead!'

'I did.'

☺ He caught a pike that was so big he took a picture of it and the negative weighed five pounds.

'I caught a twenty-pound salmon last week.'

'Were there any witnesses?'

'Yes. If there weren't, it would have been forty pounds.'

A trout fisherman was at it for two weeks before he landed his first fish. He sent off a telegram to his wife:

'I've got one. It's a beauty. Weighs eight pounds. Be home Saturday.'

The next day a telegram was delivered to his hotel from his wife:

'I've got one. It's a beauty. Weighs seven pounds. Looks like you. Come home at once.'

☺ I catch deformed fish. The ones I get always have their heads too close to their tails.

John and Steve stopped at Keith's place. 'John and I are going out on the Channel fishing. Do you want to be in it?'

'Fishing? Anyone who goes out fishing on a day like this ought to be certified. It will probably blow like the devil and a man will be as sick as a dog, get no fish, and get soaked to the skin into the bargain. Probably finish up with pneumonia or something.'

'Well, if you feel like that about it we'll be going alone. See you.'

'Hang on. What's the idea? Are you two trying to sneak off without me?'

A fisherman was bragging about a monster of a fish he caught. A friend broke in and chided, 'Yeah, I saw a picture of that fish and he was all of six inches long.' 'Yeah,' said the proud fisherman, 'but after battling for three hours, a fish can lose a lot of weight.'

An inspector from the Fisheries Department boarded a boat that had just come in.

'I want to inspect your catch.'

'We only got the one fish – this fifteen-pound cod. It was a funny thing. When we opened the cod we found it had swallowed this two-pound mackerel. But that isn't all. Inside the mackerel was this whiting.'

The inspector was not impressed.

'Sorry, but I'll want your name and address. That whiting is undersize.'

☺ Two goldfish were swimming in a bowl. 'Do you believe in God?' one suddenly asked the other. 'Of course,' it replied. 'Who do you think changes our water every day?'

The local angling club was having its annual dinner and presentation of trophies. When the members arrived they were surprised to see all the chairs spaced out two metres apart. One of them said to the caterer:

'That's a strange way to arrange seats for a party.'

'We always do it like that so that members can do full justice to their stories.'

A group fishing out in the sea struck a patch of rough weather. One of the men was so sick he lost his false teeth over the side.

Later on as they were cleaning their catch in a sheltered inlet, another member of the party, for a joke, took out his own false teeth and pretended to find them in a big bass he was cleaning. He passed them to the first man. He studied them closely and threw them over the side.

'Not mine. Some other poor sod must've lost them.'

Steve and Keith were out fishing in a boat when Keith had the first bite of the day. As the fish tugged the line he said:

'I think it's a big pike or a carp.'

After he played it for a couple of minutes he told Steve: 'Maybe it's a perch, the way it's darting around.'

'No, I think it might be a tench.'

But when he landed it: 'A miserable roach!'

It was the only bite they had, and after an hour or so they headed back to the jetty. One of their friends asked them:

'Did you have any luck?' Steve laughed and held up their single fish:

'Keith caught five different kinds of fish – pike, carp, perch, tench and roach. This is it.'

☺ Did you hear about the fisherman who used chewing tobacco for bait? When the fish would surface to spit it out, he'd knock them on the head with a stick.

All along the pier there were fishermen hauling in fish. Among them was a young schoolboy fishing with a bent pin and a ball of string. Beside him was a fish weighing over ten pounds. His mate came down to the pier and asked him about his catch:

'What kind of fish is it?'

'I don't know, but that man over there told me it was a bloody fluke.'

The bailiff confronted two men camped by a river. 'Who owns that line set in the river down there?'

'I do.'

'Don't you know that fishing is prohibited in this area?'

'Well, if you must know, I'm not fishing. I just tied a bottle of beer to the end of a line and left it in the river to cool.'

'Is that so? In all my experience, it's the first time I've ever seen a bottle of beer swimming around in circles and coming up every few minutes for air.'

Two men were talking. 'Just how big was that monster pike that got away from you?' asked one. 'Well,' replied his friend, 'I had fifty yards of new line on my reel. I dropped the hook over the side and the pike grabbed the bait and took off upstream. The last of the line ran off the reel just as the bream's tail passed the boat.'

Two Irishmen were holidaying in Scotland. After a few days they realized they had spent overspent on whisky. They were hungry and short of cash. Walking around they saw two Scotsmen on a bridge. One was holding the other over the side by the ankles. When they asked what this meant, it was explained to them that the two men were tickling trout. Sure enough, a few minutes later the man below pulled out a good-sized fish.

'Let's find a bridge of our own, Colm, and we'll try our luck.'

Presently they found a bridge and Patrick held Colm over the side by the ankles. He was there twenty minutes and having no luck when suddenly he called to Patrick:

'Jaysus. Pull me up, Pat. Quick.'

'Have you got a beauty, Colm?'

'No, I haven't, but there's a great train coming!'

After the wedding the young couple drove off on their honeymoon. Just past the river they stopped and the groom went off through the trees.

After an hour his bride went looking for him. He was fishing.

'What's going on?' she demanded.

'Are you nagging already?'

⊙ There are two types of fishermen: those who fish for sport, and those who catch something.

Back from holiday a fisherman was telling his neighbour about a big carp he caught while he was away.

'Thirteen pounds it was, and took me more than two hours to land.'

His little daughter chimed in: 'Yes, and Daddy was so good. He gave it to my kitten to eat.'

It was cold and wet and windy. Two men met in the street.

'Where're you going?'

'Football.'

'You're mad. In weather like this? Why don't you come with me?'

'Where are you off to?'

'Fishing.'

⊙ Two brothers were preparing to go fishing. 'How do you get your little brother to dig up so many worms?' the father asked the eldest boy. 'Oh that's easy, Dad. For every ten he gets I let him eat one.'

A man returned from an illicit weekend with his mistress.

His wife asked: 'How was the fishing trip?'

'Very good,' he replied. 'We caught quite a few but gave them to the local children's home. By the way, dear, you forgot to pack the flask of brandy and my aftershave.'

His wife looked at him icily: 'I put them in your tackle box.'

One moonlit night the rector, the vicar and the Catholic priest were fishing from a small boat. Presently the rector stood up.

'Excuse me, gentlemen. I have to answer a call of nature.'

Stepping out the right side of the boat, he walked across the water to the bank six metres away. After a time he returned the same way.

Then the vicar also said that he would answer a call of nature. He stepped out the right side of the boat, walked across the water to the bank, and returned in the same way a few minutes later.

This was too much for the Catholic priest, who decided that he couldn't be left out.

He stepped out the left side of the boat and at once sank out of sight. The vicar said ruefully to the rector: 'We mustn't have told him about that sandbank.'

A sailor was talking to some tourists by the harbour. 'I keep telling my kids not to go fishing here,' he said. 'The cod there are so big the little blighters can't hold them. On Tuesday I lost one about three foot six long, and yesterday I lost one more than four feet long.'

'My word,' exclaimed the visitor. 'It's really bad luck losing fish that size.'

'Fish nothing! It's kids I'm losing!'

A fisherman on holiday in the country got up very early and headed for the river. In the empty town square he heard a clock strike four and thought to himself: 'So much for these country people being early risers. The place is deserted.'

Then he saw a farm hand and called out: 'Fine morning.'

'Yes, but it wasn't half cold first thing.'

A boy's parents gave him the job of minding his four-year-old sister while they went shopping. He decided to take her fishing with him. His parents returned to find him upset. They asked him what was wrong.

'I'll never take her again. I didn't catch a thing.'

'Why didn't you explain to her that you didn't want any noise? She'd have been quiet.'

'That wasn't the trouble. She ate all the bait!'

⊙ Did you hear about the professor who collected fishing stories? Every angling club in the country welcomed him with open arms.

A fisherman in north Australia caught an enormous groper. He started to clean it, but dropped his knife down the monster's throat. He crawled in after it and was feeling around when a man came up beside him on horseback.

'Whatcha doin' there?'

'Tryin' to find me knife.'

'You've got no hope, mate. I've been in here a week tryin' to find a herd of sheep.'

A man went into a fishing tackle shop.

'You know all that expensive fishing tackle you sold me when I was in here last time?' he asked the salesman.

'Yes, sir,' nodded the assistant

'You know you told me it was well worth all the extra money because of all the fish I was going to catch with it?'

'Yes.'

'Well, would you mind telling me again? I'm getting discouraged.'

A man invited two of his mates home to show them a special surprise. As he brought them in they noticed his house was a bit dilapidated.

'Your fence is in bad shape,' one remarked.

'Yes. The whole house is practically falling to pieces,' he cheerfully agreed. 'You know how hard it is to get anything done these days. Building material is so scarce and everything.'

'What's this surprise you want to show us?' asked his other friend.

'Out here in the back garden. Look at that.'

He showed them a spanking new fishing boat.

'Isn't she a beauty? Thirty feet long, all the latest fittings. I built every bit of her myself.'

⊙ Give a man a fish and he will eat for a day. Teach him how to fish, and he will sit in a boat and drink beer all day.

Les's launch was stuck on a sandbar and he couldn't make it to his moorings. He called out to a couple of his mates in a dinghy:

'Can you stop at my place and tell the missus I won't be home until the tide comes in? I'm stuck on the sandbar.'

'OK.'

On the way home they stopped at Les's place and told his wife:

'Les won't be home for some hours. He's stuck over the bar.'

'That's nothing unusual,' she replied. 'Which pub is he at this time?'

(!) I'm not saying the water in that river is polluted, but if you catch a fish, he thanks you.

A man took his family on a holiday down the bay. With them was his wife's mother. Two days after they arrived, the old lady went missing.

The wife was very upset but her husband reassured her:

'She's probably staying the night with friends. Don't worry. If she doesn't turn up tomorrow I'll see the police.'

But the old lady didn't turn up that night, or the next day either.

Accordingly the husband went to the police station. He gave a description of his mother-in-law and the clothes she was wearing. When he had it all down, the sergeant said:

'I'm sorry to have to tell you this, but this morning we found your mother-in-law floating in the water with twelve large crabs attached to her.'

'Oh dear. The wife's going to be very upset about this.'

'What would you like us to do with her?'

'You have six, and I'll have six, and set her again tonight!'

A boastful fisherman walked into the pub. 'How did the trip go?' called one of his acquaintances at the bar. 'Not much good. We caught only one fish,' he replied.

'What did you do with it?' asked the man at the bar, incredulous that he wasn't hearing the usual tall stories.

'It was so small we got a couple of other blokes to help us throw it back.'

Two men were swapping improbable fishing stories. 'I was fishing off the pier one time when a little minnow about the size of your finger grabbed onto the hook. Next a big cod came and grabbed hold of the minnow,' said one. 'Go on,' replied his friend. 'OK. Then, just as I was reeling in the cod, a big shark came and fastened onto it.'

'Did you land the shark?'

'No. The bloody minnow let go.'

A clergyman with his two beautiful daughters was walking along the riverbank. They came upon an angler and, after exchanging pleasantries, the clergyman said:

'I too am a fisherman, but I fish for men.'

The angler eyed the girls appreciatively: 'I imagine you catch quite a few, judging by the bait you're using.'

☉ What do fish and women have in common? They both stop shaking their tails after you catch them!

An angler was telling his friend: 'I had a funny dream last night. I dreamed I was going up to heaven on a ladder. The bottom of the ladder was right in our angling club. The members who were climbing up had to put chalk marks on the side of the ladder for all the tall stories they'd told about the fish they'd caught. I looked up and saw another member coming down in a tearing hurry.'

'Who was it?'

'It was you. You said you were coming down for more chalk.'

Out in a fishing boat one of the men asked: 'Would you know how to tell your position if you were out here in a thick fog, with no compass, no sun, and a slack tide?'

'No. How?'

'You cut three feet off your best fishing line and tie your watch on the end. Then you swing it round your head three times and let 'er go.'

'How does that tell your position?'

'Because your watch would go west.'

Jim had an awful day fishing on the lake, sitting in the blazing sun all day without catching a single fish. On his way home, he stopped at the supermarket and ordered four catfish. He told the fish salesman, 'Pick four large ones out and throw them at me, will you?' 'Why do you want me to throw them at you?' 'Because I want to tell my wife that I caught them.' 'OK, but I suggest that you take the trout.' 'But why?' 'Because your wife came in earlier today and said that if you came by, I should tell you to take trout. She prefers that for supper tonight.'

A fisherman was selling his catch on the quayside. A woman walked past and stopped.

'You've got a good business here. You're making a lot of money. How is it that you're so clever?' she enquired.

'Because of the special fish I eat,' replied the fisherman.

'Can I buy some some?' she asked.

'Of couse.' He sold her the fish. Later she came back.

'That special fish you sold me at such a price. When I ate it I discovered it was only herring.'

'See? It's working already.'

☉ There are two periods when fishing is fun: before you get there and after you leave.

An angler was going off for a weekend's fishing. His wife said to him:

'Just in case you don't catch any fish to eat, take along this packet of sausages.'

'How do you cook them?'

'It's easy. The same as you do your fish.'

The weekend was not a success. The fisherman didn't get a touch. He was bad-tempered and hungry when he got home.

'Those sausages you gave me wouldn't feed the cat. By the time I skinned them and gutted them and cleaned them there wasn't enough left for tea.'

A poacher from the next town was in the pub. 'Don't put a net into this river,' the locals warned him. 'The bailiff here hates nets. He'll blow off your head with his shotgun if he catches you at it.'

The poacher thought he knew better. Early next morning he began pulling in his net when a voice behind him boomed:

'Drop that net, put your hands up and don't move or I'll blow your head off.'

The poacher did as he was bid and asked: 'Who might you be?'

'I'm the local bailiff, sonny.'

'Well that's a relief,' said the poacher. 'I was afraid you might be the owner of the net!'

The local poacher approached a farmer.

'Have a look at this trout I just caught. You can have it for the price of two pints, and I'll clean it for you for another fifty pence.'

'OK. You can clean it, but I want you to leave the eyes in.'

'Leave the eyes in? What for?'

'So it'll see me through the weekend.'

⊙ Where does a fish keep his money?
In the riverbank!

A husband and wife were game fishing together. The husband hooked a big marlin, but as he reeled it in it became tangled with a large lump of driftwood. He yelled to his wife: 'Quick! Dive in and free the line before the sharks get to him!'

A woman walking along a beach came upon a man fast asleep with a fishing rod gripped in his hand. The line was jerking so she woke him up.

'Wake up, mister. You've got a bite.'

'Oh, would you mind reeling it in for me please?' She did this and landed his fish for him.

'Could you put some fresh bait on the hook and cast it out for me, please?' She grinned and baited his hook.

'A man as lazy as you should be married and have a son to help him.'

'That's an idea. I wonder where I can find a pregnant girl.'

An Irishman went into the fishing tackle department. 'Do you have any left-handed fish hooks, please? I'm left-handed.'

'We'll go through them and see.'

The assistant brought out every box of hooks that he had and examined each one closely. By the time he finished the counter was covered with fish hooks.

'I'm afraid you're out of luck, sir,' said the assistant at last. 'There don't seem to be any left-handed fish hooks in stock at all.'

'Never mind,' said the Irishman. 'Give us a couple of dozen of those. I'll just have to fish off the left-hand side of the boat.'

A keen angler had driven by a lake many times and had seen some other anglers about, so he decided to give his luck a try. On his first day of fishing he had no luck at all but noticed that another fisherman near him that was scooping in one after another. He had to know the secret. 'Excuse me, sir, but would you mind telling me what sort of bait you are using?' he asked.

The other man looked around, a bit embarrassed. 'Well, I am a surgeon, and quite by accident I found that human tonsil works very well.'

He thanked the surgeon, thought about what sort of bait to try next time, and left.

The next day he returned to the lake, tried a different bait and still had no luck. Just as the day before, there was yet a different man reeling in fish after fish. 'Excuse me,' he asked, 'but could you suggest a bait that I could try?'

'Well, I can, but I am not sure it will do you any good. I'm a surgeon and I am using a bit of human appendix.'

'Hmm,' he thought. It seemed that the fish in this lake would require a little more effort than normal. He left, willing to give the lake one more try.

On the third day, he still had no luck. As was usual, there was yet another man near him bringing in fish left and right. He wanted to confirm what he already knew. 'Excuse me sir, but are you a doctor?'

'No, I am a rabbi,' replied the man.

One day while driving home from his fishing trip in the pouring rain, a man got a flat tyre outside a monastery. A monk came out and invited the man inside to have dinner and to spend the night. The stranded motorist gladly accepted the monk's offer, and offered the monk the fish he had caught as a thank you.

That evening the man had a wonderful dinner of fish and chips. He decided to compliment the chef.

Entering the kitchen, the man asked the cook, 'Are you the fish fryer?'

'No,' the chef replied, 'I'm the chip monk.'

⊕ What is the definition of a 'live bait'?
The biggest fish you will handle all day!

Two fishermen were talking.

'I love fishing. The fresh air. The solitude. Man against nature. Matching wits with the cunning creatures of the deep. The thrill of playing and landing your worthy adversary. Tell me. Why do you fish?'

'My son's learning the violin.'

⊙ What can you do in radiation-contaminated rivers? Nuclear fission.

An Irishman gets up really early in the morning to go ice fishing. He goes out onto the ice with his tent, his pick and his fishing rod, and starts to pick at the ice.

Then he hears a big booming voice: 'THERE ARE NO FISH UNDER THE ICE.'

The guy looks around and then starts to pick at the ice again. Then he hears the voice again: 'THERE ARE NO FISH UNDER THE ICE.'

Now the guy is getting a little edgy. He looks up towards the sky and thinks to himself, 'God, is that you?'

There is no answer, so he starts picking again. The voice bellows again: 'THERE ARE NO FISH UNDER THE ICE.'

Then the guy yells, 'God, is that you?'

The voice answered, 'NO. IT'S THE MANAGER OF THE ICE RINK.'

⊙ Bill: Hey Phil, are you going fishing?
Phil: Yeah!
Bill: You got worms?
Phil: Yeah, but I'm still going!

A priest was walking along the cliffs at Dover when he came upon two locals pulling another man ashore on the end of a rope. 'That's what I like to see,' said the priest. 'A man helping his fellow man.' As he was walking away, one local remarked to the other, 'Well, he doesn't know the first thing about shark fishing.'

A couple of young guys were fishing at their special pond off the beaten track when out of the bushes jumped the bailiff! Immediately, one of the boys threw his rod down and started running through the woods and hot on his heels came the bailiff. After about a half-mile, the guy stopped and stooped over with his hands on his thighs to catch his breath and the bailiff finally caught up to him. 'Let's see your fishing licence, boy!' the bailiff gasped. With that, the lad pulled out his wallet and gave the bailiff a valid fishing licence. 'Well, son,' said the bailiff. 'You must be about as stupid as a box of rocks! You don't have to run from me if you have a valid licence!' 'Yes sir,' replied the young man. 'But my friend back there, well, he doesn't have one …'

(!) What is the definition of a 'Treble Hook'? A hook that trebles the odds of you catching a fish but quadruples the odds of you getting it caught in your thumb.

A man is ice-fishing on a frozen lake and not having much luck. A small boy comes along, bores a hole in the ice a short distance away and starts fishing himself. After a few minutes the boy catches a huge fish. A few minutes later another large fish is caught, then another, then another. The man is mystified and, after the boy has caught his fifth fish, he goes over to investigate. 'Hey, son,' says the man. 'What's your secret?' The boy replies, 'Yu haf tu kip yr wrms wrm.' 'What was that?' says the man. The boy spits into a bucket, 'I said, "You have to keep your worms warm."'

A man walks into a fishmonger's carrying a salmon under his arm. 'Do you make fishcakes?' he asks. 'Of course,' says the fishmonger. 'Oh good,' says the man. 'It's his birthday.'

A man is taking part in a pub quiz. As a tiebreaker he has to name three fish that start with the letter 'K'. The man thinks for a moment then says, 'Killer shark, kippered haddock, and Kilmarnock.' The question master says, 'What do you mean? Kilmarnock isn't a fish.' The man replies, 'Yes, it is. It's a place.'

�) Did you hear about the Newfie who went ice-fishing? He caught fifty pounds of ice and his wife drowned trying to cook it.

�) How many Newfies does it take to go ice-fishing? Four. One to cut a hole in the ice and three to push the boat through.

Two men go on a week-long fishing trip and spend a fortune renting their gear and accommodation. All week they fish but don't catch a thing. On their last day they finally catch one small fish but then have to pack up and go home. On the drive back both men are very depressed. One turns to the other and says, 'Do you realize that one lousy fish we caught cost us fifteen hundred pounds?' The other man perks up and says, 'Really? Then it's a good thing we didn't catch any more!'

�) Fisherman to friend: 'I've caught as many as 15 trout in an hour. Can you say the same?' Friend: 'Yes. But not with a straight face.'

Old fishermen never die, they simply smell that way.

Football

What's the difference between a PG Tips monkey and a Scottish footballer? Some people can still vaguely remember the PG Tips monkey holding a cup!

David Blaine was gutted to hear that his record of forty-eight days in the box doing absolutely nothing has been broken by Darren Bent.

☉ Goalkeepers never do it near the other half.

What's the difference between Manchester City and bird flu? Bird flu made it to Europe.

☉ Police believe Osama Bin Laden to have been hiding in Newcastle's trophy room for the last seven years, let's be honest, it could be true!

Did you hear about the tight Scotsman who travelled to Laugardalsvollur Stadium, Reykjavik, for an Iceland match. When he returned home, one of his mates said, 'Was it a big gate, Jock?'
   'Too right it was!' he replied. 'One of the biggest I've ever had to climb over!'

Frank Lampard was interviewed about England's recent line-up changes. On being asked what position he would be playing he replied: 'I'm not sure – but I think I heard the coach say that I was the team's main drawback.'

Kevin Keegan says Man United only won last season's clashes with Newcastle by playing 'ugly and dirty'. Or as we know them: Wayne Rooney and Patrice Evra.

Dirk Kuyt went into Burger King and asked the assistant for two Whoppers. She replied, 'You're good-looking, and you've a great first touch.'

BUTLINS
Proud new sponsors of West Ham United.
Because our season ends in October too!

⊙ What do you say to a Spurs supporter with a good-looking bird on his arm? Nice tattoo!

Unsubstantiated reports seem to suggest that Chelsea will be releasing a new record at the end of the month, titled 'I'm forever blowing Doubles!'

An old man hands over fifty quid to the turnstile operator at Celtic Park.
Man: Two please.
Turnstile operator: Aye, will that be defenders or strikers?

⊙ What do Chelsea keeper Petr Cech and Michael Jackson have in common? Both wear gloves for no apparent reason.

A Newcastle fan saunters past a corner shop and spots a video for sale entitled *Newcastle – The Golden Years*.
Enthused, the supporter asks the shopkeeper, 'How much for the video, mate?'
'£200, sir,' replies the shopkeeper.
'£200 for a video?' says the fan. 'You're having a laugh!'
'Oh no,' the shopkeeper replies. 'The video's only a fiver, but the Betamax player will cost you £195!'

What's the difference between Spurs' Gomes and a taxi driver? The taxi driver will only let four in!

When at Sunderland Roy Keane didn't stand for any nonsense. One Saturday he caught a couple of fans climbing over the stadium wall. Absolutely filled with rage he grabbed them by the collars and said, 'Get back in there and watch the game till it finishes!'

☺ What do you call a Scotsman in the first round of the World Cup? The referee!

Rafael Benitez walks into the dressing room before the Champions' League final and there's a load of litter lying around! 'Whose rubbish on the floor?!' he says. Crouch stands up and says, 'Me, Gaffer! But I'm not bad in the air!'

Watching the depressing scenes in Portugal 2004, I was sure I was not alone in asking how the government plans to stop these people travelling abroad in 2008 and shaming our country. I mean, they have been caught on camera often enough, and we even know their names: Crouch, Rooney, Terry, Lampard...

What have General Pinochet and Spurs got in common? They both round people up into football stadiums and torture them!

☺ What have Heather Mills and Spurs' European campaign got in common? Their second leg is just for show!

Three Spurs fans were standing on the terrace moaning that their team was losing game after game.

'I blame Redknapp,' said the first, 'if he would sign eleven new players we could be a great side.'

'I blame the players,' said the second, 'if they would make some effort they might at least score a few goals.'

'I blame my parents,' said the third, 'if I'd been born in Islington I'd be watching a decent team now!!'

A blonde woman is walking past a field and notices some kids playing. She then notices that there is one kid standing by himself away from the others, so she feels sorry for him and walks over. 'Is there something wrong son?' she says. 'No,' says the boy. 'Why don't you go and join the others?' she says. 'I don't think I should,' says the boy. 'Why not?' she says. 'Because I'm the flipping goalie!' he replied.

⊙ What goes down and never comes up?
Leeds United!

Two blokes were walking through a cemetery when they happened upon a tombstone that read:

'Here lies Dave Brown, a good man and a Chelsea fan.'

So, one of them asked the other: 'When the hell did they start putting two people in one grave?'

⊙ What does Harry Redknapp do after Spurs beat Arsenal? Turn off the PlayStation!

How many Man U supporters does it take to change a light bulb? None, they all fled at the first sign that the light bulb was failing.

A man was found drowned in the River Thames today. He was dressed in a Spurs shirt, frilly knickers, stockings and suspenders and high heels.

Police have removed the Spurs shirt to save his family any embarrassment.

Jose Mourinho was called as a character witness at a football tribunal, and on being asked his profession, replied, 'I am the greatest football manager in the world!'

After the case was over he came in for a good deal of teasing from the world press. 'How could you stand up in court and say a thing like that?' they asked.

'Well,' he replied, 'you must remember I was under oath!'

Man United's Gary Neville walks into Old Trafford with a bag in his hand.

The security guard says, 'What's in the bag, Gary?'

He replies, 'Just a gun and a few grenades.'

The guard says, 'Thank heavens for that – for a minute I thought you'd brought your boots!'

How can you tell that the Elephant Man was a Villa fan? Because he looked like one.

! Someone asked me the other day, 'What time do Millwall kick off?' 'About every ten minutes,' I replied.

In a recent football match the left back took the ball right in the groin and passed out from the pain. When he woke up he found himself in the local hospital. Though still in pain, he asked the doctor, 'Doc, is it bad? Will I be able to play again?'

'Yes, you should be able to,' replied the doctor.

'Oh, great. So I can play for my club again?' said the man, feeling much relieved.

'Well, just as long as they've got a women's team,' said the doctor.

Chelsea's John Terry was sent off during a recent football match. Returning to the changing room, he had a terrible leg. It was covered in cuts and bruises and had a massive gash from the top of the thigh to the knee. He had no idea whose it was.

England keeper Scott Carson attempted suicide today. He threw himself in front of a bus but it went under him.

! Alan Shearer was nicked for speeding on his way to St James' Park today. Police said he'd do anything for three points.

Football Anagrams

Arsenal Football Club – Cruel banal footballs

Barnsley Football Club – Flabby brutal colonels

Burnley Football – Foul ball rentboy

Charlton Athletic – Halt technical rot

Chelsea Football Club – Callous fat leech blob

Derby County – Dunce by Tory

Darlington FC – Farting 'n' cold

Everton Football Club – Lovelorn, fat, cute blob

Grimsby Town – My wrong bits

Leeds United – I needed slut

Leicester City – Electric Yetis

Liverpool FC – Pelvic floor

Manchester City – I'm Shy, Can't Erect

Newcastle United – Wet dense lunatic

Nottingham Forest – Fat hogs in torment

Oxford United – An odd fixture

Portsmouth – Rum hotpots

Queens Park Rangers – Queer spankers rang

Southend – Hot nudes

Swansea – A new ass

Torquay United – Tiny rude quota

Tottenham Hotspur – To the posh tantrum

West Ham United – With nude mates

West Bromich Albion – I am two-inch slobber

Wolverhampton Wanderers FC – Old Woman perverts raw hen

Wigan Athletic – What giant lice

York City – Yo! tricky

☺ What's the worst thing about Newcastle's St James' Park? The seats face the pitch.

Officials in Afghanistan have claimed that Osama Bin Laden hasn't been killed and is still alive, by showing the Al Qaeda leader giving an interview which was said to be live.

He said, 'To prove I am still alive, Spurs were total rubbish on Saturday.'

However, a Foreign Office spokesman commented, 'That could have been recorded any time in the last twenty years.'

Paul Gascoigne has been sectioned under the Mental Health Act and sent to an institution for the deluded with no chance of recovery.

Shearer says, 'We're glad to have him back.'

Kevin Keegan stated he intended to bring a lot of new faces to Newcastle United when he was manager. Peter Beardsley is reported to have asked for one.

☺ What's the difference between Kevin Keegan and a jet engine? A jet engine eventually stops whining.

How many Manchester United fans does it take to change a light bulb?
Just one but you have to pick him up from Kent.

Sophie Ellis-Bextor has been found dead in the hotel room of a top French footballer. Police are saying little, but have confirmed they're treating it as murder on Zidane's floor.

Apparently Rangers have added a new line to their club merchandise – the Rangers Souvenir European Campaign Calendar. Unfortunately, many purchasers are already trying to get their money back because they've discovered it ends in August.

Jose Mourinho has been offered the job at Newcastle, but turned it down claiming, 'I'm not that special!'

The Football Association was considering a scheme for simplifying club badges and emblems so that they more closely reflected the clubs' names. A committee was set up to receive suggestions and, after a few weeks, the chairman called a meeting. 'Gentlemen,' he said, 'our request for new club badge designs has produced a very satisfactory response. Most of the suggestions are perfectly straightforward and logical – an ox for Oxford United, a sun for Sunderland, a heart for Heart of Midlothian, a windmill and a brick wall for Millwall. However, I'm afraid we must definitely draw the line at the proposed design received from Arsenal!'

☺ I was watching the footy while my wife was hoovering the floor. She accidently knocked the telly and Drogba fell over.

During the last Tory government it was said that Walter Smith was approached by a group of backbench Conservative MPs who were violently opposed to the European Community. It seemed they were looking for advice on how to exit from Europe as quickly as possible.

At a Celtic v Rangers match one season, things got a bit hairy in the crowd, with bottles being thrown by the two sets of supporters. One young spectator, stuck in the middle, was naturally rather concerned for his safety, so an old boy went to reassure him. 'Don't worry, son,' he said. 'It's a bit like bombs in the war. One of those won't hit you unless it's got your name on it.' 'That's what worries me,' said the young man. 'My name's Johnny Walker.'

☺ Did you hear about the Millwall fan who always booked two seats when he went to watch a game? One to sit in and one to throw when the fighting starts.

A Spurs fan arrives at a football match midway through the second half.

'What's the score?' he asks his friend as he settles into his seat. 'Nil-nil,' comes the reply. 'And what was the score at half-time?' he asks.

(!) After Rangers' last early exit from European competition Walter Smith was found wrestling with a cigarette machine. It seemed he was desperate for twenty Players.

There was once a football match between two small village teams. The visitors were surprised to see that the home team's goalkeeper was a horse. The horse played extremely well and it was mainly due to him that the home team won. After the match the visiting captain said to the home captain, 'How on earth did a horse ever learn to keep goal like that?' 'How does anyone learn,' answered the home captain. 'Practice, practice, practice!'

Two men were at a football match and it was just seconds away from kick-off.

'Man,' said the first man, 'I'm bursting for a pee, and the toilets are miles away.'

'Don't worry,' said the second man. 'You see that bloke in front of you? Just pee up his leg.'

'Are you crazy?' said the first man, 'that bloke's massive.'

'Oh,' said the second man, 'he won't notice anything.'

'How do you know?' said the first man.

'Because I've just peed up yours!' said the second man.

Two mad fans were sitting frozen and feeling awful on the terrace. They were complaining that the torrential rain and severe fog was making the game very boring to watch. They decided that they might as well go and grab a bite of something warm to eat. Just as they got up from their seats a policeman interrupted them. 'You two should go home now,' he said, 'the game was abandoned about thirty minutes ago!'

Two old men were holding up the queue outside the turnstile before the game, while one of them hunted for his ticket. He looked in his coat pockets and his waistcoat pockets and his trouser pockets, all to no avail. 'Hang on a minute,' said the gateman. 'What's that in your mouth?' It was the missing ticket! As they moved inside his mate said, 'Crikey, Cyril! You must be getting senile in your old age. Fancy having your ticket in your mouth and forgetting about it!' 'I'm not that stupid,' said old Cyril. 'I was chewing last week's date off it!'

> What do you get if you see a Leeds United fan buried up to his neck in sand? More sand.

A football hooligan appeared in court charged with disorderly conduct and assault. The arresting officer, giving evidence, stated that the accused had thrown something into the canal. 'What exactly was it that he threw into the canal?' asked the magistrate.
    'Stones, sir.'
    'Well, that's hardly an offence is it?'
    'It was in this case, sir,' said the police officer. 'Stones was the referee.'

The boss called the office boy into his private sanctum. 'How did your great-aunt's funeral go yesterday afternoon?' he asked. 'It went off all right, sir,' said the office boy, puzzled. 'Good, good,' said the boss. 'Pity they've got to do it all over again.' 'Pardon, sir?' said the office boy. 'Yes, I understand there's a replay on Saturday!'

> What's the difference between Spurs and an albatross? An albatross has two good wings!

Virgin Rail have decided to start sponsoring Hull City.
    The company think they are a suitable team because of their regular points failures.

A football player had dislocated his shoulder in a nasty challenge and was still screaming in agony when they got him to hospital. 'For heaven's sake,' said the doctor, 'don't be such a baby, you're supposed to be a big, tough defender. There's a woman having a baby next door and she's not making anything like the noise that you are.' 'That's as may be,' wailed the footballer, 'but in her case, nobody's trying to push anything back in!'

☺ Leeds fans are so fickle. The other night I heard one of them yell, 'Go United. And take the Rhinos with you!'

In a particularly rough tackle, a player was knocked unconscious. A first-aid man ran over and began to sprinkle water in his face and fan him with a towel. Slowly the player recovered consciousness and said groggily, 'How the hell do they expect us to play in all this wind and rain?'

Apparently, when Harry Redknapp was West Ham manager he offered to send the squad on an all expenses paid holiday to Florida but they declined. They'd rather go to Blackpool so they could see what it's like to ride on an open-top bus.

What is the difference between West Brom and the Bermuda triangle? The Bermuda triangle has three points …

Why do Newcastle fans plant potatoes around the edge of St James' Park? So they have something to lift at the end of the season!

☺ What happens when opposing teams cross the halfway line at Villa Park? They score!

Apparently, Newcastle are under investigation by the Inland Revenue for tax evasion. They've been claiming for silver polish for the past thirty years.

A bloke goes into Stansted Airport and manages to eventually get into the departure lounge where his flight home is being called. All around him there are overturned tables, smashed windows, broken computer terminals, upturned chairs and crowd control barriers lying on the floor.

'What's happened here?' he asks one of the ground crew.

'Oh yeah ... ' he replies. 'Absolutely hopeless ... we had the Chelsea players in here this morning filming the new Nike ad!'

☺ What do you call a Liverpool fan with an IQ of 10? Supremely gifted!

What does Paul Ince's mum make for Christmas?
Ince pies !

What do a footballer and a magician have in common?
Both do hat tricks!

☺ What's the difference between a Spurs fan and a coconut? You can get a drink out of a coconut!

A man walks into an antique shop and sees an ornamental brass rat, the sort of thing women of a certain age love to put on the mantelpiece. He thinks, 'That'll be perfect for Mother's birthday,' so he asks the shopkeeper how much it is.

'£25 for the rat, £100 for the story,' replies the man.

'Forget the story,' says the bloke, and so buys the rat for twenty-five quid. He walks off down the road, but has not gone thirty yards when a rat comes up from the gutter and starts to follow him. Soon more arrive, and in a few minutes the whole street is a sea of rats, all following the bloke, who keeps walking until he comes to a cliff. He throws the brass rat over, and millions of rats follow, one after each other, plunging to certain death. The bloke runs back to shop ...

'Aaaah,' says the shopkeeper, 'you'll be back for the story?'

'Forget the story – do you have a brass Man Utd fan?'

A Sunderland supporter goes to his doctor to find out what's wrong with him. 'Your problem is you're fat,' says the doctor. 'I'd like a second opinion,' responds the man. 'OK, you're ugly too!' replies the doctor.

What's the difference between an Everton fan and a supermarket trolley? The trolley has a mind of its own.

A Spurs and West Ham fan are strolling along when suddenly the West Ham supporter says, 'Would you look at that dead bird!' The Spurs fan looks skywards and says, 'Huh, where?'

Why aren't football stadiums built in outer space?
Because there is no atmosphere!

⊙ Which England player keeps up the fuel supply?
Paul gas coin!

Which goalkeeper can jump higher than a crossbar?
All of them, a crossbar can't jump!

⊙ Why are football players never asked for dinner?
Because they're always dribbling!

Why did the footballer hold his boot to his ear?
Because he liked sole music!

In a small town in Northern Ireland, the local Catholic team were about to take the field against the local Protestant team. 'Remember, lads,' said the coach, 'if you can't kick the ball, kick the player's shins, and if you can't kick his shins, trip him and kick his head. Now, as soon as we find the ball we'll kick off.'

'Never mind the ball,' said a voice from the back. 'Let's get on with the game.'

A man was being interviewed on television after winning £1,000,000 on the football pools. 'What are you going to do with all that money?' asked the interviewer. 'I'm going to spend the first £250,000 on wines, spirits and beer,' said the winner cheerfully, 'and the second £250,000 on horses, dogs and cards.' 'I see,' said the interviewer, somewhat taken aback. 'And then,' continued the winner, 'I shall spend £250,000 on women and loose living generally.' 'Quite, quite,' the interviewer interrupted hurriedly. 'And what will you do with the remaining £250,000?' 'Oh, I'll probably just fritter that away,' he replied.

☺ Why do Sumo wrestlers shave their legs? So they aren't mistaken for female Chelsea fans.

During the winter of 1946/47, two northern teams turned out for a Boxing Day match. The weather was atrocious. From the touchline the pitch was hardly visible at all as it had been raining, with sleet and hail, for about three days, but the rising temperature had turned the ground into a sea of mud and water. Added to this was a strong wind blowing diagonally across the field. The two captains looked at each other glumly. 'Well,' said the one who had just lost the toss, 'which end would you like?' 'I think we'll play with the tide,' said the other.

☺ What would you get if Chelsea were relegated? 45,000 more Man U fans.

Three old football fans are in a church, praying for their teams. The first one asks, 'Oh Lord, when will England next win the World Cup?'
God replies, 'In the next five years.'
'But I'll be dead by then,' says the man.
The second one asks, 'Oh Lord, when will Forest next win the European Cup?'
The Good Lord answers, 'In the next ten years.'
'But I'll be dead by then,' says the man.
The third one asks, 'Oh Lord, when will Derby win the Premier League?'
God answers, 'I'll be dead by then!'

⚈ How do you define 144 Chelsea fans?
Gross stupidity.

Dave from Liverpool is touring America on holiday and stops in a remote bar in the hills of Nevada. He's chatting to the barman when he spies an old Indian sitting in a corner complete with full tribal gear, long plaits and wrinkles.

'Who's he?' asks Dave.

'That's the Memory Man,' says the barman.

'He knows everything. He can remember any fact. Go and try him out.'

So Dave wanders over and asks: 'Who won the 1965 FA Cup Final?'

'Liverpool,' replies the Memory Man.

The tourist is amazed.

'Who did they beat?'

'Leeds,' comes the reply.

'And the score?'

'2–1.'

Dave tries something more specific.

'Who scored the winning goal?'

The Indian does not even blink:

'Ian St John.'

The Liverpudlian returns home and regales his relatives and friends with his tale, and he's determined to return and pay his respects to this amazing man.

Ten years later he has saved enough money and returns to America. After weeks of searching through the towns of Nevada, Dave finds the Memory Man in a cave in the mountains.

The Scouser steps forward, bows and greets the Indian in his traditional native tongue: 'How.'

The Memory Man squints at him and says: 'Diving header in the six-yard box.'

Michael Owen walks into a night club in Germany and sees a stunning leggy blonde beauty on the dance floor. He approaches her and says, 'Get your coat, you're coming back to my hotel with me tonight. She looks at him and replies, 'Goodness, you're a little forward!'

The Scotland manager phones Fabio Capello to find out how to improve his training methods.

'Dustbins,' says Fabio. 'Position dustbins around the training pitch and get your players to pass the ball between them, dribble round them, chip the ball over them. It'll improve all round ball control.'

The next day Fabio's phone rings. It's the Scottish manager. 'Hi, The dustbins are winning 3–1. What do I do now?'

⊙ How many Spurs fans does it take to change a light bulb? None – they're quite happy living in the shadows.

A man arrives at the gates of heaven, where St Peter greets him and says, 'Before I can let you enter I must ask you what you have done in your life that was particularly good.'

The man racks his brains for a few minutes and then admits to St Peter that he hasn't done anything particularly good in his life.

'Well,' says St Peter, 'have you done anything particularly brave in your life?'

'Yes, I have,' replies the man proudly.

St Peter asks the man to give an account of his bravery.

So the man explains, 'I was refereeing this important match between Liverpool and Everton at Anfield. The score was nil-nil and there was only one more minute of play to go in the second half when I awarded a penalty against Liverpool at the Kop end.'

'Yes,' responded St Peter, 'I agree that was a real act of bravery. Can you perhaps tell me when this took place?'

'Certainly,' the man replied, 'about three minutes ago.'

Fixed to a wall in Liverpool in the mid-1960s was a Baptist poster which read, 'What would you do if Jesus returned among us?'

Underneath the poster someone had written, 'Move St John to inside left.'

⊙ What is the difference between a battery and a Spurs fan? A battery has a positive side.

Saddam Hussein had been found guilty of war crimes and was sentenced to death by firing squad.

The court granted his last request which was to name his own firing squad ...

Mr Hussein chose Frank Lampard, Steven Gerrard and Jamie Carragher from twelve yards.

Wayne Rooney gets home late from training to find Coleen with a face like a bulldog chewing a wasp. 'Where the hell have you been?' she yells at him.

'I did exactly what we were discussing this morning,' he says, 'and been to get a new tattoo.'

He takes off his top and reveals an ornate new design on his upper arm. 'There you are babe,' he says. 'What do you think of that?'

Coleen puts her head in her hands. 'You prat!' she sighs. 'I told you to ask for a transfer!'

☺ The goalkeeper threw a party after his team won the league championship. As a special honour, he asked the manager to say grace before they sat down to dinner. Finishing up the short prayer, the manager said, '... and we thank you, Lord, in the name of the Father, the Son, and the goalie host.'

The top scorer of a Premier League team was tragically killed in a car accident. Seeing an opportunity for glory, the reserve striker went to see the manager.

'How about me taking his place?' he asked.

'Well, I'm not sure about that,' said the manager, 'we'll have to speak to the undertaker first.'

One of the lesser-known stories in Greek mythology tells of a classic football match on Mount Olympus between the Gods and the Mortals.

The Gods trounced the Mortals 8-0 and attributed their victory to the brilliance of their new centaur-forward.

◉ A bad football team is like an old bra – no cups and little support!

There was once a match in Liverpool between Anglican vicars and Roman Catholic priests.

Early in the game the Catholics were awarded a penalty. Father Flanagan placed the ball carefully, took a long run at it, and kicked. The ball sailed high into the air and missed the goal by miles.

Father Flanagan didn't utter a word. He just stood there with a grim expression on his face.

The team captain, Monsignor Ryan, came up behind him and said reprovingly, 'Father, that is the most profane silence I have ever heard!'

In church one Sunday the vicar opened his Bible to read the lesson. In a loud voice he proclaimed, 'Corinthians 7!'

A keen football fan who was dozing in the front row woke up with a start and shouted, 'Who were they playing?'

◉ Football is a game in which a handful of men run around for one and a half hours watched by millions of people who could really use the exercise.

Did you hear about the football fan who lost a £50 bet on a TV football match? He lost another £50 on the instant replay.

Two Man City fans were travelling in a car to watch City play Blackburn but they got lost along the way.

'I've no idea where we are,' said the first fan.

'Don't worry,' replied the second, 'I have an idea.' With that he stuck his arm out of the car window. 'We're in Liverpool.'

'How do you know that?' asked the first fan, amazed.

'I just had my watch nicked!' came the reply.

A Sky TV reporter goes to the post-match conference of the game between Blackburn and Hull and speaks to both managers. First, he speaks to Phil Brown. 'So, Phil, what are your hopes for Hull in the future?' asks the reporter.

Brown replies: 'Well, if we can pick up a few points here and there, hopefully we can stay in this division.'

The reporter then interviews Sam Allardyce, 'So, Sam, what are your hopes for Blackburn in the future?'

Allardyce replies: 'We'll walk this division unbeaten for rest of the season. We'll win that and the League Cup, maybe win the FA Cup along the way, and on to Europe!'

The Sky reporter interrupts, 'Sam, don't you think you're getting daft now?'

'Well, Phil started it!' replies Allardyce.

☺ Some flies were playing football in a saucer using a sugar lump as a ball. One of them says, 'We'll have to do better than this, lads. We're playing in the cup tomorrow.'

How can you tell a level-headed Liverpool supporter? He dribbles from both sides of his mouth – at the same time.

Rafael Benitez: 'Our new winger cost five million. I call him our wonder player.'
Sir Alex Ferguson: 'Why's that?'
Rafael Benitez: 'Every time he plays I wonder why I bothered to buy him!'

A father and son were eating breakfast. The father's newspaper had the headline, 'Van Gogh sold for £8 million.' The son asked, 'Is he worth it, Dad?' The father, surprised at his son's interest in fine art, replied, 'I suppose so, son. Why do you ask?'

The son said, 'Well, Liverpool paid more than that for Stan Collymore, and he was rubbish.'

Newsflash: Thieves broke into the home of a Spurs fan and stole two books. 'The thing that upsets me,' he said, 'is that I hadn't finished colouring them in yet!'

⊙ What do you call a Manchester United fan in a two-bedroomed semi? A burglar!

Two Man Utd fans in London walked past a shop and saw a sign: Shirts fifty pence, Trousers one pound.

Deciding this was great value, they decided to go in and take advantage of the offer. Before they go in, one says: 'Don't let them know we're Man U fans or they'll try to rip us off.' So they hide their scarves.

They go into the shop and asked for six shirts each and six pairs of trousers each.

The assistant asks, 'Are you Man U fans?' to which they reply, 'Yes.'

'Then bugger off. This is a launderette.'

⊙ Why do Manchester United supporters have moustaches? So they can look like their mothers.

A man walks into a pub and pounds his fist on the bar. 'All Man U fans are idiots!' he shouts. Another man in the back of the bar jumps up. 'I resent that!' 'Are you a Utd fan?' the first man asks. 'No ... I'm an idiot.'

⊙ What do you get when you offer a Manchester United fan a penny for his thoughts? Change!

Two Man Utd fans are walking down the street at 5 p.m. on a Saturday evening.
First Man U fan: I couldn't make the game at Old Trafford today, I was at a funeral. What was the score?
Second Man U fan: We drew 0–0.
Third Man U fan: Who missed our penalty?

Apparently, they've found Bin Laden, hiding in the Liverpool trophy room. He said it reminded him of his cave in Afghanistan: large, dark, empty ... and just been taken over by Americans.

☺ One of Arsene Wenger's new recruits is so fast he can eat ice cream in the rain without having it drip.

What's the difference between Rangers and a student rail card? With a student rail card you get four weeks in Europe.

☺ What's the difference between Cesc Fabregas and a Mini? A Mini can only carry three passengers.

Why does Yogi Bear support Celtic? Because he's smarter than the average bear and always outwits the Rangers.

Sam and John are at work in the timber yard when John accidentally chops his arm off with a saw. Sam wraps the arm in a plastic bag and takes John to a surgeon. Four hours later Sam is amazed to see John in the pub throwing darts. 'Wow!' thinks Sam. 'That surgeon is great.' A few weeks later John accidentally cuts his leg off. Sam puts the leg in a plastic bag and takes John back to the surgeon. That evening he's amazed to see John playing football. 'Wow!' thinks Sam. 'That surgeon is amazing.' A few weeks later John cuts his head off. Sam puts the head in a plastic bag and carries John to the surgeon. Next day the surgeon calls Sam and says, 'I'm sorry, but John is dead.' 'Don't blame yourself,' says Sam. 'I'm sure you did all you could.' 'I'm not blaming myself,' says the surgeon. 'I'm blaming you. If you'd put some holes in that plastic bag the poor bloke wouldn't have suffocated!'

☺ I won't say that the play-offs are long, but when they started the season, Blair was still Prime Minister.

First fan: 'I wish I'd brought the piano to the stadium.'
Second fan: 'Why would you bring a piano to the football game?'
First fan: 'Because I left the tickets on it.'

⊙ Why aren't the England football team allowed to own a dog? Because they can't hold on to a lead.

Oxo were going to bring out a Euro 2004 commemorative cube painted red, white and blue in honour of the England squad. But it was a laughing stock and crumbled in the box.

⊙ What's the difference between the Invisible Man and Scotland? You've got more chance of seeing the Invisible Man at the World Cup finals.

It's a cup tie, ten minutes to go, Notts Forest are down 1–0 and they've used all their subs. For once in his life Stuart 'Psycho' Pearce comes off second best in a tackle. The physio shouts out to Brian Cloughie, 'He can't go back on, he's taken a knock to the head, he doesn't know who he is.' Cloughie replies, 'Tell him he's Pele and put him up front!'

⊙ What's the scariest position? Ghoulie.

The chairman of a Premier League club was retiring after many years of loyal service. At the dinner given in his honour by the club, the team captain, who had had a few, rose to make his speech.

   'It is said,' he began, 'that when a child is brn, its guardian angel gives it a kiss. If the kiss is on the hands, the child will become a musician or an artist. If the kiss is on the head, it will become a great thinker or scientist. If on the lips, it will grow up to be a singer or an actor. Now I don't know where Bill here was kissed, but he's certainly been a damn good chairman!'

🙂 How many clever Spurs fans does it take to change a light bulb? Both of them.

What has Old Trafford on a Saturday afternoon at 4.45 p.m. got in common with Wormwood Scrubs? They're both full of cockneys trying to get out!

How many Man United fans does it take to change a light bulb? 560,001. That is, 1 to change it, 60,000 to say they've been changing it for years and 500,000 to buy the replica kit.

Where do football directors go when they are fed up? The bored room!

🙂 Why do managers bring suitcases along to away games? So that they can pack the defence!

What should a football team do if the pitch is flooded? Bring on their subs!

What did the bumble bee striker say? Hive scored!

🙂 What part of a football pitch smells nicest?
The scenter spot!

What's the chilliest ground in the premiership? Cold Trafford!

🙂 How did the football pitch end up as a triangle?
Somebody took a corner!

Why didn't the dog want to play football? It was a boxer!

What did they call Dracula when he won the league? The champire!

Why did the goalpost get angry? Because the bar was rattled!

What lights up a soccer stadium? A soccer match!

⊙ What part of a football ground is never the same?
The changing rooms!

What is a goalkeeper's favourite snack? Beans on post!

What is the difference between Jon Pertwee and Ray Parlour? Ray Parlour still looks like Worzel Gummidge.

Two boys are playing football in a park in London when one of them is attacked by a Rottweiler. Thinking quickly, his friend rips a plank of wood from a fence, forces it into the dog's collar and twists it, breaking the dog's neck. All the while, a newspaper reporter who was taking a stroll through the park is watching. He rushes over, introduces himself and takes out his pad and pencil to start his story for the next edition.

    He writes, 'Spurs fan saves friend from vicious animal.'
    The boy interrupts: 'But I'm not a Spurs fan.'
    The reporter starts again: 'QPR fan saves friend from horrific attack.'
    The boy interrupts again: 'I'm not a Rangers fan either.'
    The reporter asks: 'Who do you support, then?'
    'Arsenal,' replies the boy.
    So the reporter starts again: 'Evil Arsenal fan kills family pet.'

⊙ How long did Tony Adams play for Arsenal?
Donkey's years.

What's the difference between a pyromaniac and Leeds United? A pyromaniac wouldn't throw away all his matches!

What's the difference between a Leeds fan and a chimp? One's hairy, stupid and smells, and the other is a chimpanzee.

A very religious young boy is going to the Vatican with his mum to see the Pope. The boy is a bit worried about whether or not they will see the Pope among the thousands of people. So his mum says, 'Don't worry son, the Pope is a big football fan so I'll buy you an Arsenal strip, the Pope will see the famous Arsenal colours and he'll talk to you.'

So they buy the strip and the boy wears it while they are standing in the crowd as the Pope goes along in his Popemobile. Next thing Pope Benedict stops the Popemobile and gets out to talk to a different little boy wearing a Leeds United top. Then he gets back into the mobile and it drives right past the Arsenal fan.

The little boy is very upset and is in tears. 'Don't worry,' says his mum. 'I'll buy you a Leeds United strip, we'll come back tomorrow and then the Pope is guaranteed to stop and talk to you.'

So they are back the next day now wearing the Leeds United shirt. The Popemobile comes along and the boy is all excited. Next thing the Popemobile stops, then Pope Benedict gets out, bends down to talk to the little boy and says, 'I thought I told you to get lost yesterday!'

⊙ Who is the strongest team in the Premiership? West Brom, as they're holding everyone else up!

How many Evertonians does it take to change a light bulb? None, they just sit in the dark and blame it all on Liverpool.

There was once a fanatical Spurs supporter who thought of nothing but football all day long. He talked about football, read about football, watched nothing but football on television and attended matches as often as he possibly could. At last his poor wife could stand it no longer. One night she said, 'I honestly believe you love Spurs more than you love me!'

'Blimey,' said the fan, 'I love Hartlepool United more than I love you!'

A tourist is in North London one Saturday and he decides he would very much like to go to a football match, so he asks a man in the street if there are any local matches being played that afternoon.

'Well,' replies the man, 'the Arsenal ground is very close but they're playing away today. If you feel you really must see a match, the Tottenham ground is not that far away. You go straight down this road and you'll see two queues, a big queue and a small queue.

'You should go to the small queue because the big one is for the fish and chip shop.'

⊙ Two Spurs fans are walking along. One of them picks up a mirror, looks in it and says, 'Hey, I know that bloke.' The second one picks it up and says, 'Of course you do, you thick git – it's me!'

⊙ There was trouble on the terraces at The Hawthorns one Saturday afternoon. A huge West Bromwich Albion fan picked up a tiny spectator wearing the blue and white colours of Millwall, the visiting team. As he was about to hurl him to the ground, one of his mates yelled, 'Hey, Derek, don't waste him! Chuck him at the referee!'

Last year, my aged great-aunt, who is more than a bit senile, gave me a Doncaster Rovers season ticket for Christmas. Not wanting it, I took it down to the ground, and nailed it to the gates. A couple of weeks later, I had a change of heart, and decided that it was stupid to give something as valuable as that to any old stranger, so I went to retrieve the prized item. When I returned, however, it was too late. Some creep had nicked the nail.

☺ What's the best thing to come out of Derby?
The A52.

A primary teacher starts a new job at a school on Merseyside and, trying to make a good impression on her first day, explains to her class that she is a Liverpool fan. She asks her students to raise their hands if they, too, are Liverpool fans. Everyone in the class raises their hand except one little girl. The teacher looks at the girl with surprise and says: 'Mary, why didn't you raise your hand?'

'Because I'm not a Liverpool fan,' she replied.

The teacher, still shocked, asks: 'Well, if you're not a Liverpool fan, then who are you a fan of?'

'I'm a Manchester United fan, and proud of it,' Mary replied.

The teacher could not believe her ears. 'Mary, why are you a United fan?'

'Because my mum and dad are from Manchester, and my mum is a United fan and my dad is a United fan, so I'm a United fan too!'

'Well,' said the teacher, in an annoyed tone, 'that's no reason for you to be a United fan. You don't have to be just like your parents all of the time.

'What if your mum was a prostitute and your dad was a drug addict and car thief, what would you be then?'

'Then,' Mary smiled, 'I'd be a Liverpool fan.'

A schoolboy Man U fan goes into sports shop to buy a Man U football in the window. He asks the shop assistant behind the counter how much it is. The assistant tells him it's £25.

The little boy replies, 'I have only got £5 pocket money,' so the assistant tells him to come back when he's saved up more.

So the boy thinks and says to the assistant, 'I'll do you a deal. Blindfold me and pick any football off that shelf and I bet I can guess what football team is on the ball. If I get it right you have to give me the Man U ball.'

The assistant thinks he'll never do it, so he agrees. He blindfolds the little lad and he gets the ball off the shelf, puts it in front of the boys face and the boy shouts, 'It's Wolves!' The assistant is shocked, 'How did you know that?'

The boy says, 'I could hear the sound of a pack of wolves in the woods.' So the assistant says 'OK, let's have another go.'

So he gets a ball from the shelf puts it in front of the boy's face. The boy shouts, 'It's Arsenal!'

The assistant says, 'Wow, how did you get that?'

The boy says, 'I could hear the guns on a bloody war field.'

The assistant in total shock says, 'Right, get this one and you can have the ball and the Ronaldo boots.' So he gets the ball puts it in front of the boy's face. The boy shouts, 'It's West Brom.'

'Blimey! How did you get that one?' says the assistant.

The boy replies, 'Well, it's going down.'

David Seaman was walking down the street one day when he heard screams from a nearby building. He looked up to see smoke billowing from a fourth storey window with a woman leaning out holding a baby.

'Help, help!' she screamed, 'I need someone to catch my baby!'

A crowd of onlookers had gathered, but no one was confident of catching a baby dropped from such a great height. Then Seaman stepped forward.

'I'm the ex-England goalkeeper,' he shouted to the woman. 'I'm famous for my safe hands. I've still got it. Drop the baby, for me it will be like catching a ball.'

'OK!' screams the woman. 'I'll trust you. I've no choice! Here she comes!'

So, with the flames roaring all around her, the woman throws the baby from the window. However, the edge of the baby's shawl catches on the woman's watch with the result that the child goes spinning off to one side, tumbling head over heels and with her little arms and legs flailing.

The woman screams and the crowd gasps, all sure that the baby will perish because she will fall out of reach of the man. Seaman remains motionless as the child descends, spinning and tumbling further and further away from him as she comes. Then when the baby is only feet from hitting the ground Seaman dives across the pavement, catches the baby in his outstretched right hand, pulls her in towards his chest and shields her body with his left hand and arm.

The crowd erupts with cheers and the woman, still in danger herself, nearly faints with relief. Seaman, still clutching the child to his chest in his right arm, waves to the crowd of onlookers to acknowledge their appreciation. Then, slowly and gracefully, he turns away from them, bounces the baby twice on the ground, and kicks her sixty yards down the road.

David Beckham

Alex Ferguson goes on *Who Wants to be a Millionaire?*

He gets to the £500,000 question and Chris Tarrant asks him, 'What animal lives in a sett? Is it a rabbit, a cuckoo, a sheep or a badger?'

Fergie thinks for some time and says, 'That's a hard one, I'll have to go fifty-fifty.' Tarrant instructs the computer and Fergie is left with cuckoo and badger.

Fergie still isn't sure so he tells Chris: 'I think I'll phone a friend.' Tarrant is surprised when Fergie nominates the 'boy wonder' Beckham to take the call.

Beckham answers the phone and is presented with the question and the two remaining options by Fergie. Beckham states with assured authority, 'It's a badger, boss.' Fergie asks if he's sure and gets confirmation from 'the gifted one'. Fergie gives his reply to Tarrant and walks away with half a million.

Next day in training Fergie says to Beckham, 'How come you were so sure of the answer last night?' Beckham says, 'That was easy, boss – everyone knows that a cuckoo lives in a clock!'

⊙ The Manchester United players are in the dressing room on Saturday, just before the game, when Roy Keane walks in. 'Boss,' he says, 'there's a problem. I'm not playing unless I get a cortisone injection.' 'Hey,' says Becks, 'if he's having a new car, so am I.'

David runs into a bar in a terrible state and orders a large brandy followed by another large brandy. Once his nerves are calmed, he sheepishly asks the barman, 'Excuse me, mate, but do you know how tall penguins grow?'

The barman shrugs his shoulders.

'I dunno, a couple of feet, I suppose.'

'Are you sure?'

'Yeah, pretty sure.'

'Oh dear,' says David. 'I think I just ran over a nun.'

Posh and Becks are sitting in front of the television watching the six o'clock news. The main story is a man threatening to jump off the Clifton Suspension Bridge on to the busy road below.

Posh turns to Becks and says: 'David, I bet you £5,000 that he jumps!' to which Beckham replies '£5,000? Done! I bet that he doesn't.'

So they shake hands on the bet and continue watching. Sure enough, the man jumps and hits the road below with a loud thud. Beckham takes £5,000 out of his back pocket and hands it to Posh.

But she refuses. 'I can't take your money, David,' she says. 'The truth is, I was cheating. I saw the five o'clock news, so I knew he was going to jump.'

'No, babe, fair's fair,' says David. 'That money is yours fair and square. I was cheating just as you were. I saw the five o'clock news, too. I just didn't think he would do it again.'

As part of his medical upon joining Real Madrid, David had to undergo a psychiatric test to establish his response to certain questions.

'What would happen,' asked the psychiatrist, 'if I cut off your left ear?'

'Well,' says David, 'I'd be half deaf, I suppose.'

'Very good. And what would happen if I then cut off your right ear?'

'Oh, well, in that case I'd go blind.'

'Why do you think you'd go blind if I cut off both your ears?'

'Easy,' replies David. 'My bandana would slip over my eyes.'

☉ David Beckham walks into a pub. The landlord says 'A pint of your usual, David?' Beckham replies, 'No, just a half, then I'm off.'

Posh takes her car into a garage to have some dents removed. The mechanic, knowing she isn't the brightest Spice Girl in the world, decides to play a joke on her. 'You don't need me to take those dents out,' he says. 'Just blow up the exhaust pipe and the metal will pop back into place.' So she takes the car home and tries it.

David spots her from the house, opens a window and shouts, 'What are you doing? You have to wind the windows up first!'

David Beckham is celebrating: 'Fifty-seven days, fifty-seven days!' he shouts happily.

Posh asks him why he is celebrating. He answers: 'Well, I've done this jigsaw in only fifty-seven days.'

'Is that good?' asks Posh.

'You bet,' says David. 'It says three to five years on the box.'

A thief drives off with Posh's new Porsche. David sees it all happen. 'Victoria, Victoria, someone's stolen your car!' 'Oh my God,' says Victoria. 'Did you get a description of him?' 'I did better than that,' says David. 'I wrote down the number of the number plate!'

⊙ David Beckham walks into a pet shop and asks for a pound of bird seed. 'How many birds do you have?' asks the pet shop owner. 'None yet,' says David, 'but I'm hoping to grow some.'

Posh Spice walks into a posh restaurant with a frog attached to her forehead. She sits down at her table and orders her food from the waiter. As he brings out her lunch, the waiter can't contain his curiosity. 'I don't wish to be rude,' he says, 'but how on earth did you get that thing on you?'

'Well,' answers the frog, 'it started out as a wart on my bum ...'

David Beckham goes shopping, and sees something interesting in the kitchen section of a large department store. 'What's that?' he asks.

'A Thermos flask,' replies the assistant.

'What does it do?' asks Becks.

The assistant tells him it keeps hot things hot and cold things cold.

Really impressed, Beckham buys one and takes it along to his next training session. 'Here, boys, look at this,' Beckham says proudly. 'It's a Thermos flask.'

The lads are impressed. 'What does it do?' they ask.

'It keeps hot things hot and cold things cold,' says David.

'What have you got in it?' asks Roy Keane.

'Two cups of coffee and a choc ice,' replies David.

Jaap Stam, Andy Cole and David Beckham noticed that Alex Ferguson always left work a little early. So one day they met and decided that when Ferguson leaves, they'll all leave early too. Later in the day they see Ferguson leave early so they do too. Jaap Stam goes home and goes to rest so he can get an early start. Andy Cole goes home and cooks dinner for his family. David Beckham goes home and walks to his bedroom. He opens the door slowly and sees his wife, Posh Spice, in bed with Alex Ferguson, so he shuts the door and leaves quietly. The next day Jaap Stam and Andy Cole are talking and plan to go home early again. They ask David Beckham if he wants to leave early again and he says, 'No way! Yesterday I almost got caught!'

⊙ David and Brooklyn are walking down the street when they see a sign in a fast-food restaurant saying, 'Free Big Mac'. 'Why?' David asks his little boy. 'What did he do?'

David Beckham boards an aircraft and goes straight through into the First Class seats. A stewardess comes along to him and tells him he is booked in Economy Class, but he refuses to move out of First.

The bloke sitting next to Becks whispers to the stewardess, 'I'm a psychologist, and if you'll let me speak privately with Mr Beckham, I'm sure this can be sorted out.' A minute later, David stands up, gets his bag out of the rack and walks back into Economy.

The stewardess is amazed, and asks the psychologist how he had persuaded Beckham to move.

'Oh,' he says, 'I just told him the First Class section isn't going to New York!'

Posh and Becks were recently seen in a car park trying to get into their BMW with a coat hanger.

Posh: 'David, I can't seem to get this door unlocked!'

Becks: 'Well, Victoria, you'd better get a move on and try a bit harder. It's starting to rain and the top's down.'

David and Victoria go to see the doctor for their annual medicals. David goes in first and once he's finished, the doctor asks him to send Victoria in.

'Before we start, Mrs Beckham, I need to speak to you about your husband,' says the doctor in a concerned tone of voice. 'To be honest I am a bit worried about him. I asked him how everything was going and he said that he'd never felt better, everything was fantastic.'

'What's so worrying about that?' asks Victoria.

'That's what I am coming to. He said that when he got up this morning he went to the bathroom, opened up the door and God turned on the light for him. And when he left the bathroom, he shut the door, and God turned the light off for him too. Now I'm afraid that delusions like that simply are not normal.'

Victoria rolls her eyes towards heaven.

'Oh dear, oh dear,' she says, 'it sounds like he's been peeing in the fridge again ...'

Worried that his reputation for not being the sharpest pencil in the box is begin-ning to affect his career, David decides to go back to school for a bit. After the first week, Posh goes to pick him up at the end of the day and gets talking to one of his teachers. 'How's he doing?' she asks. 'Very well,' says the teacher. 'He's made straight A's.' 'That's marvellous!' says Posh. 'Absolutely,' says the teacher. 'His B's are a bit wonky, but we'll start on those next week.'

☺ David is a bit worried about his marriage, so he goes to see a marriage counsellor. 'Did you wake up grumpy this morning?' she asks. 'No,' replies David. 'I let her sleep.'

David Beckham walks into a library.

'I'll have a cheeseburger and fries, please.'

The librarian looks at him strangely. 'Sir,' she says, 'this is a library.'

David looks embarrassed and whispers as quietly as he can, 'Sorry! I'll have a cheeseburger and fries.'

Slightly embarrassingly, David finds himself suffering from constipation. He goes to the doctor, who perscribes a course of suppositories. A week later, all is not well, so he goes back to the doctor. 'Have you been taking the suppositories I gave you?' he asks. 'What do you think I've been doing, doc?' replies David. 'Shoving them up my bum?'

David is sitting in a restaurant and the waitress comes over to take his order. 'I'll have a quickie, please,' he says. Offended, the waitress slaps him in the face and walks away. David can't understand what he's done wrong, so he flags down another waitress. 'Could I have a quickie, please?' he asks her. Again he gets slapped in the face and the waitress walks away. David is feeling quite bemused when a lady at the next table leans over to him and says, 'I think you'll find it's pronounced "quiche".'

⊙ On his first flight to Madrid, David is told that chewing gum is a good way to stop his ears popping. As they land, he calls over the air stewardess and says, 'This gum worked a treat, but do you know how I'm supposed to get it out of my ears?'

David is involved in an unfortunate car accident. He lies injured in the road when, like an angel from above, a policeman comes up to him. 'Don't worry Mr Beckham,' he advises. 'A red cross nurse will be here soon.' 'Aw,' replies David, 'couldn't I have a blonde happy one?'

Posh Spice has the Spice Girls round for lunch. As they arrive, she invites them in, offers them drinks, runs to the window and shouts, 'Green side up!' They finish their drinks and then lunch is served, but before she tucks in, Victoria runs to the window again and shouts, 'Green side up!' As the coffee arrives, Victoria stands up, runs to the window, but before she can shout anything, Baby Spice asks Victoria, 'Are you going to shout "Green side up?"' 'Yes, I am.' 'Why?' 'Because David is laying some turf!'

David is discussing his forthcoming holiday with a mate. 'I'm thinking of going to the equator,' says David.

'Aren't you worried that the weather will disagree with Victoria?'

'Trust me,' says David. 'It wouldn't dare.'

David Beckham hears a knock at the door. He opens it to find an old lady in some distress. 'I'm very sorry, Mr Beckham, but I think I've just run over your cat. I'll be more than happy to replace it.' 'OK,' says David, 'are you any good at catching mice?'

⊙ The Beckham family go on an expensive safari holiday in Africa. 'Dad,' shouts Brooklyn, 'I just passed an elephant!' 'Really?' says David. 'How did you get the toilet seat down?'

David Beckham comes home from training with a note from Alex Ferguson, indicating that 'David seems to be having some difficulty with the differences between boys and girls,' and would Posh Spice, 'Please sit down and have a talk with David about this.'

So Posh takes him quietly by the hand upstairs to her bedroom, and closes the door. 'First, David, I want you to take off my blouse ...' so he unbuttons her blouse and takes it off. 'OK, now take off my skirt ...' and he takes off her skirt. 'Now take off my bra,' which he does. 'And now, David, please take off my knickers.' And when David finishes removing those, she says, 'David, PLEASE don't wear any of my clothes any more!'

A parachutist jumps out of a plane flying at 30,000 feet. He has a wonderful flight, enjoying the exhilaration of his jump right up until the moment that he discovers his parachute is broken. Hurtling towards the ground he desperately tries to fix the parachute, when all of a sudden he sees David Beckham on the way up.

'Hey, David,' he shouts, 'do you know anything about parachutes?'

'Sorry, mate,' David cries out, 'not a thing. Do you know about gas cookers?'

'You don't love me any more, David,' says Posh.

'Yeah I do,' he says in return.

'Prove it!'

'OK, I'll buy you anything you want.'

'Will you buy me a mink?'

'Of course I will. On one condition.'

'What's that?'

'You have to keep the cage clean.'

Posh Spice goes to an old people's home in an effort to cheer up the residents. She is dismayed, however, to find that nobody recognises her. Getting a little shirty, she turns to one of the old ladies.

'Do you know who I am?' she asks.

'Oh no, dear. But don't worry. If you ask matron, she'll tell you.'

☺ Victoria is having difficulty getting her heavy, lumpy luggage onto a plane. An air stewardess helps her stuff the bag into an overhead locker. 'Do you always carry such heavy luggage?' she asks Posh Spice. 'You must be joking,' she says. 'Next time I'm riding in the bag and David can buy the ticket.'

Beckham was feeling a little thirsty after training, so headed off to the drinks machine.

In went the first fifty pence and out came the Lucozade. David decided to put another fifty pence in and out came another. For a third time, in went another fifty pence and again out came another drink.

By this time, there was quite a queue forming and Gary Neville, who happened to be behind, exclaimed:

'Come on, Becks, we're dying back here. How many do you want?'

Becks: 'Hold up a minute, lads, I'm winning big time here!'

An English ventriloquist come to Madrid where he performs his act at an English pub. Unknown to him, David Beckham is in the audience, and embarrassingly enough he and his dummy start telling all their favourite David Beckham jokes. After a while, poor David can stand it no more. He gets up and starts heckling the ventriloquist. 'I'm sick of this. Don't you understand that it's guys like you that make me a figure of fun? Do you ever stop to think how I might feel about your incessant jokes?'

'I'm sorry, mate,' says the ventriloquist. 'It's just a bit of fun.'

'Keep out of it, you,' replies David, 'I'm talking to the little bloke on your knee.'

David is driving down the motorway when his mobile rings. It's Victoria.

'David, be careful. There's just been a report on the radio that there's a car driving the wrong way down the motorway.'

'They got their report wrong, it's not just one car, it's thousands of them!'

Alex Ferguson is on his way to training one morning and, as usual, stops by David Beckham's house to give him a lift. He knocks at the door, only for it to be answered by a pale and drawn-looking Beckham.

'Och, David. You're no looking too good this morning.'

'For sure, Mr Ferguson, I am under the weather.'

'Ah no worries, you can have the day off today. Is there anythin' I can get youse?'

David asks Alex for some groceries and off Fergie goes. On his way home he stops at Tesco's and who should he bump into but Arsene Wenger.

'A-ha, Monsieur Ferguson. What are you doing 'ere?' asks the Arsenal boss.

'Ah've just got these here carrots for David Beckham.'

'Ah, Monsieur. You are indeed an exceptional businessman!'

Posh and Becks go to see Brooklyn perform in his school play. Halfway through, Brooklyn steps forward to say his main speech and falls straight through a hole in the floorboards. 'Don't worry,' says David to Posh, 'it's just a stage he's going through.'

Alex Ferguson calls David Beckham into his office. 'David,' he says, 'I'm worried about your performance the last few games. You've been hopeless, completely off form.'

'Sorry, boss,' says David. 'I've not been myself lately. I've got problems at home.'

'Oh dear,' says Ferguson, 'What's up? Victoria and the boys OK?'

'Oh they're fine,' says David. 'It's just that something's really bugging me and I'm losing sleep and everything. I can't concentrate on my football and it's really getting me down.'

'Whatever's the matter, David?' says Fergie.

'Well, boss,' says David, 'it's pretty serious. You see I'm really stuck with this jigsaw and ...'

'A jigsaw?!!!' shouts Alex. 'You're useless every time you play because of a jigsaw?!!!'

'Yeah, boss, but you don't understand, it's really doing my head in!' says David. 'It's really hard and it's this picture of a tiger and it looks really good on the box and I'm sure I've got all the bits and everything but I just can't get it right and it's doing my head in and I even had my hair cut to try and cool my brain down and ...'

'David, David, David,' says Ferguson. 'You've got to get a grip. It's affecting our games and nothing is as important as Manchester United's success.'

'Yeah, boss,' says David, 'but it's this picture of a tiger and it looks really good on the box and I really want to finish it but it's really hard.'

'David,' he says, 'Bring the tiger jigsaw in and let's have a look at it. We've got to get you back to playing football.'

'Oh thanks, boss,' says David, 'that'd be really helpful because it's really hard and it's a picture of a tiger and it's doing my head in, that tiger is.'

So David brings the jigsaw into Ferguson's office. 'Here it is, boss,' he says, showing Ferguson the picture on the box. 'Look, boss, it's this tiger, right, and it's a really good picture and ...'

'Will you just shut up, and empty the pieces over my desk,' says Ferguson. Beckham then empties all the pieces from the box all over Ferguson's desk.

Ferguson looks at what's on his desk. He looks up at David Beckham. 'David,' he says, 'put the Frosties back in the box.'

David is driving down a country lane when he sees a flashing light in the rear-view mirror. He pulls over and a policeman approaches the car. 'I thought you ought to know, sir, that there is a woman about a mile back who claims to be your wife. She says she fell out of the car when you turned a corner.'

'Thank heavens for that,' says David. 'I thought I'd gone deaf.'

David jumps into a cab.

'Take me to the football ground,' he says.

'We're already at the football ground,' says the cabbie.

'Really?' says David, handing him a twenty-pound note. 'Well, don't drive so fast in future ...'

☺ Poor Brooklyn is stuck on his maths homework. 'Dad,' he yells, 'will you help me with my homework?' 'I don't know, son,' says David. 'It wouldn't really be right, now, would it?' 'Probably not, Dad,' replies Brooklyn. 'But have a go anyway.'

David makes a panicked call to the emergency services.

'Help me, help me,' he yells. 'My house is on fire!'

'Where do you live, sir?' asks the voice on the other end.

'Oh, I can't remember the address.'

'Then how on earth do you expect us to get to you?'

'Come on,' shouts David. 'Don't you have any of those big red trucks?'

As a young boy, David Beckham gets a holiday job painting white lines on the road. On the first day, the foreman is very pleased as he's painted five miles of white lines. The next day is less impressive, only three miles. On the third day, the foreman is forced to take David to one side. 'Look, son,' he says, 'how come you painted five miles on your first day, three on your second day and only a mile today?'

'Because,' David replies, 'I keep getting further away from the can of paint!'

Posh walks in the living room one day back from a shopping spree.

She goes over to David, gives him a bag and says, 'Here's a gift.'

David opens the bag and it's a new Manchester United scarf to add to his collection.

'Thanks, ' David says.

Posh walks into the kitchen and about two minutes later hears David scream, 'AGGGH!!!'

Posh runs in and says, 'What's wrong, David?'

'It's this scarf, it's too tight!'

David turns up at football practice one day with a ferret on a lead. 'Nice ferret, David,' says Rio Ferdinand.

'Thanks, Rio,' says David. 'I got it for Victoria.'

'Nice swap,' says Rio.

Posh and Becks's limo broke down and the driver asked them to check that the hazard warning lights were working. So they got out and walked round the back to take a look.

'Are they on?' shouted the driver.

They replied, 'Yes, no, yes, no, yes, no ...'

☺ David decides to treat Brooklyn and Romeo by taking them to Disneyworld. They fly to Florida, jump in the car and start driving. After a while, David sees a big sign saying 'Disneyworld Left'. 'Oh well,' he shrugs, turning the car round and heading back to the airport.

David walks into a hardware shop and asks for some four by twos. 'I think you mean two by fours, mate,' says the bloke behind the counter. 'Hang on,' says David, 'I'll go and ask Victoria.' He nips out to the car to check, comes back and says, 'Yeah, mate, you're right. Two by fours.' 'OK, how long do you need them?' 'Hang on,' says David, 'I'll go and check.' He goes out to the car, comes back and says, 'A long time. We're building a house.'

A police officer sees a car swerving all over the road, so he puts his sirens on and makes it pull over. Funnily enough the driver is David Beckham. 'Excuse me, Mr Beckham,' says the copper, 'but I couldn't help noticing that you were swerving all over the road. Is there some sort of explanation?'

'There certainly is, officer,' says David. 'I was driving along and this huge tree appeared in front of me. I swerved to the left, but there was another tree. So I swerved to the right – you guessed it, another tree! It's a nightmare.'

'I think you'll find that that's not a tree,' says the slightly exasperated officer. 'That's your air freshener!'

① Posh Spice is just hours away from giving birth to Romeo. In a state of high excitement, David calls the hospital. 'My wife's in labour,' he says. 'Her contractions are only a couple of minutes apart.' 'Is this her first child?' asks the midwife. 'Don't be daft,' says David. 'I'm her husband.'

Mrs Beckham wants to buy a microwave. So she goes in and asks the salesman, 'How much for that microwave?'

The salesman replies, 'We don't sell microwaves to thick Beckhams.'

So the next day she dyes her hair red, dresses in disguise, and goes in and asks the same question. The sales clerk answers, 'We don't sell microwaves to Beckhams.'

So the next day she puts on a bowler hat, suit, wig and false beard and goes and asks the same question. The sales clerk replies the same way. Posh then asks how he knows she is Mrs Beckham. The clerk says, 'That isn't a microwave. It's a TV.'

David is chatting to his friend Phil Neville. 'I'm thinking of taking Victoria on safari in Africa,' he says. 'Wow,' says Phil. 'That's brave. What would you do if she was attacked by a vicious wild lion?' 'Do? I wouldn't do anything,' says David. 'Nothing?' asks Phil, slightly aghast. 'No,' replies David. 'It's the law of the jungle. I'd leave the lion to fend for itself.'

David needs to increase his level of fitness if he is to excel at Real Madrid, so he goes to a Spanish doctor. 'What I would advise you to do,' says the doctor, 'is run five miles a day for the next fifty days and then come back and see me.' Sure enough, fifty days later, the doctor receives a phone call from David. 'I thought I told you to come back and see me,' he says. 'I can't,' replies David. 'I'm two hundred and fifty miles from home and I don't know the way back.'

☺ A policeman is startled to see David Beckham whizz pass him on the motorway at seventy mph, happily knitting at the wheel. He chases after him, pulls up beside the speeding car and shouts, 'Pull Over!' 'No,' cries David. 'Pair of socks!'

☺ David alights from a train feeling a bit queasy. Victoria, who meets him, asks why he feels sick. 'I always feel sick if I'm facing towards the back of the train,' he explains. 'Couldn't you just ask to swap with the person opposite you?' asks Victoria. 'I thought about doing that,' he replies, 'but there was nobody sitting there.'

Man Utd are playing Chelsea at Old Trafford one Saturday afternoon. Fifteen minutes into the game George Weah is adjudged to have fouled Jaap Stam at a corner and furiously shouts and remonstrates at the ref. Upon seeing this, Beckham goes up to Weah, puts a finger up to his lips and says, 'Shhhhh.' Then he bursts out laughing and runs off leaving Weah somewhat bewildered. Ten minutes later Dwight Yorke puts the reds one up after sloppy defending and George is furious at his defence and shouts at them to get their act together. Once again Beckham comes up to Weah, says, 'Shhhh,' starts wetting himself laughing and runs off again. Weah turns to his equally puzzled team-mates but they all shrug their shoulders in confusion too. Just before half-time old George loses his cool again and shouts at a linesman and for a third time Beckham repeats his strange act. The half-time whistle goes and as the players walk off, Roy Keane goes to Beckham and says, 'Hey Becks, what's all that about with Weah then?' Beckham whispers something in Keane's ear and the Irishman looks to the heavens and says to Beckham, 'No, you twat, he's a Liberian!'

David Beckham, Rio Ferdinand and Paul Scholes are having their lunch break. Rio gets his sandwiches out and says, 'If I have corned beef sandwiches one more time, I swear I'll kill myself.' Paul gets his ones out and says, 'Oh no, not egg and cress. Honestly, if I get them again, I swear I'll do myself in.' David gets his sandwiches out and says, 'Oh no, not cheese and pickle. One more cheese and pickle sandwich and I'm a goner.'

Next day they all stop for lunch. Rio gets his sandwiches outs, sees they're corned beef, can't take it any more and runs out in front of a bus. Similarly, Paul sees he's got egg and cress and does the same. David opens his lunch box, sees with dismay, a pile of cheese and pickle sandwiches and runs into the road himself. The following week, after the funerals, the three women in the footballers' lives are consoling themselves. 'I'll never understand it,' says Rio's mum. 'I thought he liked corned beef sandwiches.' 'Me too,' says Paul's wife. 'I could have sworn he loved egg and cress sandwiches.' 'It's a mystery to me too,' says Victoria. 'David always made his own lunch.'

By a strange quirk of fate, Posh Spice finds a magic lamp. She rubs it and out pops a genie. 'You have released me from the prison of the lamp,' says the genie. 'As a reward, I shall grant you one wish. What does your heart desire?' 'After some deliberation and knowing that she has all the money she could ever need, Posh decides to make a noble wish. 'I wish that peace could descend upon all the countries of the world.' 'I am afraid that some things are beyond even my control,' said the genie. 'Wish again.' 'OK,' says Posh, 'In that case I wish that people would stop thinking that my husband is so daft.' 'I see,' says the genie. 'Let me have another look at that map of the world ... '

After downing more beers than is good for him, a big, mean-looking bloke stands up in the pub and shouts, 'Right, everyone on the left-hand side of the pub is stupid.' Seeing that he's getting no reaction he yells, 'And everyone on the right-hand side of the pub is a wimp.' Suddenly he sees David Beckham standing up. 'Think you're hard enough then, do you?' says the bloke. 'Not really,' replies David. 'It's just that I'm sitting on the wrong side of the pub.'

The England team have to go to the doctor's for a special memory test. First up is Rio Ferdinand.

'What's two times two?' asks the doctor.

'Ha!' says Rio. 'Easy. It's three thousand and eighty-two.'

'Hmmm, OK,' says the doctor, turning to Emile Heskey.

'What do you think two times two is?'

'Um, is the answer Tuesday?'

'Er, nearly, Emile,' replies the doctor.

He turns to David Beckham. 'And you, David do you know what two times two is?'

David scratches his head and suddenly looks enlightened.

'Is it four, doctor?'

'Brilliant!' exclaims the doctor. 'How did you work that out?'

'Oh, it was quite easy really,' replies David. 'I just subtracted three thousand and eighty-two from Tuesday.'

David was attacked by muggers. Despite being in the peak of fitness, he was no match for the three men who eventually overpowered him and found thirteen pence in this pocket. 'Are you trying to tell us you put up all that resistance for thirteen pence?' ask one of the muggers. 'Of course not,' says David. 'I thought you were after the three grand in my jockstrap!'

Victoria checks into a hotel and the porter offers to take her bags to her room. As the door closes Posh gets on her high horse. 'Young man,' she says. 'This is not the room I requested. There's no en-suite bathroom, no window.' She looks around. 'There's not even a bed.' 'No, Mrs Beckham,' says the porter. 'This is the lift.'

David Beckham walks down the street pulling an old length of string behind him. A fan sees him and says,

'Hey, David, why are you pulling that piece of string?'

'Well,' says David, 'it's a lot easier than pushing it.'

① David goes to the doctor with a cucumber up his nose and a pickled onion in his ear. 'I'm not feeling too well, Doc,' he complains. 'I'm not surprised,' says the doctor. 'You're clearly not eating properly.'

Brooklyn was asking his mum what certain words meant.

'What's the opposite of joy, Mum?' he asks.

'The opposite of joy, Brooklyn, is sadness.'

'Oh I see. So what's the opposite of anger?'

'Well, I suppose that the opposite of that one is happiness.'

'Right,' says Brooklyn. 'And what's the opposite of woe?'

'Hey,' interrupts David. 'I think I know this one. Is it giddy up?'

David comes home very late one night, a little the worse for wear. Posh is not impressed. 'Where have you been?' she yells. 'I've had the most amazing night out,' says David, oblivious to his wife's fury. 'We went to this bar and it was so exclusive, everything was made of gold. The seats were made of gold, the glasses were made of gold, even the urinals were made of gold!' 'That is the biggest cock and bull story I've ever heard,' says Posh. 'If such a place existed, I'd have heard of it. Where is it?' 'No idea,' says David, 'I'm too drunk to remember.' 'Well you'd better tomorrow, or you'll be in trouble.' Next day, David gets the phone book and calls around all the bars in the area, asking each one if they have all the gold decor. Finally, he finds the right bar and shouts to Victoria, 'Here, I've found it. Have a word with the landlord.' So Victoria comes to the phone, puts on her poshest voice and says, 'I know this might sound like an odd question, but do you have a golden urinal in your establishment?' The landlord puts the phone down and she hears him call, 'Hey, Fred, I think I've found out who peed in your saxophone last night!'

David Beckham's sister gives birth to twins, but unfortunately ends up in a coma after the birth. A week later she wakes up and her first question is about her children. 'Don't worry, they're fine,' the doctor tells her. 'Your brother's even given them names.' David's sister groans inwardly. 'What did he call the girl?' she asks. 'Denise,' replies the doctor. That's not too bad, she thinks. 'And what about the boy?' 'Denephew.'

☺ What is the difference between an aeroplane kit and David Beckham? One is a glueless kit, the other is a clueless git!

Young David wants to earn himself a bit of pocket money, so he offers his services around the neighbourhood doing odd jobs. His neighbour says to him,

'OK, I'll give you twenty pounds if you paint my porch while I'm out at work.'

'Right you are,' says David, thrilled,and sets to work.

When the neighbour comes back from work that evening, he finds David looking as pleased as punch.

'Did you get the work done?' he asks him.

'Absolutely,' replies David, 'in fact I gave it two coats. Oh just one thing – it's actually a Ferrari!'

David Beckham is strolling down the road carrying a plastic bag, when an old tramp comes up to him.

'What have you got in the bag?' asks the tramp.

'Pork pies,' replied David.

'I'll tell you what,' says the tramp. 'If I can tell you how many pork pies you've got in the bag, you have to give me one.'

'If you can tell me that,' retorts David, 'I'll give you both of them.'

David takes Posh out to a swanky restaurant.

'What would you like, darling?' he asks her.

'I think I'll have the asparagus.'

David lowers his voice.

'Don't be stupid. They don't serve sparrows here – and my name's not Gus!'

St Peter is standing at the Pearly Gates when up walks Wolfgang Amadeus Mozart. Peter puts one hand up and says,

'Stop. I need proof of identity before you can go in.'

'Fair enough,' says Mozart. 'I'm Wolfgang and this is one of my tunes.'

And he whistles a few bars of 'Eine Kleine Nachtmusik'.

'Good enough for me,' says Peter. 'In you go.'

A little later, William Shakespeare walks up. Peter puts up a hand and says,

'Stop! I need proof of identity before letting anyone in.'

'In truth,' says Shakespeare, 'I am the bard of Stratford. To be or not to be, that is the question!'

'Lovely,' says Peter. 'In you go.'

Soon enough up walks David Beckham.

'Stop! I need proof of identity before I let you in.'

'What do you mean you need proof of identity? I'm David Beckham. Everyone knows who I am.'

'Sorry, sir,' says Peter. 'Even Mozart and Shakespeare had to give proof of identity.'

'Who?' asks David.

'In you go, Mr Beckham.'

☺ Romeo Beckham got his first chance to play for Man U at Old Trafford, so he asked his dad what number he should wear and his dad thought for a minute and said ... 'Romeo, Romeo, wear four out there, Romeo.'

David Beckham buys himself a fridge. Keen that his celebrity client should be satisfied with his purchase, the salesman calls him up to check everything is OK.

'How's the new fridge, Mr Beckham?'

'Oh, fine I suppose,' says David, 'but I do find it difficult cutting the ice into squares so that it fits in the tray.'

David Beckham turns up for training wearing different-coloured boots – one's black, and the other one's brown. Ferguson stops him and says: 'Go home and change your boots.' 'I can't, boss,' says Beckham, 'the ones I've got at home are just like the ones I'm wearing.'

Having retired from the heady world of football, David decides that it is time to take his family to the countryside and follow a simpler lifestyle. He decides to rear his own chickens. It turns out that his neighbour is also a chicken farmer.

'I'll tell you what,' says the neighbour to David. 'Chicken farming isn't easy. To help you get started, I'll give you a hundred chickens.'

'That's very kind of you,' says David and takes his hundred chickens.

Next day, the neighbour stops by and asks how things are going.

'Not too well,' David's forced to admit. 'All the chickens are dead.'

'Really! That is strange. But never mind, I'll give you another hundred chickens. See how you get on with those.'

So David takes another hundred chickens, but when the neighbour stops by again the next day, he has to say that these chickens have died too.

'What do you think is going wrong?' asks the neighbour.

'Well, I'm not sure,' replies David. 'But I think I might be planting them too close together.'

A policeman sees a flash sports car doing a very slow four miles per hour on quite a fast road, so decides to pull it over to check that everything is OK. To his surprise the driver is David Beckham.

'You seem to be driving very slowly, Mr Beckham. Is everything all right?'

'Fine officer,' he replies. 'It's just that the sign back there says that the speed limit is four miles per hour … .'

'Er, no, that's not the speed limit, that's the name of the road. You're on the M4.'

At this point he notices Posh sitting in the passenger seat, trembling, her face as white as a sheet.

'What's wrong with her?' asks the policeman.

'Oh nothing,' answers David sheepishly. 'We just came off the A316 … '

David Beckham was speaking at a management conference and in response to a question said,

'Well, the great thing about them is they're only two calories and leave your mouth feeling fresh for an hour.'

A voice from the back called out, 'David, we wanted you to speak about tactics!'

☺ David goes to his coach and says:
'Coach, coach, I keep seeing spots in front of my eyes.'
'Have you seen a doctor, David?'
'No coach, just the spots.'

David Beckham was driving his Ferrari around when he almost crashed into a truck. The trucker got out and went up to David and started shouting at him.

David said, 'Yeah, yeah can I just go now?'

The trucker marked out a circle and said to him, 'I need to get something out my truck. Don't go out of the circle till I get back.'

He went to his truck and came back with a sledgehammer. He walked up to David's car and smashed the windscreen. He turned around and David started laughing. So he got a stake and popped the tyres. David started laughing harder. He poured lighter fluid on the car and set it alight. David was peeing himself!

The trucker said to him 'What are you doing? I've just fucked up your Ferrari.'

And David said 'I know ... but each time you turn around I jump out the circle!'

One hot summer's day Posh come home to find David painting the front door.

'You're doing a great job, darling,' she tells him. 'But tell me, why are you wearing your leather jacket and your raincoat?'

David points at the tin.

'It says here, "For best results, put on two coats!"'

David's personal trainer decides that he's a little bit overweight, so he puts him on a diet.

'What I want you to do,' he says, 'is eat normally for three days then skip a day. Carry that on for a month, and then come back to see me.'

Sure enough, a month later David comes back looking much leaner and fitter than he was.

'That's a great diet,' he says, 'but you know, I thought I was going to drop dead on that fourth day.'

'What,' asks the trainer, 'from hunger?'

'No,' says David. 'From skipping.'

David Beckham walks into a beauty salon to get a hair cut with his headphones on. The hairdresser asks him to take them off for the haircut and he replies, 'I can't, I'll die.'

She proceeds to cut his hair and it looks awful. Six weeks later he comes in for another haircut. The hairdresser pleads with him to take his headphones off. Once again Becks replies, 'I can't, I'll die!' So he receives another awful haircut.

Six weeks later David turns up at the salon and once again the hairdresser says, 'Please take your headphones off – I can make your hair beautiful if you would just take off the headphones.'

'I can't, I'll die!' he moans. The hairstylist proceeds to cut his hair. While doing so Becks falls asleep. The hairstylist quickly thinks to herself – I will remove the headphones and replace them before he wakes up. I'll make his hair look wonderful.

Seconds after doing this he falls off the chair. The hairdresser checks and he isn't breathing. Dying to know what was keeping him alive, she places the headphones on her head. She hears Posh Spice's voice, saying, 'Breathe in, breathe out, breathe in, breath out.'

David and Victoria are playing Trivial Pursuit.

'If you're in a vacuum,' asks Victoria, 'can you hear your name if someone calls it?'

David thinks for a bit. 'Erm,' he manages after a while, 'is it on or off?'

A policeman is walking down the road when he sees David Beckham pushing a wheelbarrow full of penguins.

'Ello, ello,' he says, 'what have we here?'

'Don't worry, officer,' says David. 'I'm just taking this wheelbarrow full of penguins down to the zoo.'

'Well, sir,' says the copper, 'mind you do.'

Next day, the same policeman is walking down the same street, when he sees David Beckham with the same wheelbarrow full of the same penguins, only this time they all have buckets and spades.

'Excuse me, Mr Beckham,' he says, 'but I thought I asked you to take that wheelbarrow full of penguins to the zoo.'

'I did,' replied David. 'But we had such a good time I thought we'd go to the beach today!'

⊙ What did David Beckham have for breakfast this morning? Who cares.

David is on a plane when, mid-flight, the captain is taken ill.

Fortunately David saves the day by landing the plane at the nearest airport. But it is a difficult landing and David only manages to avert an accident by the skin of his teeth.

'That's the shortest runway I've ever seen,' says David to one of the air stewardesses.

'I agree,' says the air stewardess. 'But it sure is wide.'

Fed up of Posh nagging him to cut down the trees at the bottom of the garden, David goes to a hardware store.

'I want a saw that will cut down six trees in an hour,' he tell the assistant, who sells him a top-of-the-range chainsaw.

Next day, David comes back. 'I want a refund,' he says. 'It took me all day to cut that tree down.'

Concerned and eager to locate the problem, the assistant starts up the chainsaw.

'What's that noise?' asks David.

On his first night in Spain, David decides to treat himself to a traditional Spanish meal, so he takes himself off to one of Madrid's finest restaurants and orders the house speciality. The waiter brings him a plate with two large, meaty-looking rissoles.

'What's this?' he asks.

'These, Senor Beckham, are cojones.'

'What are cojones when they're at home?'

'They are the testicles of the bull that lost in today's bullfight.'

Not one to turn down a new experience, David tucks in and, to his surprise, finds his meal quite delicious. So good, in fact, that he returns the next night and orders the same thing. When his meal comes, however, he finds that the cojones are much smaller. He beckons the waiter over and asks for an explanation.

'Well, you see, Senor Beckham, it is not always the bull who loses ... '

David's on the train and the guard approaches him asking for his ticket. David searches his pockets in an increasing state of agitation and finally has to admit, 'This is terrible. I think I have lost my ticket.'

'Don't worry about it, Mr Beckham,' says the guard. 'I'm sure you're not a fare dodger.'

'You don't understand,' says David. 'I've got to find it otherwise I won't know where to get off!'

⊙ If David Beckham were to become one of the Spice Girls which one would he turn out to be? Waste of Spice!

David sees a little, grey-haired old man in the street and decides to cheer up his day by going and talking to him.

'All right, mate,' he says. 'I couldn't help but notice how happy you look. What's your secret?'

'Well,' says the man. 'Every day, I smoke a hundred cigarettes and drink a bottle of whisky. I don't do any exercise, and I only eat bacon and eggs.'

'That's amazing,' says David. 'How old are you?'

'Thirty-six!'

Tributes had been pouring in over the sad news of the death of Sir Stanley Matthews.

Kevin Keegan said he was 'a legend'.

Alan Hansen described his talent as 'sublime'.

Bobby Charlton called him 'a Brazilian in an England shirt'.

Gary Lineker was quoted as saying, 'He was the last great gentleman of the game.'

David Beckham said, 'It's a real shame. Posh and I loved his Turkey Drummers.'

David Beckham's footballing prowess suddenly deserts him and so Posh sends him out to get another job. He goes for an interview on a building site.

'Can you make tea?' asks the foreman.

'Oh yes,' says David. 'I can make tea.'

'Can you drive a fork-lift truck?'

'What?' asks David. 'How big is this teapot?'

Snow White, Arnold Schwarzenegger and Saddam Hussein are having a conversation. Snow White says, 'I am the most beautiful, divine woman in the world, but how do I know?'

Arnie says, 'I am hunkiest man in the world, but how do I know?'

Saddam says, 'I'm the most despised person in the world, but how do I know?'

'I know,' says Snow White, 'let's ask the Wise Man.' So off they go. Snow White comes out of the wise man's house and says: 'Yes, it's true, I am the most beautiful divine woman in the world.'

Arnie comes out and says 'Yes, it's true, I am hunkiest man in the world.'

Saddam comes out and says, 'Who's David Beckham?'

David Beckham walks into a sperm donor bank. 'I'd like to donate some sperm,' he says to the receptionist. 'Certainly, sir,' she replies. 'Have you donated before?' 'Yes,' replies Beckham, 'you should have my details on your computer.' 'Oh, yes, I've found your details,' says the receptionist, 'but I see you're going to need help. Shall I call Posh Spice for you?' 'Why do I need help to donate sperm?' asks Beckham. 'Well,' the receptionist replies, 'it says on your record that you're a useless tosser.'

Becks, Posh and Brooklyn enter a raffle. To her delight Posh wins first prize – a huge bottle of perfume.

Funnily enough, Brooklyn comes in second and wins himself a football.

Third prize goes to David and he goes home the proud owner of a new toilet brush.

Next day, Brooklyn says to his mum, 'Mum, do you like your new perfume?'

'Yes, darling, it's lovely,' says Posh. 'How about your new football?'

'Oh, it's brilliant. What about your new toilet brush, Dad, is that good?'

'Not really,' says David, 'I think I'll go back to using paper.'

Cristiano Ronaldo

Rumours are circulating that Ronaldo dived from his car just before it hit the barrier. When police arrived at the scene the footballer was heard to complain that the wall wasn't back ten yards.

Police are investigating why the so called 'world's best player' can't take a corner.

The strange thing about Ronaldo's car crash is that, even though he only slightly injured his leg in the accident, he rolled out of the car clutching his head.

Sir Alex Ferguson has claimed that Ferrari did not offer Ronaldo enough protection.

! Why did the chicken cross the road? Because Cristiano Ronaldo mounted the kerb.

! How does Ronaldo change a light bulb? He holds it in the air and the world revolves around him.

! What's the difference between Ronaldo and God? God doesn't think he's Ronaldo.

Why did the chicken cross the road?

Arsene Wenger: 'From my position in the dug-out I did not see the incident clearly so I cannot really comment. However, I do think that he gets picked on by opposition players and fans who are clearly chickenophobic.'

Sam Allardyce: 'It's always the same against the so-called big four. That chicken crossed the road perfectly, and the ref has bottled it, making him go back to the kerb.'

David O'Leary: 'To be fair, he's just a baby chicken really and crossing the road is just a big exciting adventure for him. He'll enjoy the experience as long as it lasts and learn from it, but I don't seriously expect him to cross it this season.'

Alex Ferguson: 'As far as I'm concerned he crossed the road at least a minute early according to my watch.'

George Graham: 'I want a good, solid team of chickens who'll cross the road in a straight line when they're told and how they're told. There's no room at this club for a prima donna chicken running around aimlessly – he's not worth it!'

Gianfranco Zola: 'He'll just be one of the chaps. I like, he attractive passing chicken. He love West Ham, this chicken. His technique in crossing the road is marvellous.'

Glenn Hoddle: 'The chicken was hit by the lorry when crossing the road because in a previous life it had been a bad chicken.'

Brian Clough: 'If God had wanted chickens to cross roads he'd have put corn in the tarmac. Anyway, I'm more interested in Wild Turkey.'

Ron Atkinson: 'Spotter's badge, Clive. For me, Chicko's popped up at the back stick, little eyebrows, and gone bang! And I'll tell you what – I've got a sneaking feeling that this road's there to be crossed.'

Ruud Gullit: 'I am hoping to see some sexy poultry.'

Gordon Strachan: 'I'm really proud of the wee fella. Let's face it, if it had been one of the big chickens everyone would be saying how well he'd done, but as it's one of the wee chickens it must be luck.'

Kevin Keegan: 'OK, so the chicken's dead, but I still feel, hey, he can go all the way to the other side of the road.'

Joe Royle: 'I can't understand why they're letting female chickens cross roads these days. They should be at home laying eggs.'
Bobby Robson: 'Goose, what turkey, is there a duck somewhere, where am I?'

For Sale: West Ham BANNERS – Come complete with interchangeable slogans
E.g:- 'Pardew OUT', 'Roeder OUT', 'LET ME OUT' etc.. £15:00

⊕ Phil Thompson went to the Liverpool Xmas party last season dressed as a pumpkin. Come midnight he still hadn't turned into a coach.

A little Welsh lad is practising his free kicks at Derby. He has one of those portable walls which he moves around to change the angle so he can shoot from different areas of the field. He takes fifty kicks at goal, every one finds the back of the net. Nigel Clough is watching in the stands and walks down to talk to the young man.

'How old are you, son?' asks Nigel.

'Eleven,' replies the young fellow.

'Well, I am very impressed with your shooting,' says Clough, 'and I must say if you continue in this vein of form, when you get older you may be good enough to play for the Derby first team ...'

'Get lost!' said the boy. 'It's bad enough being Welsh!'

The fire brigade phones Harry Redknapp in the early hours of Sunday morning. 'Mr Redknapp, sir, White Hart Lane is on fire!'

'The cups, man! Save the cups!' cries Harry.

'Uh, the fire hasn't spread to the canteen yet, sir.'

⊕ How do you confuse a Manchester United fan? Show him a map of Manchester.

A woman goes to see the doctor. 'Doctor, doctor, I'm very worried about my son,' she said. 'All he does is play football all day; then he comes in covered in mud and walks all over my clean carpet.'

'I rather think you may be overreacting,' said the doctor reassuringly. 'Sons often behave like that.'

'I know, doctor,' said the woman, 'but it's not just me that's worried about him. His wife is too.'

A football widow decided to take an interest in the game in order to share her husband's pastime. One Saturday afternoon she accompanied him to the local match. It was a good game: plenty of open play, good attacking movements and strong defence.

She was enjoying the game when suddenly all the players except one froze and stood like statues. The active player grabbed the ball and shoved it up his jersey.

Then he too remained motionless. The woman looked at the referee to see what action he was going to take, but he too was in a statue-like position.

'Whatever are they doing?' she asked.

'Oh, they're posing for the "Spot-the-Ball" competition', replied her husband.

☺ Wolves are being predicted to stay in the Premiership for three seasons. Autumn, winter, spring.

Wife: 'Football, football, football! That's all you ever think about! If you said you were going to stay at home one Saturday afternoon to help with the housework, I think I'd drop dead from the shock!'

Husband: 'It's no good trying to bribe me, dear.'

A woman was reading a newspaper one morning and said to her husband, 'Look at this, dear. There's an article here about a man who traded his wife for a season ticket to Arsenal. You wouldn't do a thing like that, would you?'

'Of course I wouldn't!' replied her husband. 'The season's almost over!'

The Oxford and Cambridge University student teams were due to play when one of the Oxford men had to drop out at short notice. 'Why don't we use Johnson, the head porter at Balliol?' suggested the Oxford captain to the selection committee.

'I've seen him play in a local amateur team and he's a brilliant striker – absolutely unstoppable. We can get him a set of colours and as long as he doesn't speak to anyone, we should be able to get away with it.'

The committee thought this might be a little unethical but in desperation they agreed to the plan. They rigged out the Balliol porter and put him on the left wing. He was, as the Oxford captain had said, unstoppable, and they beat Cambridge 9–1, Johnson having scored eight of the goals single-handed.

Afterwards in the bar, the Cambridge captain approached Johnson and said sportingly, 'Well done, old boy! A magnificent effort! By the way, what are you studying at Balliol?'

The porter thought for a moment, then said brightly, 'Sums!'

⊙ Have you heard about the Bobby Zamora computer virus? It infects your PC, and makes it really hard to find the net.

A player was being ticked off by the coach for missing a very easy goal kick.

'All right,' said the player, 'how should I have played the shot?'

'Under an assumed name,' snapped a defender.

A match took place recently in Oxford between a local amateur team and a side made up of university tutors and professors. Before the match the two captains faced each other while the referee flipped the coin to decide who would have choice of ends.

The local team won the toss and, as the captain shook hands with his opposite number, he said sportingly, 'May the best team win!'

The university captain sighed, removed his monocle and polished it on his jersey, 'You mean, may the better team win!'

A famous soccer international was talking to another guest at a party.

'I've been persuaded to write my autobiography,' he said, 'but I don't want it published until after I'm dead.'

'Really?' said the guest. 'I shall look forward to reading it.'

ⓘ Why should you never run over a Liverpool supporter when they are on a bike? It's probably your bike.

A famous English footballer had just been transferred for a record sum of money and was being interviewed on television.

'Do you realize,' said the interviewer, 'that the money you will receive as a result of this transfer, together with your income from endorsements, personal appearances, lecturing and so on will mean that you'll have earned more in one year than the Queen gets?'

'Well, I should hope so!' said the footballer. 'She's a rubbish left back.'

'Is your goalkeeper getting any better?' asked a fan to his friend.' Not really,' he replied. 'Last Saturday he let in five goals in the first ten minutes. He was so fed up when he failed to stop the fifth that he put his head in his hands – and dropped it!'

ⓘ 'My wife would make a great goalie,' one man said to his friend. 'I haven't scored for months.'

It was only the fourth week of the season and United's new goalkeeper had already let in twenty-seven goals. He was having a drink in a pub one night when a man approached him and said,

'I've been watching you play, son, and I think I might be able to help you.'

'Are you a trainer?' said the young goalkeeper hopefully.

'No,' said the stranger, 'I'm an optician.'

I'm not saying our goalkeeper is rubbish but ...

- He suffers from repetitive strain injury in his back from continually having to bend over and pick the ball out of the back of the net ...

- He is the hero of the other team's supporters club.

- He once saved a penalty and eight fans were taken to hospital suffering from shock.

An amateur team in the west of Ireland played a match against a team from the local monastery.

Just before the kick-off the visiting team, all of whom were monks, knelt down solemnly on the pitch, put their hands together and indulged in five minutes of silent prayer.

The monastery then proceeded to trounce their hosts 9–0. After the match the home team captain said,

'Well, lads, we've been out-played before but this is the first time we've ever been out-prayed!'

A teacher at a blind school is taking the soccer team to an away game. They stop for a roadside break and the team has an impromptu practice in a nearby pasture. The bus driver comes over to the teacher and asks how he taught blind kids to play soccer. 'We made a special ball for them with a bell in it,' replies the teacher. Just then a farmer comes along, 'Hey!' he shouts. 'Are you the guy with those damn blind kids from the bus?' 'Yes,' says the teacher. 'What about it? You got something against blind kids?' 'Not ordinarily,' says the farmer. 'But right now they're kicking the hell out of my best milk cow!'

☺ What's the difference between a chocolate orange and the European Cup? The European Cup isn't Terry's!

⚠ When did John Terry start playing football?
When he was just a slip of a lad.

What's big and blue and goes beep, beep, beep? The Chelsea open-top bus reversing back into the garage.

Missing: 1 x Bottle.
Last seen: twenty-first of May 2008, Moscow.
If found please return to: John Terry, Stamford Bridge, London.

⚠ Heard about the John Terry tyre? Excellent durability but not so good in the wet.

John Terry always listens to the same song before a game – 'Born Slippy'.

⚠ John Terry is going to start making his own brand of vodka – and like him it's bottled in Russia.

Police are called to Old Trafford. A man in full Chelsea strip is standing on top of the main stand, threatening to throw himself off.

The police negotiator says to him, 'Come on, mate, it's not that bad, don't do it!'

'You don't get it!' says the Chelsea fan. 'For years I've been a Chelsea supporter, and this year I was convinced we would win everything. Instead, we were kicked out of the FA cup by Barnsley ... we lost the Carling Cup final to Spurs ... then we lost the Premiership to Man U, and then we went to the Champions League final and United beat us again! I can't take it any more!'

'OK, mate, I do understand your pain,' replied the negotiator, 'but I don't understand one thing ... why are you here at Old Trafford? Why aren't you jumping off the main stand at Stamford Bridge?'

The Chelsea fan looked at the policeman and replied, 'Have you seen the QUEUE?'

The Verve have released a tribute song to John Terry after his Champions League penalty blunder.

It's called 'The Studs Don't Work'.

What's the difference between O. J. Simpson and Bulgaria? O. J. Simpson had a more credible defence!

① John Terry was unfortunate to miss out on an Adidas Football Boots sponsorship deal following defeat in the Champions League final. However, it's not all bad news. He has been offered a very nice deal by a company who make slippers.

Zidane, Ronaldo and Terry are at the pearly gates of heaven when St Peter opens the gate. He turns to Zidane and asks, 'Why do you deserve eternal happiness in heaven, my son?'

Zidane replies, 'I am an artist: I inspire young people to be great footballers and in turn take them away from a life of crime.' St Peter nods, impressed.

He turns to Ronaldo and asks the same question. Ronaldo retorts, 'When I play football, I treat everyone as an equal: I see no ethnic or racial divides. The boy from Rio is the same as the superstar from Madrid.'

Once again, St Peter is impressed and nods.

Next he turns to Terry and says, 'I suppose you want your ball back?'

A tourist at a Paris brasserie sits down to eat his croissant. He glances at an unfamiliar sachet which is branded 'Zidane'. 'What is this?' asks the tourist. The waiter replies, 'Monsieur, zat iz ze finest French butter.'

Why do all Portuguese children have long ears?

Because every time their parents go to the Spanish border with them, they lift them up by the ears and say: 'Look, over there, that's where the World Champions live.'

A German family head out one Saturday to do some shopping. While in the sports shop the son picks up an England football shirt and says to his sister, 'I've decided to be an England supporter and I would like this for my birthday.' His big sister is outraged by this and promptly whacks him round the head and says, 'Go talk to your mother.' So off goes the little lad with the white and red football shirt in hand and finds his mother. 'Mum?'

'Yes, son?'

'I've decided I'm going to be an England supporter and I would like this shirt for my birthday.' The mother is outraged at this, promptly whacks him around the head twice and says, 'Go talk to your father.' Off he goes with the football shirt in hand and finds his father. 'Dad?'

'Yes son?'

'I've decided I'm going to be an England supporter and I would like this shirt for my birthday.' The father is outraged and promptly whacks his son around the head four times and says, 'No son of mine is ever going to be seen in THAT!' About half and hour later they're all back in the car and heading towards home. The father turns to his son and says, 'Son, I hope you've learned something today?'

The son says, 'Yes, Dad, I have.'

'Good son, what is it?'

The son replies, 'I've only been an England supporter for an hour and already I hate you Germans!'

☺ Rafa Benitez has two signings lined up for the summer: a Japanese international and an Italian. He believes they should fit in well on Merseyside. They're called Nickamotor and Robatelli.

Some years ago an important European match between England and Scotland was taking place in Milan. The referee was Hungarian. His command of English left a good deal to be desired and the players of both teams were taking the mickey out of him at every opportunity. Finally the Hungarian's patience ran out. 'You British!' he shouted. 'You think I know damn nothing about the game! Let me tell you I know damn all!'

Football chants

'When the ball hits your head and you sit in row Z, that's Zamora.'
(to the tune of 'Amore'.)

'We're gonna deep-fry your pizzas!'
(Scotland supporters sung to Italy fans.)

'Neville Neville, your play is immense
Neville Neville, you play in defence
Neville Neville, like Jacko you're bad,
Neville Neville, the name of your dad'
(Sung to the tune of David Bowie's 'Rebel Rebel', to honour Gary and Phil Neville.)

'Don't blame it on the Biscan
Don't blame it on the Hamman
Don't blame it on the Finnan
Blame it on Traore ...
He just can't, he just can't, he just can't control his feet'
(To honour the hapless Djimi Traore during his time at Liverpool. Sung to the tune of 'Blame it on the Boogie'.)

'He's big, he's red
His feet stick out the bed
Peter Crouch, Peter Crouch'
(Liverpool fans celebrate Peter Crouch's physique.)

'Two Andy Gorams
There's only two Andy Gorams'
(after keeper Andy Goram was diagnosed with schizophrenia.)

Football limericks

There was a young player from Tottenham,
His manners he'd gone and forgotten 'em.
One day at the doc's
He took off his socks,
Because he complained he felt hot in 'em.

There was a young player from Crewe
Who seldom found that much to do.
For an hour or so
He ran to and fro
And after he ran fro and to

There was a young striker from Clyde
Who hated his eggs boiled or fried.
When asked to say why,
'It's just because I
Am a poacher by trade,' he replied.

Little Jack Horner once took a corner
And belted the ball so high.
With the keeper upset,
if went straight in the net.
So he said, 'What a good boy am I!'

A striker from somewhere in Kent
Took free kicks which dipped and then bent.
In a match on the telly
He gave one some welly
And the keeper the wrong way he sent.

There was a young player called Kelly
Who couldn't play 'cos of his belly
When he ran on the pitch,
He caused a big ditch,
So he just watches games on the telly.

There once was a footballing cat
Who played in a black bowler hat.
When he ran down the wing
He could not see a thing
And you can guess what the crowd thought of that!

There was a young striker from Spain
Who hated to play in the rain.
One day in a muddle
He stepped in a puddle
And got washed away in a drain.

A team of footballers from Stroud
Had supporters who shouted too loud.
When all ceased their din,
Goals just rocketed in,
So now they're a much quieter crowd.

A football pitch groundsman from Leeds
Went and swallowed a packet of seeds.
In less than an hour
His head was in flower
And his feet were all covered in weeds.

A player who turned out for Dover
Had no shirt, so he wore a pullover.
But the thing was too long
And he put it on wrong,
So that all he could do was fall over.

FOOTBALL

There was a young striker from Reading
Who bumped his brow on a door at a wedding.
It made his head swell
But he said, 'Just as well,
'Cos now I'll improve on my heading.'

A footballer in from the States
Was paid at very high rates.
But when he lost touch
He wasn't worth much.
Now he just kicks around with his mates.

There was a goalkeeper called Walter
Who played on the island of Malta.
But his kicks were so long
And the wind was so strong,
That the ball ended up in Gibraltar.

Was it City, United or Town
Got promoted and then went back down?
It was one of the three,
But it mystifies me,
Which is why I walk round with a frown.

There was a young player from Clyde
Took a penalty kick that went wide.
That next match his brother
Well, he missed another
And now neither can get in the side.

The wonderful Wizard of Oz
Retired from football because,
When he tried to run fast
His legs didn't last
'Cos he wasn't the wizard he was.

A footballing lad named Paul
Could do fabulous things with a ball.
In one of his tricks,
With a series of flicks,
He managed to knock down a brick wall.

A striker who came from Devizes
Did little to help to win prizes.
When asked for a reason,
He said, 'Well, this season
My boots were of two different sizes.'

Mary had a little lamb
Who played in goal a lot.
It let the ball go through its legs
So now it's in the pot.

Referees

Definition of a good referee:
1) Must be fair.
2) Must be consistent.
3) Must make correct judgements.
4) Must be able to stay in control.
5) Must award your team at least two penalties and give out two red cards to opposition players.

Reasons to become a referee:

- You love football, but can't quite understand the rules.
- You have the strange desire to run aimlessly around in the wind, rain and snow.
- You love the sound of verbal abuse.
- You find it hard to make decisions and whenever you do you're always wrong.

Offside definitions

- Definition 1: The Bermuda Triangle area of the pitch that 'innocent' players are drawn towards.

- Definition 2: The offside rule is there to attract to football those people who can already explain how to play cricket.

- Definition 3: A player is offside if they are nearer to the opponent's goal line than both the ball and the second last player except on alternate Saturdays when in addition the second last player must be facing in the opposite goal's direction in which the ball is directed.

A player is not offside if they are in their own half of the field, or they are level with the second last opponent, or the player, opponent and referee form a triangle as perceived by an imaginary linesmen positioned on the celestial meridian.

All offside regulations are immediately found to be in favour of the defending team if shortly after the ball is played they all stop, in unison, and raise their right arm to the linesman and appeal for an offside decision.

Referee: 'Penalty!'
Home captain: 'Who for?'
Referee: 'Us!'

A well-known footballer and his wife recently decided to take a holiday at a nudist camp. He was asked to referee the camp football match but, surprisingly, he declined the offer. 'Why did you refuse to referee that match?' asked his wife.

'I wasn't too happy about where I had to carry the spare whistle,' replied the husband.

'Just a minute, ref!' yelled the goalkeeper. 'That wasn't a goal.'

'Oh, wasn't it?' shouted the referee. 'You just watch the *Sport's Night* on TV tonight!'

Did you hear about the England international player who had a date with a referee's daughter? She penalized him three times for handling, interference and trying to pull off a jersey.

Referees at Celtic versus Rangers matches always have a particularly hard time. One poor unfortunate, officiating at his first fixture, was checking in with the team managers before the kick-off.

'Well, that seems to be about everything,' said the Rangers boss.

'Now, if you'd just like to give us the name and address of your next of kin, we can start the match.'

The angry captain snarled at the referee, 'What would l happen if I called you a blind fool who couldn't make a correct decision to save his life?' 'It would be a red card for you,' replied the referee. 'And if I didn't say it but only thought it?' asked the captain. 'That's different. If you only thought it but didn't say it, I couldn't do a thing,' said the ref. 'Well, we'll leave it like that, then, shall we?' smiled the captain.

The shrill blast of the whistle and the pointing finger of the referee stopped the player in his tracks. The referee beckoned him over and produced notebook, pencil and yellow card. 'It's a yellow card for you,' said the referee, waving the card at the footballer. 'You know what you can do with your yellow card!' shouted the player. 'You're too late, mate,' replied the referee. 'There are three red cards there already!'

'Your team's rubbish! We beat you 9–2 last Saturday, even though we had a man short!'

'What do you mean "a man short"? You had ten players and the referee, didn't you?'

Football and the Irish

The manager of an Irish club was talking to a young player who had applied for a trial with the club. 'Do you kick with both feet?' asked the manager. 'Don't be silly!' said the trialist. 'If I did that, I wouldn't be able to stand up, would I!'

In the heat of the game, one of the players threw a vicious punch. The victim was all set to get stuck into him when the referee rushed up and held him back. 'Now then, O'Hara! You know you mustn't retaliate!'

'Come on ref!' said O'Hara. 'He retaliated first!'

At recent Irish League match between Newry and Larne, the visitors were awarded a penalty and the captain summoned his best player and said, 'I want you to take this one, Patrick. Just think hard as you kick, think which way the wind is blowing, and think which direction the keeper's going to jump.' 'Holy Mother!' said Patrick. 'Do you expect me to think and kick at the same time?'

'Is your new striker fast?'

'Is he fast! He's so fast, the rest of the team have to run twice as fast just to keep up with him!'

It is said that in Ireland, if it looks like rain before a match, they play the extra time first.

The manager and coach of an Irish team were discussing the players they had on their books and the manager asked, 'How many goals has O'Halloran scored this season?'

'Exactly double what he scored last season,' replied the coach. 'Eleven.'

'I don't care about results!' said an Irish team manager being interviewed on television. 'Just so long as our team wins!'

Two Irish team managers promised their players a pint of Guinness for every goal they scored during an important match. The final score was 119-98.

Three football codes prevail in Ireland: rugby, which is defined as a thugs' game played by gentlemen; soccer, a gentleman's game played by thugs; and Gaelic football, a thugs' game played by thugs!

'I just don't understand it,' an Irish footballer complained.
'One match I play very well, then the next match I'm terrible.'
'Well,' said his wife, 'why don't you just play every other match?'

Golf

An elderly man and his wife were playing golf when on the fifteenth green she fell to the ground with a heart attack. Her husband ran to get help while she lay there. He soon returned, but instead of comforting his wife he began lining up a putt.

'What are you doing?' she said. 'I thought you went to get help.'

'It's OK, dear,' he replied. 'I found a doctor on the second hole and he said he'd help.'

'The second hole! How long is that going to take him to get here?'

'Don't worry, dear. Everyone's agreed to let him play through!'

☉ Golfers do it best when they are below par.

A man comes across four golfers in a bunker. One of the golfers is lying on the sand and the other three are arguing. 'What's the matter?' asks the man. One of the golfers turns to him and says, 'These swine will do anything to win a game. My partner's just had a stroke and they want to add it to our score.'

A terrible golfer hits his ball into a large bunker. 'Which club should I use for this one?' he asks his caddie as he prepares to step into the sand. 'I wouldn't worry about the club,' replies the caddie. 'Just make sure you take in plenty of food and water.'

Harry and Tom are on the golf course when Harry slices a shot deep into a wooded ravine. He takes his eight iron and clambers down the embankment in search of his lost ball. After fifteen minutes hacking at the underbrush, Harry spots something glistening among the leaves. He gets closer and discovers that it's an eight iron in the hands of a skeleton. Harry calls out to Tom, 'Hey! I've got trouble down here!' 'What's up?' shouts back Tom. 'Bring me my wedge!' replies Harry. 'You can't get out of here with an eight iron!'

On their honeymoon a husband confesses a secret to his new wife. 'Darling, I'm a golf addict,' he says. 'You'll never see me at the weekends and all our holidays will be at golfing resorts.' 'I've got a confession too,' replies his new wife. 'I'm a hooker.' 'That's not a problem,' replies the husband. 'Just keep your head down and your arm straight.'

☉ What's a golfer's favourite letter? Tee!

Two men were talking in the golf club bar: 'Did you hear about John? Fined £1,000 for hitting his wife with a three iron.'
  'Really? That sounds a bit steep!'
  'It wasn't the hitting so much. The judge fined him for using the wrong club.'

A grandfather and his young grandson were playing a round of golf together. On a severely dog-legged par four, the grandfather said, 'When I was your age, I would aim right over those trees and hit the green every time.'
  The grandson thought about the comment for a moment and decided to give it a try. He hit a perfect drive, but it landed smack in the middle of the fifty-foot trees.
  The grandson looked sadly at his grandfather, who said, 'Then again, when I was your age, those trees were only seven feet tall.'

☉ Why was the computer so good at golf?
It had a hard drive!

The course had just opened and a man was visualizing his shot when an announcement came over the loudspeaker: 'Would the gentleman on the ladies' tee kindly move back to the men's tee'. The golfer was oblivious, continuing with his routine. Again the announcement, 'Would the MAN on the LADIES' tee please move back to the men's tee!' The man's concentration broken, he lowers his club and shouts back, 'Would the announcer please shut up and let me play my second shot!'

A vicar played golf with one of his elderly parishioners and was well beaten. As he walked dejectedly back to the clubhouse, the old man tried to cheer him up: 'Never mind, reverend. You'll be burying me soon!'

'Yes,' said the vicar bitterly, 'and even then it will be your hole!'

Keith and Dick are out playing golf and Tom brings his Yorkshire terrier along with him. Every time Keith hits a good shot the little dog gets on its hind legs and gives him a round of applause. 'That's very impressive,' says Dick. 'But what does it do when you hit a bad shot?' 'He turns three or four somersaults,' replies Keith. 'But it depends on how hard I kick him.'

⊙ What do you call 143 white men chasing after one black one? PGA Tour.

Every Friday, Bob and Tom play golf. Tom is a terrible putter, so Bob always wins. One Friday, though, Tom doesn't miss any! He sinks every shot on the green. Bob can't believe his eyes. After the round, Bob asks, 'What's happened? You can't seem to miss today.' 'Order up the beer, while I go to the toilet,' Tom says. When Tom returns, the front of his trousers are all wet. 'What the heck happened to your trousers?' a confused Bob asks. 'I'll get to that in a minute. First, let me tell you about my new and improved game,' says Tom. 'Last week, I went to the eye doctor and he said I needed bifocals. So when I look down, I see a little ball and a big ball. I look over and I see a little hole and a big hole. I put the little ball in the big hole, and I can't miss.' 'But what about your trousers?' Bob asks again. 'I looked down and saw a little one and a big one,' Tom explains. 'I figured the little one couldn't be mine, so I put it away.'

A group of elderly golfers had waning enthusiasm for another round. 'The hills are getting steeper as the years go on,' complained one.

'The bunkers seem to be getting bigger, too,' added one of the others.

'And the fairways seem so long these days,' said a third.

The oldest among them nodded his head. 'At least we should be thankful we're still on the right side of the grass!'

☺ In Scotland a new game was invented: gentlemen only, ladies forbidden. And thus GOLF entered the language.

A vicar, a doctor and a lawyer were waiting one morning for a particularly slow group of golfers. 'What's wrong with this lot?' demanded the lawyer. 'I've never seen such poor players,' added the doctor. The vicar grabbed a passing green-keeper and asked what the problem with them was.

'That's a group of blind firemen,' the greenkeeper replied. 'Last year they lost their sight saving our clubhouse from burning down, so we always let them play for free when they want.' The three players considered this for a moment. 'I'm going to pray for these men tonight,' announced the vicar. 'And I'll contact an eye specialist to see if anything can be done for them,' said the doctor. The lawyer was silent for a moment, then said, 'Why can't they play at night?'

Tom and Dick are on the golf course. 'That's a funny-looking golf ball you've got there,' says Tom. 'It's the latest thing,' replies Dick. 'It's fantastic, a completely unloseable golf ball. If it goes in the bushes, it lights up. If it lands in the water, a flag pops up. If you lose it at night, it emits a bleeping sound till you track it down.' 'That's amazing,' says Tom. 'Where did you get it?' 'I found it,' replies Dick.

☺ Golfer to caddy: 'I'd move heaven and earth to be able to break a hundred on this course.' Caddy: 'Try heaven. You've already moved most of the earth.'

A group of golfers were searching the rough for one of their balls. After a few minutes of searching the golfer who sliced his ball into the undergrowth called out that he'd found his ball. 'He's a cheat,' calls back one of the others. The other golfers gather round. 'That's a pretty serious accusation you're making. Why do you say he's a cheat?'

'Because I've got his ball here in my pocket!'

⚎ A golfer is thrashing through the bushes, looking for a lost ball. An old lady watches him as she sits on a bench, knitting. After half an hour the golfer is just about to give up when the old lady says, 'Excuse me. But is it against the rules if I tell you where it is?'

A guy was just about to tee off when he was approached by a man who handed him a card which read: 'I am a deaf mute. Would you please allow me to play through?' The guy angrily shook his head as he handed the card back and said, 'NO, you cannot play through!' Figuring the man could lip read, he added, 'I can't believe you would attempt to use your handicap to your own advantage. You should be ashamed of yourself!' The deaf man walked away, while the guy whacked his ball onto the green and then walked off to finish the hole. As he was about to put the ball in the hole, he was knocked out cold when a golf ball hit him in the head.

Coming to a few minutes later, he looked around and saw the deaf mute giving him a stern look, one hand on his hip and the other holding up four fingers.

Rick tees off, but it slices horribly, hits a tree and bounces out of bounds into the road. He decides it's not worth going to look for the ball, tees up another ball and plays on. About half an hour later the club manager catches up with him further round the course. 'Rick, wait. Did you see what happened to your lost ball?'

'Well, I saw it hit a tree and bounce into the road but I didn't see anything after that.'

'Well, let me tell you. It hit a car and bounced into a school bus, where it hit the driver on the head, knocking him out. The bus skidded and went down an embankment where it burst into flames. Three kids are in intensive care in the hospital!'

'That's terrible,' wails Rick. 'What should I do?'

'Well, I think that if you just opened the face of the club a bit more ...'

A man was just about to tee off when he remembered that he had forgotten to tell his wife that the washing machine repair man was coming. So he pulled out his mobile to make a quick call home. A little girl answers the phone – 'Hello?' 'Hello, Sweetheart, it's Daddy. Is Mummy there?'

'No,' comes the reply :'She's upstairs with Uncle Fred!'

The man pauses, then says, 'But darling, you haven't got an Uncle Fred.'

'Yes I do, and he's upstairs in the bedroom with Mummy.'

'OK then. What I want you to do is go upstairs and shout through the bedroom door to Mummy and Uncle Fred that my car has just pulled up outside in the driveway.'

'All right, Daddy.'

A few minutes later the little girl comes back to the phone. 'I did what you said Daddy.'

'And what happened?'

'Well, Mummy jumped out of bed and ran around screaming, then she tripped on the rug and fell through the front window and now she's dead!'

'Oh no! What about Uncle Fred?'

'Well, he got up and ran straight out of the other window and landed in the swimming pool and he drowned so he's dead too.'

There is a long pause. 'Swimming pool? Is that 374 6712?'

What safety precautions should you take if lightening interrupts your round? Walk round with a one iron over your head. Not even God can hit a one iron!

A lady golfer runs into the clubhouse, 'Help, help, I've been stung by a bee, and I'm allergic to bee poison!'

'Where?' asks the club pro.

'Between the first and second holes,' she replies.

'Then your stance is too wide!'

A father felt the time had come in his son's life to sit him down for the 'big talk'. 'Soon, son,' the father said, 'you will begin to have urges and feelings you've never experienced before. Your hands will sweat and your heart will pound. You'll find you're preoccupied and unable to think about anything else. Don't worry though, son,' continued the father, 'I want you to know it's perfectly normal ... it's called golf.'

A man is playing the best golf of his life. He hits a magnificent tee shot which takes him halfway to the hole. However, there is a branch of a tree hanging down which is just in the way. He wonders whether to play safe with an iron, or go for it with a wood. As he's playing so well he chooses the wood. He gives the ball an almighty whack, it rockets off, hits the branch and rebounds into his head, killing him instantly. A short while later he is standing at the pearly gates in front of St Peter. St Peter is looking through his book, but he can't seem to find the man's name. 'How did you get here again?' asks an exasperated St Peter. 'I got here in two,' the man replies.

Tiger Woods pulls up at a posh country golf course for a round. He goes up to the imposing front door and rings the bell. After a while a club member sticks his head round the door, looks him up and down and asks him what he wants. Tiger explains he fancies a round on their course. 'I'm sorry,' says the snooty member. 'I think you'll find a more suitable club for you about a four-iron down the road.' Tiger is enraged. 'Don't you know who I am? I'm Tiger Woods, the best golfer ever!' The member slaps his head. 'Of course. So sorry. Tiger Woods, eh? Well, for you it's only a six-iron.'

ⓘ My brother went to the doctor's and said, 'Some days, I think I'm a golf ball.' The doctor said, 'Well you've come a fair way to see me ...'

John Smith was definitely not the best of golfers. One day he decided to go to a new golf course where no one knew him, just to get away and see if it was possible for him to do better elsewhere.

He hired a caddy to guide him around the course. After another day of his usual slices, duff shots, misread putts and bad temper, he was totally discouraged and upset.

Turning to the caddy he said, 'I must be the world's worst golfer.'

'Not really, sir,' replied the caddy. 'From what I understand there's a guy by the name of John Smith from across town who is the worst player ever!'

A novice golfer treats himself to a day at a posh course, complete with professional caddy. All day he plays badly, slicing shots and hacking around the course. At he end of the day he turns to the caddy and says, 'I've played so badly today that I think that I'm going to go and drown myself in that lake over there.'

The caddy looks back at him and says, 'I don't think you could keep your head down that long!'

⊕ My brother went to the doctor and said, 'Some days, I get the strange feeling that I'm a golf club.' The doctor said, 'Can I join?'

A blonde walks into a golf shop and starts going through all the shelves. The assistant comes over to ask if he can help. 'I'd like some green golf balls, please,' says the blonde. 'I'm afraid we don't stock those. May I ask madam why she wants green balls?' 'So I can see them easier in the bunker, stupid,' she replies.

This man wrote into the *Daily Mirror* for some advice. He said, 'Dear Marge, I must get this off my chest. I did this awful golf shot, and the ball didn't go anywhere near the green. In fact it landed on this bloke's head and killed him. What shall I do?'

Marge replied, 'Try and get more rhythm in your swing.'

Pat had such a bad round of golf that he went home and beat his wife to death. Overcome with remorse, he phoned the police and confessed his crime. A few minutes later a police car screeched to a halt outside his house and two policemen came up the path. Pat answered the door.

Police: 'Are you the man who beat his wife to death?'

Pat: 'I am.'

Police: 'And how did you kill her?'

Pat: 'I hit her with my five iron.'

Police: 'How many times did you actually hit her?'

Pat: 'Seven ...no, wait. Put me down for five.'

The expectant women and their partners were attending their antenatal class. The instructor was teaching the women how to breathe properly and was instructing the men on how to give the necessary assurances at this stage.

'Ladies,' the instructor said, 'you must remember that exercise is very good for you. Walking is especially beneficial. Gentleman, it wouldn't hurt you to go walking with your partner.'

The room was very quiet as everyone was paying careful attention to what the instructor had to say. Suddenly, a man in the middle of the group raised his hand.

'Yes, Mr Jones?' said the instructor.

'Is it OK if she carries a golf bag while we walk?'

(!) Two men are nearing the end of their round when one turns to the other and says: 'Do you know, I only play golf to annoy my wife. She thinks I'm having fun!'

Stevie Wonder and Jack Nicklaus are in a bar. Jack asks Stevie how the music business is treating him. 'Pretty well,' says Stevie. 'My last album went platinum. How's the golf going for you?' 'Not too bad,' replies Nicklaus. 'I'm still playing OK. I'm not winning as much money as I used to, but I'm doing all right.' Stevie nods and says, 'I find that when I'm not playing too well if I just stop for a bit it seems to be better next time I play.' Jack Nicklaus is amazed. 'I didn't know you played golf!' 'Have been for years,' says Stevie. 'But how do you manage, being blind?' asks Jack. 'Well,' says Stevie, 'what I do is get my caddy to stand in the fairway and call to me. Then I hit the ball towards the sound of his voice. Then when I get to the ball my caddy moves further towards the hole again and calls out and I hit the ball that direction.' 'How do you putt, though?' asks Nicklaus. 'I get my caddy to put his head on the ground right by the hole and putt towards the sound of his voice.' 'What's your handicap?' Jack asks. 'I play off scratch,' says Stevie. Jack is amazed and asks Stevie if he'd like to play a round. 'Ok,' he replies, 'but I only play for £100, 000 a hole because people don't take me seriously.' Jack thinks about this a while, then agrees: 'When do you want to play, then?'

'Any night next week is fine,' replies Stevie.

A brash American is playing golf on a Spanish course. His shot lands beside a lake, and he impatiently demands that the caddy tells him what club to use. The caddy hesitantly starts to offer advice in broken English: 'Last month Mr Kevin Costner here ...same shot ... he choose six iron ...' The golfer rudely grabs the six iron, takes a swing, and plops the ball straight down into the middle of the lake. He turns on the caddy, 'Hey, stupid. The six iron wasn't enough. I went straight in the water.' The caddy replies, 'That's what Kevin Costner did too!'

⊕ Man to caddy: 'Why do you keep looking at your watch?'
'It's not a watch. It's a compass.'

The golf club secretary was very apologetic, 'I'm terribly sorry, sir, but we have no time open on the course today.'

'Wait just a minute,' the member argued. 'If I told you that Prince Andrew and a friend wanted a game, would you find a starting time for them?'

'Most definitely,' she answered.

'Well, since I happen to know that the Prince is in Scotland at the moment, we'll just take his time,' said the member.

⊕ Two golfers come to a river halfway through their round. One turns to the other and says: 'Look at those idiots over there, fishing in the rain ...'

A man received a ransom note stating that if he ever hoped to see his wife alive again, he was to bring £50,000 to the seventeeth hole of the country club at ten the next morning.

The next day, he didn't arrive until almost 12.30. Jumping out from behind some bushes, a masked man yelled at him, 'What took you so long? You're over two hours late.'

'Give me a break, would you!' whined the man. 'I do have a twenty-seven handicap!'

A Jewish man went to a golf course one day where they prided themselves on the range of caddies they had. The man asked the head caddy if he had anyone who could caddy Jewish style. The head caddy asked around, but no one could help. In the end a new caddy came forward and said he could do it. The Jewish man and his new caddy went off towards the first hole, when the caddy whispered, 'Look, I don't know what Jewish style is. I just said I'd do it because I'm new here and I'd like to impress my boss. I'll do the round for half price if you'll teach me Jewish style on the way round.'

'You learn fast!' the man replied.

☺ Did you hear about the golfer who spent so much time in a bunker that he started to get letters addressed to Hitler?

Sitting in the clubhouse enjoying a drink after their game, one golfer turned to his friend and said, 'I'm so sorry to hear your uncle passed away last week. From what I've learned, it was while the two of you were playing golf. Apparently you carried him all the way back to the clubhouse. That must have been pretty difficult for you, considering he weighed well over two hundred pounds.'

With a saddened look on his face, his friend replied, 'Carrying him wasn't that difficult. The hard part was putting him down and then picking him up after each stroke.'

☺ Angry golfer to wife: 'One day you'll drive me out of my mind.'
Wife: 'That would be a putt, dear.'

A schoolteacher was taking his first golf lesson. 'Do you spell it p-u-t or p-u-t-t?' he asked the club pro. 'P-u-t-t is correct,' he replied. 'Put means to place a thing where you want it. Putt means a hopeful attempt to do the same thing.'

☺ A reporter was interviewing Jack Nicklaus. He said, 'Jack, you are spectacular. Your name is synonymous with the game of golf. You really know your way around the course. What is your secret?' To which Jack replied, 'The holes are numbered!'

A man and his wife played regularly on the same course, but in all the years of playing Mrs Jones had never been able to get over the water on the sixth hole, always falling short of the green and landing in the lake. Eventually the club pro was called, who recommended that Mrs Smith have hypnotherapy for what had obviously become a mental block. Mrs Smith duly went to see the hypnotist who put her in a trance and suggested to her that when she came to the sixth hole she should not see the water, but instead imagine it was a beautiful green fairway all the way up to the green.

A few months later the club pro was chatting in the bar to another couple, and mentioned that he hadn't seen Mrs Smith for a while. 'Oh, it's a terrible tragedy,' said the woman, 'she drowned on the sixth!'

A man dragged himself into the emergency room with multiple bruises, concussion, two black eyes and a nine iron wrapped around his throat. Shocked by all of this, the doctor asked him what happened.

'My wife and I were having a nice quiet round of golf,' he explained. 'We reached a difficult hole and both of us sliced our balls into a cow pasture. We went to look for them and while I was searching around I noticed a cow that had something white near its rear end.'

'I went over to it,' he continued, 'and lifted its tail. Sure enough, there was a golf ball with my wife's monogram on it stuck right in the middle of the cow's backside. That's when I made my biggest mistake.'

'What do you mean? What did you do?' asked the doctor.

'I pointed to the cow's bum and yelled out to my wife, "Hey, this one looks like yours!"'

A man went to the doctor with a strange complaint.

'Well it's like this, doc, whenever I play golf, I fall in love with the beautiful, lush fairways and greens we are playing on, and I just burst into song.'

'What's wrong with that?' said the doc.

'Well, all I ever sing when we're on the course is "The Green Green Grass of Home" and it's annoying my colleagues.

'But there's more ... When we get back to the clubhouse, in the bar is the lucky black cat that lives at the club. I see it, then at the top of my voice I start singing "What's new, pussy cat?" and all I get is a barrage of complaints from the other members in the bar.'

'Can't you sing some different tunes?' said the doctor.

'Well no, I just can't seem to sing anything else, but then it gets worse because when I get home, it continues and when I'm asleep and dreaming, I always sing "Delilah", and my wife is increasingly getting really angry and suspicious. But I just can't seem to stop singing these same tunes.'

'Ah, yes I see, I am beginning to suspect that you have the early symptoms of Tom Jones syndrome.'

'Well, I've never heard of that, is it common?' asked the man.

'It's not unusual,' replied the doctor.

ⓘ What's the difference between a golf ball and the G spot? A man will spend five minutes looking for a lost golf ball.

Two friends were playing when one hit in to the rough and landed on a stony track. The owner of the ball asked if he could move it, 'It's too rough and rocky here and it'll ruin my clubs.' But his friend refused to let him move his ball, saying, 'You've got to play from where you lie.' 'But it'll destroy the clubs.' 'Tough'

Shrugging his shoulders, the man went to play the ball. Sure enough, he hit the rocks and sparks flew everywhere. He tried again and the same thing happened. He swung again, and miracle of miracles, the ball flew straight onto the green. 'That's an amazing shot,' marveled his friend. 'What club did you use?'

'Your five iron,' he replied.

A fellow was getting ready to tee off on the first hole when a second golfer approached and asked if he could join him. The first said that he usually played alone, but agreed to the twosome. They were even after the first few holes. The second guy said, 'We're about evenly matched, how about playing for five quid a hole?' The first fellow said that he wasn't much for betting, but agreed to the terms. The second guy won the remaining sixteen holes with ease. As they were walking off number eighteen, and while counting his eighty pounds, the second guy confessed that he was the pro at a neighbouring course and liked to pick on suckers. The first fellow revealed that he was the parish priest. The pro got all flustered and apologetic, offering to return the money. The priest said, 'You won fair and square and I was foolish to bet with you. You keep your winnings.' 'Is there anything I can do to make it up to you?' the pro asked. The priest replied, 'Well, you could come to Mass on Sunday and make a donation. And, if you want to bring your mother and father along, I'll marry them.'

☺ Old golfers don't die, they just lose their drive.

☺ Old golfers don't die, we just lose our distance.

☺ Old golfers never die, they simply putter away.

Three guys are golfing with the club pro. The first guy tees off and hits a dribbler about sixty yards. He turns to the pro and says, 'What did I do wrong?' The pro says, 'Loft.' The next guy tees off and hits a duck hook into the woods. He asks the pro, 'What did I do wrong?' The pro replies, 'Loft.' The third guy tees off and slices into a pond. He asks the pro, 'What did I do wrong?' The pro says, 'Loft.' As they're walking to their balls, the first guy finally speaks up. He says to the pro, 'The three of us hit completely different tee shots, and when we asked you what we did wrong you answered the same exact answer each time. What is loft?'

The pro replies, 'Lack Of F****** Talent.'

☺ Why do golfers carry two pairs of trousers? In case they get a hole in one!

A golfer, well known for his bad temper, entered the pro shop and plunked down a wad of money for a new set of woods. The staff was all anxious to see what would happen after he used them for the first time, convinced he would come in and demand his money back.

Much to their surprise, the next time he came in, he was all smiles. 'They're the best clubs I've ever owned,' he declared. 'As a matter of fact, I discovered that I can throw them at least thirty yards further than my last ones!'

☺ Did you hear about the Spanish golfer who was shot? It was a hole in Juan!

After attending a business meeting, a Jewish, a Catholic and a Mormon man were enjoying drinks at a bar. Bragging about his virility, the Jewish man said, 'I now have four sons. One more and I'll have a basketball team.' The Catholic man chuckled at the Jewish man's accomplishment and stated, 'That's nothing. I have ten sons. One more and I'll have a football team.' 'You guys don't have a clue. I have seventeen wives. One more and I'll have a golf course,' the Mormon man proudly declared.

Gym, fitness and exercise

If yo momma's arms were dinosaurs, they'd be tricepaflops.

☺ A newcomer walks into a gym and asks if he can be taught to do the splits. The trainer asks, 'Are you flexible?' To which he replies, 'Can't make it Tuesday or Friday.'

A bloke walks into his gym and tells his trainer he has been on steroids and they have produced an extra penis for him. His trainer looks shocked, and asks 'Anabolic?' The bloke replies, 'No, just the penis.'

☺ What exercise do hairdressers do in the gym? Curls!

Why didn't the blonde make the gymnastics team? When they asked for a cart-wheel, she stole a tyre from the hot-dog vendor!

What's the difference between an aerobics instructor and a well-mannered professional torturer? The torturer would apologize first.

☺ Why did the aerobics instructor cross the road? Someone on the other side could still walk.

What do aerobics instructors and people who make bacon have in common? They both tear hams into shreds.

⊙ How many aerobics instructors does it take to change a light bulb? Four! ...Three! ....Two! ...One!

I joined an aerobics class for overweight men. We meet in the church basement. Well, actually we were on the first floor when we started last week.

⊙ What do you call an aerobics instructor who doesn't cause pain and agony? Unemployed.

What's the difference between an aerobics instructor and a dentist? A dentist lets you sit down while he hurts you.

I'm into low impact aerobics. Very low! I lie on the couch and just watch.

⊙ His idea of exercise is to sit in the bath, pull the plug, and fight the current.

I've been working out every day this week. My TV remote is broken, and getting up out of the chair fifty times a night is really tough.

The first machine the health club put me on was the respirator.

⊙ I enjoy long walks, especially when they're taken by people who annoy me.

Exercise must be good for you. My wife's tongue has never been sick a day in her life.

My wife was forced to quit her aerobics class because she broke a toe. Unfortunately, it wasn't hers.

☺ My idea of exercise is ripping the wrapper off a Snickers.

An ethical lawyer, an honest politician, and a merciful aerobics instructor all fall out of an airplane. Which one hits the ground first? It doesn't matter none of them exist.

I have a new incentive to do sit-ups. I put M&Ms between my toes.

☺ He's into heavy lifting. He carries his lunch to work.

Yo mama is so fat the only exercise she gets is running after the Mr Whippy van.

The doctor is really subtle. He suggested that I lend my body to someone who will exercise it.

☺ There's nothing like getting up at 5 a.m., jogging six miles, and then taking an ice-cold shower. There's nothing like it, so I don't do it.

He's developing a more active lifestyle. Now he sits and watches aerobics shows on television.

I really need exercise. I get winded just winding my watch. I'm not in great shape. I blacked out putting my socks on yesterday.

Every time I get an urge to exercise, I sit down with a bag of chips and wait until the urge goes away.

Exercise wouldn't be a problem with me if I had a different body to do it with.

⊙ If it weren't for car parks, some of us wouldn't do any walking at all.

After we do our aerobics, we always check the scales. The Richter Scale, that is.

The doctor said, 'Walking is healthier than driving.' I said, 'When was the last time you saw a postman who looked healthier than a truck driver?'

⊙ I bought a rowing machine, but I haven't used it yet. I haven't been able to tear the box open.

I get all the exercise I need these days just by bending down to pick up those blank subscription cards that fall out of magazines.

A woman was hit by a truck. In her dying breath, she was heard to say, 'Thank goodness. No more aerobics.'

⊙ How can one believe in survival of the fittest when you look at some of the people running around in jogging shorts?

I asked the instructor at the health club what I could do for my body, and he said, 'Schedule it for demolition.'

⊙ I owe my athletic physique to my wife and clean living. 'Clean the car ... clean the attic ... clean the garage.'

I prefer sit-ups to jumping jacks. At least I get to lie down after each one.

☺ I exercise religiously. I do one sit-up and then I say, 'Amen!'

Don't forget, your brain needs exercise, too. Therefore, spend lots of time thinking up excuses for not working out.

☺ I met a friend jogging in the park. Well, he was jogging and I was sitting on a bench.

I gave up exercising when I broke my nose doing push-ups.

My figure used to be my fame and helped me get ahead, but that was fifteen years ago, and now my fame has spread.

☺ When I was younger, I looked forward to getting up early in the morning to exercise. Now, getting out of bed in the morning is my exercise.

Books on exercise are selling by the thousands. And there's a reason for this. It's a lot easier to read than it is to exercise.

☺ His idea of vigorous exercise is to lift his feet while his wife is vacuuming.

I get enough exercise by stumbling about a mile each day looking for my glasses.

What's harder to catch the faster you run? Your breath!

I went to a gym. They offered me free membership for life if I posed for a 'don't let this happen to you' poster.

☺ A gym is just a PE class that you pay to skip.

Did you hear about the man who was sacked on his first day working at the gym? A customer asked him for help to define his abs. 'Sure,' he replied 'disgusting, sloppy, gelatinous.'

What time of year do you jump on a trampoline? Spring time!

☺ I like being married for two reasons: 1) I got really tired of dating, and 2) I got really tired of exercising.

How does a physicist exercise? By pumping ion!

Hiking and walking

A hiker is walking up to the shelter when he sees another hiker with a rod and reel fishing in the privy. He walks over and asks, 'What in the world are you doing in there?' The hiker says, 'I dropped my jacket in and I'm trying to get it out.'

The first hiker looks in at the jacket and says, 'You're not actually going to wear that are you?' The second hiker shakes his head in disbelief at such a ridiculous question and replies, 'Heck, no! There's a Snickers in the pocket!'

☺ A hiker comes to the river crossing up north and wants to get across, sees another hiker on the other side and yells over, 'HOW DO I GET TO THE OTHER SIDE?' The other hiker looks upriver, then downriver and yells: 'YOU ARE ON THE OTHER SIDE!'

A hiker hobbles into the doctor's office and says, 'Doctor, I've hiked all the way here from the mountain and my right leg is killing me, can you take a look at it?'

'Sure,' says the doc and he puts his stethoscope to the hiker's right shin bone. He hears a small voice say, 'Doc, can you lend me fifty pence?'

Then he listens to the hiker's right knee and hears, 'Hey, Doc, can you lend me a quid?'

Then he puts the stethoscope to the hiker's right thigh and hears, 'Doc, can you lend me a fiver?'

The doctor puts down the stethoscope and sighs, shaking his head gently from side to side.

The hiker says, 'Well, did you find out what's happened to my leg?'

The doc says, 'Yes; I really hate to tell you this, but your leg is broke in three places!'

There were two men out hiking when they came upon an old, abandoned mine shaft. Curious about its depth they threw in a pebble and waited for the sound of it striking the bottom, but they heard nothing. They went and got a bigger rock, threw it in and waited. Still nothing. They searched the area for something larger and came upon a railway sleeper. With great difficulty, the two men carried it to the opening and threw it in. While waiting for it to hit bottom, a goat suddenly darted between them and leapt into the hole!

The men were still standing there with astonished looks upon their faces from the actions of the goat when a man walked up to them. He asked them if they had seen a goat anywhere in the area and they said that one had just jumped into the mine shaft in front of them! The man replied, 'Oh no. That couldn't be my goat, mine was tied to a sleeper!'

Last summer, a husband took his wife camping for the first time. At every opportunity, he passed along outdoor-survival lore. One day they got lost hiking in the deep woods. He tried the usual tactics to determine direction: moss on the trees (there was none), direction of the sun (it was an overcast day), etc. Just as the wife was beginning to panic, he spotted a small cabin off in the distance. He pulled out his binoculars, studied the cabin, turned, and led them right back to our camp. 'That was terrific,' his wife said. 'How did you do it?' 'Simple,' he replied. 'In this part of the country, all the TV satellite dishes point south.'

☺ When I found the skull in the woods I immediately called the police, but began to wonder, who was this person and why did he have antlers?

While hiking in the woods, Nate and Sam found this huge rock which had an old iron lever attached to it. Etched into the rock was the following inscription: 'If this lever is pulled, the world will come to an end!' Nate wanted to pull the lever and see what would happen, but Sam, being a paranoid pessimist, greatly feared this. He said to Nate that if he tried to pull the lever, he'd shoot him. In a daring attempt, Nate lunged for the lever, and sure enough, Sam shot him! What is the moral of this story? Better Nate than lever!

Hiking: how to build a fire

- Split dead limb into fragments and shave one fragment into slivers.

- Bandage left thumb.

- Chop other fragments into smaller fragments.

- Bandage left foot.

- Make structure of slivers (include those embedded in hand).

- Light match.

- Light match.

- Repeat 'a Scout is cheerful', and light match.

- Apply match to slivers, add wood fragments, and blow gently into base of fire.

- Apply burn ointment to nose.

- When fire is burning, collect more wood.

- Upon discovering that fire has gone out while out searching for more wood, soak wood from can labelled 'kerosene'.

- Treat face and arms for second-degree burns.

- Re-label can to read 'petrol'.

- When fire is burning well, add all remaining firewood.

- When thunderstorm has passed, repeat steps.

There were three explorers, hiking through what is now known as Canada. 'You know,' said one of the explorers, 'we should name this place we're hiking through.'

'I know,' said the second explorer. 'We'll each pick a letter and then make a name out of that.'

'OK,' said the one, 'I'll go first. C, eh. N, eh. 'D, eh.'

And that's how they named Canada.

☺ A man came back from a long business trip to find that his son had a new three-hundred-pound mountain bike. 'How'd you get that, son?' 'By hiking.' 'Hiking?' 'Yeah, every night, Mum's boss came over and gave me twenty pounds to take a hike.'

One day three men were hiking along and came upon a raging, violent river. They needed to get to the other side, but had no idea of how to do it. The first man prayed to God, saying, 'Please God, give me the strength to cross this river.' Poof! God gave him big arms and strong legs and he was able to swim across the river in about two hours. Seeing this, the second man prayed to God saying, 'Please God, give me the strength and ability to cross this river.' Poof! God, gave him a rowing boat and he was able to row across the river in about three hours. The third man had seen how this worked out for the other two, so he also prayed to God, saying, 'Please God, give me the strength, ability and intelligence to cross this river.' And poof! God turned him into a woman. He looked at the map, then walked across the bridge.

Two guys are out hiking. The first guy says, 'Did you see that?' 'No,' the second guy says. 'Well, a bald eagle just flew overhead,' the first guy says. 'Oh,' says the second guy.

A couple of minutes later, The first guy says, 'Did you see that?'

'See what?' the second guy asks.

'Are you blind? There was a big, black bear walking on that hill, over there.'

'Oh.'

A few minutes later the first guy says: 'Did you see that?'

By now, the second guy is getting aggravated, so he says, 'Yes, I did!'

And the first guy says: 'Then why did you step in it?'

Hockey

⊙ Why did the referees stop the leper hockey game? There was a face-off in the corner.

How do hockey players kiss? They just pucker up.

What do you need a credit card for in ice hockey? Charging!

⊙ What tea do hockey players drink? Penaltea!

Horse racing

A man was walking down the road leading a horse when he bumped into his friend. His friend looked at the horse and asked, 'What are you going to do with that?' The first man replied, 'Race it.' 'Well, by the looks of it you're going to win!' replied his friend.

💬 If horse racing is the sport of kings, how come there are no famous royal jockeys?

A jockey was given an eye test and was presented with a new pair of glasses. The optician said they would cost two hundred pounds. 'Too much!' cried the jockey. 'They're bi-focal,' said the optician. 'I don't care if they're by Kauto Star. It's too much.'

The trainer was giving last-minute instructions to the jockey and appeared to slip something into the horse's mouth just as a steward walked by. 'What was that?' enquired the steward. 'Oh nothing,' said the trainer, 'just a polo.' He offered one to the steward and had one himself. After the suspicious steward had left the scene the trainer continued with his instructions: 'Just keep on the rail. You are on a certainty. The only thing that could possibly pass you down the home straight is either the steward or me.'

💬 His horse lost the race, and the owner was irate. 'I thought I told you to come with a rush at the end,' he screamed at the jockey. 'I would have,' answered the jockey, 'but I didn't want to leave the horse behind!'

A man drove his car into a deep ditch on the side of a country road. Luckily a farmer happened by with his retired race horse named Kelvin. The man asked for help, and the farmer said Kelvin could pull his car out. So he backed Kelvin up and hitched him to the man's car bumper. Then he yelled, 'Pull, Daisy, pull.' Kelvin didn't move. Then he yelled, 'Come on, pull, Boxer.' Still, Kelvin didn't move. Then he yelled really loud, 'Now pull, Billy, pull hard.' Kelvin just stood. Then the farmer nonchalantly said, 'OK, Kelvin, pull.' Kelvin pulled the car out of the ditch. The man was very appreciative but curious. He asked the farmer why he called his horse by the wrong name three times. The farmer said, 'Oh, Kelvin is blind, and if he thought he was the only one pulling he wouldn't even try.'

☺ What's a racehorse's favourite sport? Stable tennis!

A preacher wanted to raise money for his church and, being told there were fortunes in racehorses, he decided to purchase one and enter it in the races. However, at the local auction, the going price for horses was so steep he ended up buying a donkey instead. He figured that since he had it, he might as well go ahead and enter it in the races, and to his surprise the donkey came in third. The next day the racing sheets carried the headlines, 'Preacher's Ass shows'. The preacher was so pleased with the donkey that he entered it in the races again and this time he won! The papers said, 'Preacher's Ass out in Front!' The bishop was so upset with this kind of publicity that he ordered the preacher not to enter the donkey in another race. The newspaper printed this headline, 'Bishop Scratches Preacher's Ass'. This was just too much for the Bishop and he ordered the preacher to get rid of the animal. The preacher decided to give it to a nun in a nearby convent. The headlines the next day read, 'Nun has the Best Ass in Town!' The bishop fainted. He informed the nun that she would have to dispose of the donkey and she finally found a farmer who was willing to buy it for ten pounds. The paper stated, 'Nun Peddles Ass for Ten Pounds!' They buried the bishop the next day.

☺ That horse is so slow the post office should buy him.

A man's car stalls on a country road. When he gets out to fix it a horse in the nearby field comes up alongside the fence and leans over by him. 'Your trouble is probably in the carburettor,' says the horse. Startled, the man jumps back and runs down the road until he meets a farmer. He tells the farmer his story. 'Was it a large white horse with a black mark over the right eye?' asks the farmer. 'Yes, yes,' the man replies. 'Oh, I wouldn't listen to her,' says the farmer, 'she doesn't know anything about cars.'

☺ My horse was right up there with the winning horse when the race started.

A champion jockey is about to enter an important race on a new horse. The horse's trainer meets him before the race and says, 'All you have to remember with this horse is that every time you approach a jump, you have to shout, "ALLLLEEE OOOP!" really loudly in the horse's ear. Providing you do that, you'll be fine.' The jockey thinks the trainer is mad but promises to shout the command. The race begins and they approach the first hurdle. The jockey ignores the trainer's ridiculous advice and the horse crashes straight through the centre of the jump. They carry on and approach the second hurdle. The jockey, somewhat embarrassed, whispers, 'Aleeee ooop!' in the horse's ear. The same thing happens the horse crashes straight through the centre of the jump. At the third hurdle, the jockey thinks, 'It's no good, I'll have to do it,' and yells, 'ALLLEEE OOOP!' really loudly. Sure enough, the horse sails over the jump with no problems. This continues for the rest of the race, but due to the earlier problems the horse only finishes third. The trainer is fuming and asks the jockey what went wrong. The jockey replies, 'Nothing is wrong with me. It's this bloody horse. What is he deaf or something?' The trainer replies, 'Deaf?? DEAF?? He's not deaf he's blind!!!'

☺ He's been playing the horses for a long time. As a kid, he was the only one on the merry-go-round with a racing form.

A trainer had a filly that won every race in which she was entered. But as she got older she became very temperamental. He soon found that when he raced her in the evening, she would win easily, but when she raced during the day she would come in dead last. He consulted the top vets and horse psychologists to no avail. He finally had to give up because it had become ... a real night mare.

⊙ It would have been a photo finish, but by the time my horse finished, it was too dark to take a picture.

A man turned up at the Grand National with a six-year-old horse that had never raced before, but which he entered for the big race. The horse won easily and the bookmakers paid a whopping price. The racing stewards suspected foul play and questioned the owner. 'Is this horse unsound?' they asked. 'Not a bit,' said the owner. 'In that case,' asked the stewards, 'why have you never raced him before?' 'Well,' said the man, 'we couldn't even catch him until he was five years old.'

⊙ The chronic gambler paused before taking his place at the betting windows, and offered up a fervent prayer to his Maker. 'Blessed Lord,' he muttered with intense sincerity, 'I know you don't approve of my gambling, but this once, Lord, just this once, please let me break even. I need the money so badly.'

A man wakes up in the morning and it is 5.55 a.m. The temperature is 55 degrees and the humidity is 55%. He turns on his TV to channel 5. He gets up and it is 5th May. He heads to work and his car has 55,555.5 miles on the odometer. He gets to work goes to the 5th floor. He has five messages. IT DAWNS ON HIM. He rushes to the bookies. In the fifth race is a horse called, Double Five. He understands fate has spoken. He bets his entire bank account and maxes out all his credit cards. The race is run ... double five came in fifth.

A woman went to a psychiatrist and said she was in great distress over her husband. 'He thinks he's a horse. He sleeps standing up and he neighs instead of speaking. He even insists on being fed oats in a bag,' said the woman. 'It's terrible!' 'How long has this been going on?' asked the doctor. 'Six, maybe eight months,' she replied. 'You have let things go too far,' said the doctor. 'Your husband will require a great deal of treatment and it will be very expensive.' 'I don't care about the expense,' said the wife. 'I will pay you anything, anything at all to make my husband stop thinking he's a horse.' 'But it will cost many thousands of pounds, can you afford this amount of money?' asked the doctor. 'Why of course we can,' said the woman. 'He's already won three races at Cheltenham this year.'

The next time that horse runs will be from a bottle of glue.

A horse walked up to the racetrack betting window and plopped his money down. 'I want to bet fifty pounds on myself to win the fifth race,' said the horse. 'I don't believe it!' said the astonished clerk. 'You don't believe what?' said the horse. 'That I can talk?' 'No,' replied the clerk. 'You don't stand a chance of winning the fifth race!'

☉ I bought a horse. In its first race it went out 25 to 1. The only problem is that all the other horses left at 12.30.

Riding the favourite at Cheltenham, a jockey is well ahead of the field. Suddenly he's hit on the head by a salmon sandwich and a pork pie. He manages to keep control of his mount and pulls back into the lead, only to be struck by a tin of caviar and a dozen Scotch eggs. With great skill he manages to steer the horse to the front of the field once more when, on the final furlong, he's struck on the head by a bottle of Chardonnay and a Bakewell tart. Thus distracted, he only manages second place. Furious, he immediately goes to the stewards to complain that he's been seriously hampered.

☺ His horse came in so late the jockey was wearing pyjamas.

A man went to the races and while there he saw a Roman Catholic priest. The priest went over to a horse and sprinkled it with holy water. The horse went on to win the race, streaking ahead of the opposition. Before the next race he saw the priest go over to another horse and sprinkle it with holy water. Like the first horse it went on to win its race. The man decided that if the priest sprinkled another horse with holy water he was going to bet every penny he had on that horse. Sure enough, the priest went over to another horse and sprinkled it with holy water. So the man went to a bookie and bet every penny he had on this horse. The race started and the horse that the priest sprinkled with holy water dropped dead about a hundred yards after the start of the race. The man was devastated. So he went over to the priest and said, 'What's going on here? The last two horses you sprinkled with holy water went on to win their races, and this last one you sprinkled dropped dead after only a hundred yards. I had put every penny I had on its nose!' The priest replied, 'You're not Roman Catholic, are you?' The man admitted that he was not and asked, 'But, how do you know that?' The priest said, 'Because you clearly don't know the difference between giving a blessing and administering the last rites!'

Before I go racing, I always talks to people who know horse flesh: the trainers, the jockey, my butcher.

☺ My horse would have placed in the race, but he kept looking back for his plough.

I found a way to make a horse stand perfectly still. Place a bet on him.

When do vampires like horse racing? When it's neck and neck.

How do you make a small fortune on the horses? Start with a large fortune.

☺ He bet on a horse that had excellent breeding. After the horse left the starting gate, he turned around to close it behind him.

A young stallion came from a long line of winners, and looked to be following in his illustrious ancestors' footsteps. However, in actual races he was a little too timid, and could never quite bring himself to pass a mare. So one day the trainer went to him and told him he'd have to be castrated. The young horse, knowing that it was either this or the glue factory, took it philosophically. After all, having the operation was almost a certain guarantee of a long and illustrious racing career. After a short recovery period, the horse was again run, and found to be just as good. But the first time he actually ran in a race, he only went about ten paces, before getting a dejected look on his face, turning around, and ambling back to the starting gates. 'What's the matter?' asked the trainer. 'You were doing so well!' 'Yeah, well how would you feel,' replied the horse, 'if five thousand people took one look at you and shouted, "They're off!"?'

☺ I bet on a great horse yesterday! It took seven horses to beat him.

Racecourse: A place where windows clean people.

Horse sense: that innate sense that keeps horses from betting on people.

☺ Man, to friend, 'I don't fancy the chances of that horse you bet on.' Friend, 'Why's that?' Man, 'I just saw the jockey buy a book to read on the journey.'

The horse I bet on was so slow, the jockey kept a diary of the trip.

What has four legs and flies? A dead racehorse.

(!) A trainer is buying a horse from a breeder. 'And is he well bred?' asks the trainer. 'I'll say he's well bred,' says the breeder. 'In fact he's so well bred, if he could talk, I doubt he'd speak to either of us.'

Jockeys

He looks like he went to a blood drive and forgot to say when.

His best sport is the limbo. He's so good he can limbo under a rug.

It must be tough on him going through life without ever seeing a parade.

He's so short he wasn't born and raised, he was born and lowered.

(!) He's really generous with his time. He recently did a benefit for 'Save the Shrimp'.

During the tour, some of the students needed to go to the bathroom, so it was decided that the boys would go with one teacher and the girls with the other.

One of the boys came running out of the men's bathroom and told the teacher waiting outside that he couldn't reach the urinal. Having no other choice, the teacher went inside and began lifting the little boys up by their armpits, one by one.

As she lifted one up, she couldn't help but notice that he was unusually well endowed for an elementary school child. 'You must be in the fifth year,' the teacher said.

'Oh no, ma'am,' he replied, 'I'm in the seventh, riding Silver Arrow. Thank you for the lift though.'

⚠ He won't be riding tonight. He injured himself when he fell off a ladder while he was picking strawberries.

He's the shortest player in the game. He's so short he can keep his feet warm just by breathing hard.

He got a new advertising contract acting as a spokesman for a chain of miniature golf courses.

⚠ I won't say he's overweight, but his stomach crosses the start before the horse does.

A group of fourth and fifth-year students were taken on a trip to the local racetrack to learn about thoroughbred horses and the industry.

Hunting

A man was fined for using last year's hunting licence. Up before the magistrate, he was asked to defend himself: 'I was only shooting at the ones I missed last year,' he said plaintively.

Did you hear about the hunter who bought a jacket with a Velcro zip? He accidentally rubbed up against a moose and got dragged through the woods for five miles.

A hunting foursome paired off. Late at night, one returned dragging a huge stag.
'Where's Bill?' enquired the other two.
'He had a heart attack a couple miles back in the woods.'
'You mean you left Bill to drag the deer back here?'
'Yeah. It was a tough decision, but I figured that nobody would steal Bill.'

☉ I'll never go moose hunting again. I didn't mind carrying the big gun, but the two-hundred-pound decoy was a real drag.

A group of hunters fully equipped with rifles, ammo and camping supplies came upon a young boy armed only with a slingshot.
'What are you hunting for?' asked an older hunter.
'I don't know. I ain't seen it yet,' said the boy.

A hunter was boring his guests with tales of his safari. Pointing to a tiger rug, he related, 'It was either him or me.'
'It was a good thing it was the tiger, Keith,' said an acquaintance. 'You would've made a rubbish rug.'

First hunter: 'We've been here all day and haven't bagged a thing.'
Second hunter: 'Yeah, let's miss two more each and then head home.'

ⓘ Two men went duck hunting. Five hours passed with no luck. Finally, one of the men said to the other, 'Maybe we ought to try throwing the dogs a little bit higher.'

A motorist ran over the hunter's favourite pointer dog. He went to the hunter's house and told the hunter's wife what happened. She said, 'He's out in the field, so you'd better tell him. But break it to him gently. First tell him it was me you ran over.'

A young man out on his first trip was telling his companion what a great hunter he was. When they arrived at their cabin, he bragged, 'You get the fire started and I'll go and shoot us something for dinner.'

After a few minutes, he met a grizzly bear. He dropped his gun, headed for the cabin, with the bear in hot pursuit. When he was a few feet away from the cabin, the hunter tripped over a log. The bear couldn't stop and skidded through the open cabin door. The young man got up, slammed the door, and yelled to his friend inside, 'You skin that one, and I'll go and get us another one!'

Two hunters were out in the woods, and they were lost. 'How will we get home?' asked the younger one. The other one considered for a while: 'We'll shoot into the air and help will come.' So they took turns shooting until one said, 'This doesn't seem to be working and we're almost out of arrows!'

ⓘ How do you catch a unique rabbit? Unique up on it!

ⓘ How do you catch a tame rabbit? Tame way!

One Sunday, a vicar decided to skip church and go hunting in the nearby forest. He soon spied a gigantic grizzly bear that had stopped to get honey from a beehive. The vicar aimed a shot at the bear, but in his excitement he missed. The bear, enraged by the shot, jumped up and charged at the vicar. The vicar used his only option: he dropped to his knees and prayed. 'Dear God,' he said. 'Please let this bear be a good Christian, a better one than I am.' As the bear drew closer, it dropped to its knees and said, 'Dear God, thank you for this meal I am about to receive.'

Two men were hunting. One managed to shoot a deer, which limped off into the undergrowth. He whispered to his companion, 'Wait here and don't make a sound,' and crept off to find the wounded animal. He finds the deer, dead, a little way away, when suddenly he hears his companion scream. He runs back to the man who is sitting down: 'Why did you scream?' The other man says, 'I was sitting here when a snake bit me. I managed to stifle my scream, but I had to let it out when two squirrels then ran up my trouser leg and said, "Should we eat them here or take them home?"'

(!) Three statisticians are hunting when they see a deer in the clearing. One of them shoots and misses by ten feet to the left. The next one misses by ten feet to the right. The third one jumps up and yells, 'We got him!'

Two men are out hunting in the woods and all of a sudden one of them keels over and lies motionless on the ground. The other man grabs his mobile and dials the emergency services. The operator picks up and says, 'Emergency, please state your emergency,' and the man says, 'I'm out here hunting with my friend and he just keeled over, I think he's dead!' The emergency operator says, 'OK, just calm down. Now the first thing we need to know is if he's really dead.' The man says, 'OK, hold on.' The operator hears silence on the phone for a second and then she hears a loud 'BANG!'

The man comes back on the line, 'Now what?'

⊙ A hunter goes into a butcher's shop and asks for a duck. 'I'm sorry,' says the butcher. 'We're out of duck. How about a chicken?' 'Oh, yes,' replies the hunter. 'And how do I tell my wife I shot a chicken?'

Two moose hunters charter a sea-plane to fly to their destination in the Alaska wilderness. When the plane arrives at the lake, the pilot says: 'In three days, I'll meet you two guys back here with *one* moose.' The plane took off and the men set up camp. The first day they shot nothing. The second day, one man shot a moose and on the third day, the second man shot another moose. The plane came to pick them up as scheduled, but when he saw them the pilot said: 'What are you doing? I told you to be here with only one moose, not two.' The hunters told the pilot that last year, the pilot let them take two mooses home. The pilot wanted to stay competitive with rival pilots and made an exception this time to let the hunters bring both mooses. With the extra weight, the plane barely got off the lake, then hit a tree and crashed. One hunter crawled over to his friend to see if he was hurt. He shook him, until he came round. 'Where are we?' he asked, dazed. The first man answered: 'About a hundred feet from where we crashed last year.'

Two hunters hire a moose costume in the hope they can get close enough to a bull moose to kill it. They creep up on a huge bull moose but find that the costume's zip is stuck. Suddenly there's a loud bellow and the hunter in the front of the costume sees that the bull moose is approaching them with a huge erection. 'What are we going to do now?' asks the hunter in the back of the costume. 'I'm going to nibble some grass,' replies the other. 'You'd better brace yourself.'

Two Irishmen are out hunting duck. One shoots at a flying bird and it falls dead at his feet.

'You could've saved yourself a shot there,' says the other. 'From that height the fall alone would've killed it.'

Three hunters were lost in the jungle and were captured by natives. The tribes-men decided they were going to make sacrifices of them. They were all asked if they wanted one last thing before they were killed. The first man asked for a beer. He got one, drank it, wiped his lips and was promptly strangled by a native. The man who killed him then dragged away his body, saying he'd make a good canoe cover. The next man asked for a cigarette which he smoked before being killed as well. Another native took his body too to make a good canoe cover. Finally it was the last man's turn. He asked for a fork. When it was brought he took it and stabbed himself all over his body, filling himself with holes. As he lay dying he fixed the native chief with a stare: 'You're not making a canoe cover out of me!'

☺ A woman goes into a hunting shop. 'I'm here for a gun for my husband,' says the woman. 'We've got plenty of choice,' says the shopkeeper. 'What gauge did he ask you to get?' 'He didn't,' replies the woman. 'He doesn't even know I'm going to shoot him.'

Two rednecks were out hunting when they encountered a scantily clad young woman lounging against a tree.
    'What y'all boys doing?' she enquired.
    They (being manly men) responded, 'Well ma'am, we're huntin' wild game.'
    'Well I'm wild, and I'm game!' she replied suggestively.
    So they shot her.

Two hunters are dragging a dead deer back to their truck when a man approaches them and says, 'Y'know it's much easier if you drag it the other way – then the antlers won't dig into the ground and slow you up.' The hunters try this method and make good progress. The first hunter says to the other, 'That guy really knew what he was talking about, didn't he?' 'Yes,' replies the second hunter. 'But on the other hand we are getting further away from the truck.'

The members of a fox hunt had been specifically requested to bring only male hounds. One member, however, brought a female hound – the only hound that the member owned. Reluctantly, the female was allowed on the hunt.

The hounds were released, and took off in a dash. In only a few seconds, they were out of sight altogether. The confused hunters stopped to question a farmer in a nearby field. 'Did you see some hounds go by here?'

'Yes,' replied the farmer.

'Did you see which way they went?'

'No,' answered the farmer, 'but it was the first time I've ever seen the fox running in fifth place!'

☺ Obituary: Mr Thomas Gunner died in a hunting accident last Thursday. He is survived by a wife, two sons, and a rabbit.

A lawyer was out hunting when he shot a duck flying overhead. The lawyer hurried to where the duck had fallen, only to find a farmer standing there with his foot on the dead bird. 'Give me my duck,' demanded the lawyer, but the farmer shook his head: 'No, it fell on my land, so it's my duck.' 'But I shot it,' protested the lawyer, 'so it should be mine.' They argued back and forth for half an hour until the farmer said, 'Look, we're never going to resolve this by arguing. Here in the countryside we settle matters with the three-kick method. Do you want to try it?' The lawyer didn't know what that was, so the farmer explained: 'What we do is have three kicks to hurt the other one. The first one to give in loses. I'll have my three kicks first if that's OK.' The lawyer looks at the farmer, who is well into his sixties, and thinks, 'I'm a young, fit guy. He won't hurt me, and I'll boot him into the next field,' so he agrees to let the farmer go first. The farmer swiftly boots the lawyer in the groin. He falls to the floor, and as he tries to get up the farmer kicks him in the face, breaking his nose. Staggering upright, he feels a terrible pain in his knee where the farmer aims his final kick. Eventually, composing himself, the lawyer snarls at the farmer: 'Right, you're going to pay now!' 'No,' says the farmer, 'I give up. You can have the duck!'

Three Indians were told by their chief to go hunting to bring back food for their squaws. The three left, and only a couple of minutes later the first Indian comes back with a deer. The chief is amazed, 'How did you get that deer?' 'Me see track, me follow track, me shoot deer,' replied the Indian. Then the second Indian comes back with a bison. Impressed, the chief asks him how he got the bison. The Indian replies, 'Me see track, me follow track, me shoot bison.' Hours pass and finally the third Indian comes back all bruised and bleeding. The chief asks, 'What happened to you?' 'Me see track, me follow track, me get hit by a train!'

A car drives up to a farmer's house, a man gets out, knocks on the door, and the farmer opens it. 'A friend told me you have a mule that points out pheasants,' said the stranger. 'Is that true?' 'Certainly is,' said the farmer, 'would you like to see him work?' The stranger said, 'Sure!' Soon they were walking through a field, when the mule suddenly stopped and struck a beautiful point. The farmer walks ahead of the mule and up goes a big flock of pheasant. This goes on a half-dozen more times – the mule points, the farmer scares up the birds. Finally, the stranger says, 'That's enough, I've got to have that mule!' 'He's not for sale,' said the farmer. 'I'll give you £50,000.00 for him,' said the stranger. Well, the farmer couldn't refuse such a big offer, so he sold him. The next night, the farmer's phone rang ... it was the stranger. 'What the hell's wrong with this damned mule you sold me?' he screamed. 'All he's done all day is stand belly deep in my pond!' 'Well,' said the farmer, 'I guess I should have told you ... he'd rather fish than hunt!'

☺ I'm against fox hunting. In fact I'm a hunt saboteur. I go out the night before and shoot the fox.

A young man from the city goes to visit his farmer uncle. For the first few days, the uncle shows him the usual things; chickens, cows, crops, etc. However, it's obvious the nephew is getting bored so the uncle suggests he goes on a hunt. 'Why don't you grab a gun, take the dogs, and go shooting?' This cheers up the nephew and off he goes with the dogs in trail. After a few hours, the nephew returns. 'Did you enjoy it?' asks his uncle. 'It was great!' exclaims the nephew. 'Got any more dogs?'

Jim owned one of the best bird-hunting dogs ever seen. It had won many trophies over the years. One day, Jim got a call from a friend named Dave, who asked if he could borrow the dog to go pheasant hunting on Saturday. Jim told him that he never loaned his dog to hunt, and asked Dave if he had ever hunted with a dog. 'Oh yes, I grew up hunting with a dog.' 'Well then, you're a good friend, I suppose you can use him,' Jim agreed. Saturday, Dave showed up, and Jim brought out his champion dog and loaded him in the car. 'Good luck,' Jim said, 'hope you brought plenty of shells, see you later.' That evening, Dave came back to Jim's, and Jim came out to meet them. 'Well, how many did you get?' he asked. 'We didn't get any,' Dave shouted. 'That's unbelievable,' Jim exclaimed. 'Yeah, it was the funniest thing, we got there, I loaded my gun, I let out your dog and we started hunting. All of a sudden, your dog stopped. He had his head pointing straight forward, his ears were straight forward, his back was straight as an arrow, his tail was pointing straight back, one paw was lifted up off the ground, and he just stood there. Couple of quick kicks in the bum stopped him doing that any more.'

☺ The Alaskan hunters usually dined on deer in the evenings – it was far too cold to hunt bear.

Pete is taking his friend hunting but when they get to his favourite hunting spot, they notice 'No Trespassing' signs posted everywhere. He tells his friend to wait in the car and walks up to the nearby farmhouse. The farmer answers the door, and Pete says, 'Sir, I've been hunting on this property all my life, but I notice that you now have "No Trespassing" signs posted. I wanted to see if it was still OK for me to hunt here.' The farmer tugs on his beard for a bit, and replies, 'I'll make a deal with you. We have this cow out back that we have to kill for food, but we've grown too attached to it. If you go out back and shoot my cow, I'll let you hunt on my property.' Pete walks back to the car and decides to play a joke on his friend. 'That miserable old bugger won't let us hunt on his property,' he says. 'I'm going to shoot his damn cow!' He then walks over to the side of the house and ... BAM! Suddenly, two more shots ring out behind him and his friend runs up, shouting, 'I got the dog and cat too! Quick, let's get the hell out of here!'

A young man walks into a bar in Alaska. After many drinks, he announces to the whole bar that he is proud to be a new Alaskan. One of the old timers at the bar laughs at him and asks him if he has gone through the 'ritual' yet. The lad asks what the 'ritual' entails. The old timer says, 'Well, to be an Alaskan, you have to kill a polar bear and make love to an Eskimo.' The young man says that he hasn't done either yet, so he and the old timer continue to drink heavily together and the old timer answers his questions about the 'ritual'. The young man stands up and wobbles out of the bar drunk as can be.

About four hours later, he struggles back into the bar, all scratched and cut up. He summons all of his strength and shouts out, 'Where's this Eskimo I have to kill?!'

☉ What has a hundred balls and screws rabbits?
A shotgun cartridge.

A man takes his wife hunting for the first time. He impresses upon her the need to claim a kill quickly before anyone has the chance to step in and bag your deer. The wife is suitably impressed by this and they both stalk off into the woods. A little while later the wife shoots and makes a kill. The brush is too thick for the husband to see what's going on but he can hear his wife arguing with another man. 'This is my kill,' shouts his wife. 'There is no other hunter in the vicinity and I can categorically prove that my bullet killed this deer.' 'I'm not arguing with you,' says the man. 'But can I take my saddle off your deer, before you take it home?'

While visiting the country, a city boy decided that he wanted to go hunting. The farmer loaned the boy his gun and cautioned him against killing any farm animals. The city boy headed off and, before long, saw a goat. He managed to creep into range and finally shot it. Not knowing anything about animals, he had no idea what he had killed, so he ran to the farmhouse and described his kill to the farmer. 'It had two saggy udders, a beard, a hard head and it stunk like hell!' the boy said. 'Holy cow!' exclaimed the farmer. 'You've shot my wife!'

In the market for a new bird dog, the avid duck hunter ended his search when he found a dog that could miraculously walk on water to retrieve a duck. Being so shocked by his find, he was certain that none of his friends would believe him.

Deciding to break the news to a close friend of his, who was a pessimist by nature, he invited him to go hunting with him and his new dog. Waiting by the shore, they spotted a flock of ducks flying by. They fired and a duck fell. Responding quickly, the dog jumped into the water. However, he didn't sink, but instead walked across the water and retrieved the duck, never getting more than his paws wet. The pessimistic friend saw all of this, but never uttered a word.

On the journey home, the hunter asked his friend, 'Did you happen to notice anything unusual about my dog?'

'I'll say I did,' he replied. 'He can't swim!'

Hurling

How do you make a Kilkenny fan run? Build a Job Centre.

What do haemorrhoids and Cork fans have in common? They're both a complete pain in the bum and never seem to go away completely.

⊙ How many Galway fans does it take to change a light bulb? Yeah, as if they have electricity in Galway.

What's the difference between the Cork hurling team and the Ryder Cup team? There's only one Langer in the Ryder Cup team.

⊙ What do you say to a Dublin fan with a job? Can I have a battered sausage and chips please!

You're trapped in a room with a tiger, a rattlesnake and a Limerick fan. You have a gun with two bullets. What should you do? Shoot the Limerick fan twice.

What do the Kerry hurling team and Mike Tyson have in common? They're both out after round one.

⊙ What do you call a Kilkenny man in Kilkenny on a Monday morning? Unemployed.

What's the difference between the Offaly goalie and Pamela Anderson? Pamela Anderson's only got two t*ts in front of her.

The reporter asked one man if he was disappointed that England had lost.

The man replied, 'Not at all, I'm Irish, I'm from Waterford.'

The reporter then asked, 'But would you not support England when Ireland are not in the competition?'

The man replied, 'Jaysus, no way.'

Reporter: 'Why not?'

Man: 'Eight hundred years of oppression!!'

Reporter: 'Is there ever any time you would support England?'

Man: 'Maybe if they were playing Kilkenny!!!'

Hurling dictionary

Stomached: surprised e.g. 'Jaynie, when he came up behind me I was awful stomached.'

Mighty: very good.

Welt: swing at.

Lamp: a good thump.

Crowd: e.g. 'That crowd from Ardrahan are a right shower.'

Schkelp: a good thump

Bullin' angry: e.g. 'The centre half back was bullin' after I lamped him.'

Bull thick: very angry.

Bushted: e.g. 'Jayz, me arm is bushted!'

Bomber: a very popular nickname for a GAA player.

A hang: sangwidge consumed with tay on the sides of roads after matches in Croker.

Warp: hit something hard as in 'I'll warp you!'

Blast: a great amount of anything.

Rake: also a great amount of anything, usually pints of Guinness.

Namajaysus: what was that for, referee?

Mullocker: untidy or awkward players.

Horsed: bout of rough play or intimidatory tactics as in 'we horsed them out of it'.

Row: fight involving four or more players swinging hurleys like lunatics.

Massive row: row involving both team, substitutes and supporters jumping fences.

Running row: a massive row that continues out in the parking area and/or dressing room areas.

A hape: a big quantity (heap).

In the paw: to catch the ball.

A Brawl: a collection of bodies in disagreement with each other.

A Dinger: usually a fast wing forward who can leave his opponent for dust.

Martial arts

A blind man goes into a ladies' bar. Sat at the bar he turns to the woman next to him and says, 'Do you want to hear a blonde joke?'

The woman replies, 'As you are blind I feel it's only fair to warn you, this is a ladies' bar, I'm blonde and a champion at karate, my two friends are blonde and are professional wrestlers and the barmaid is blonde. Now do you really want to tell that joke?'

The blind man thinks for a moment, 'No, I don't want to have to explain it four times.'

⊙ How many Ninjas does it take to screw in a light bulb? No one will ever know because Ninjas don't need light.

You might be a martial artist if ...

- You find yourself casually standing in a half cat stance.

- You trip, go into a roll and come up in a fighting stance. In church.

- You answer your boss, 'Ussss.'

- You put your hands together in a martial arts bow position (one hand open, the other closed) after grace at the dinner table.

- You tie your bathrobe belt in a square knot. Then check to make sure the ends are exactly even.

- When you're outside doing landscaping or gardening you 'practice' with all the neat weapons.

⁇ Why don't Ninjas get needles?
Because they always slip the jab.

There was this little guy sitting in a bar, drinking his beer, minding his own business when all of a sudden this great big dude comes in and WHACK!! knocks him right off the bar stool and onto the floor. The big dude says, 'That was a kung-fu chop from China.' The little guy thinks, 'GEEZ,' but he gets back up on the stool and continues what he was doing when all of a sudden, WHACK!! the big dude knocks him down AGAIN and says, 'That was a karate chop from Japan.' The little guy, not wanting any trouble, and thinking, 'This guy is nuts', gets up off the floor, grabs his beer and moves a few seats further down the bar, and continues to sip at his beer. All of a sudden, WHACK!! without warning, he feels this foot kick him in the head and he goes sprawling to the floor once again. The big dude says with a smile, 'That's kickboxing from Thailand.' The little guy, having had enough of this gets up, brushes himself off and quietly leaves. He had been gone for about an hour when he returned, and without saying a word, walks up behind the big dude and WHACK! knocks the big dude off his stool and lays him out cold! The little guy looks at the bartender and says, 'When he comes to, tell him that's a crowbar from Homebase.'

An old grandmother took her grandchild to a karate competition. Noting that the organizer seemed understaffed she approached the table. 'Good morning,' she said to the director, 'you look a little shorthanded. Anything I can do to help?' 'Well yes, we are short of fighters for the under ninety kg division,' the director replied. 'Sorry,' the grandmother said, 'I don't know anything about karate.' 'That's OK,' said the director. 'We need referees, too.'

⁇ What's Bruce Lee's favourite drink? Wah-tahhhh!

Why don't Ninjas get married? Because they're too deadly for the ring.

Why did the wrestler bring a key to fight? To get out of a headlock!

Two kung-fu masters were carrying on about their respective skills. 'Why, my reflexes are such that you will not believe,' boasted Master Foo and, drawing his sword, he sliced at a passing fly, which promptly dropped dead in two pieces.

'That's nothing,' said Master Koh. Drawing his sword, he made two deft cuts at another passing fly.

Master Foo was highly amused. 'What are you talking about?' he sneered. 'That fly is still flying.'

'Ah yes,' replied Master Koh, 'but now it can never have children.'

What do you get when you fuse a Ninja and a Viking? A dead Viking.

What did the Ninja say to the pirate? Nothing. He was sent to kill him.

⊙ Ninjas never wear headbands with the word 'ninja' printed on them.

Ninjas invented the internet. All of it.

⊙ Ninjas can crush golf balls with two fingers. Any two fingers.

Ninjas always move to America when making a new start as a non-assassin.

⊙ What food do Ninjas eat? Kung food.

What did Bruce Lee catch? Kung flu!

Knock, knock,
Who's there?
Carrot
Carrot who?
Karate Chop.

Motorsport

During the 2009 French Grand Prix the finishing results for Australia's Mark Webber and Germany's Sebastian Vettel were terrible ... Les Miser Red Bulls!

⊙ What does NASCAR stand for?
    Non Athletic Sport Centred Around Rednecks.

David Coulthard sees an old woman with a walking stick
'Do you want a lift home?' he says.
'No thanks, sweetheart. I'm in a bit of a hurry so I'll walk,' she replies.

Ferrari took a decision for the British GP to hire a couple of Scousers as pit crew members when they found out they can remove all four wheels in under 0.8 seconds. But to their dismay, after 1.5 seconds, the car was resprayed and sold to McLaren.

⊙ What's the difference between Jacques Villeneuve and a bus driver? One is a highly skilled professional driver, and the other is in Formula 1.

Lewis Hamilton was looking to find him a woman so David Coulthard decided to help him out. He told Lewis that the next time he's on the beach to put a potato in his trunks and the ladies will gather round. Lewis goes out for three straight days with no luck. He's about to leave when he sees Coulthard and says, 'I don't understand, I did what you said and now NO women will come anywhere near me!' Coulthard looks at him and just points and says, 'The potato goes in the front!'

☺ What is the funniest motorbike? A Yamahahahaha!

Michael Schumacher and David Coulthard are in a desert. Evening comes, they set up their tent. Both go to sleep. Coulthard wakes up in the middle of the night. Schumacher isn't in the tent. He can hear something coming from outside the tent. Coulthard peeps out and sees Schumacher running around the tent like crazy, a big lion after him. Coulthard shouts: 'Run faster, he's gonna catch you!' Schumacher replies: 'Don't worry, I lead by three laps!'

What's the difference between David Coulthard and Tiger Woods? Tiger can drive further than two hundred yards!

☺ Have you heard? Jenson Button is in hospital! Apparently he hasn't passed anything for almost two years!

Lewis Hamilton calls the police in a panic, and says, 'They stole my dashboard, they stole my steering wheel, they stole my brake pedal, hell, they even stole my accelerator pedal ...'

Then, before the police can ask where he is, he says, 'Hey, never mind, I'm in the back seat.'

☺ Did you hear about Lewis Hamilton visiting that Korean sports psychologist about his losing streak? He has been seeing Dr Winn Wan Soon for about two months now.

Two rally drivers are driving through Transylvania on a remote stage when Count Dracula suddenly jumps on their car. 'Quick, show him your cross!' says the navigator. The driver shouts, 'Hey, Dracula! Get off the bleeding car!'

A rally driver gets lost and walks into a village shop for directions. 'Can you tell me the quickest way to Lincoln?' he asks. The shopkeeper says, 'Are you walking or driving?' The man replies, 'I'm driving.' 'Oh good,' says the shopkeeper. 'Because that's definitely the quickest way.'

⊙ A women rally driver is driving the wrong way up a one-way street. A cop pulls her over and says, 'Where are you going?' The woman replies, 'I don't know. But I must be late – everyone is coming back!'

A racing driver is out on the motorway having an evening drive in his sports car. He decides to open her up and the needle jumps to 120 mph. Suddenly he sees a flashing blue light behind him. He thinks about outrunning the police, accelerates for a few seconds, then comes to his senses and pulls over. The officer comes over to check his licence. 'I've had a tough shift,' says the officer. 'And this is my last pull over. I don't feel like more paperwork so if you can give me an excuse for your driving that I haven't heard before you can go!' 'Er, last week my wife ran off with a police officer,' says the racing driver. 'And when I saw your car I was afraid he was trying to give her back!' 'Have a nice night,' says the officer.

A cross-country racer is fiddling under the bonnet of his car. A tramp walks by, stops, and looks at him. 'Piston broke,' explains the driver. 'Ah yes,' says the tramp. 'So am I.'

A rally driver is driving down a deserted road. He pulls up to an intersection, and rolls through the stop sign. From nowhere a cop pulls him over. 'Do you know why I pulled you over?' asks the cop. 'Hey, I slowed down didn't I?' says the driver. The cop replies, 'You must come to a full stop at the sign.' 'Stop. Slow down. What's the difference?' argues the man. 'I'll show you,' says the cop, who then pulls out his baton and starts beating the man over the head. 'So,' he says. 'Do you want me to stop, or slow down?'

The manager of a new Irish F1 team is so appalled at his driver's basic road knowledge that he sends him for a retake of his driving test. The instructor asks him what a yellow line means. 'It means you can't park there at all,' says the Irishman. 'And what does a double yellow line mean?' asks the instructor. The Irishman replies, 'It means you can't park there at all ... at all.'

⊙ Every young woman should hang on to her youth. But not while he's driving.

Racing driver, to mechanic, 'Could you check the battery? I think it's flat.' Mechanic, 'What shape did you want it to be?'

⊙ Did you hear about the F1 driver who died with his boots on – sadly one was on the accelerator at the time.

Ross Brawn returns to his car in the paddock after a Grand Prix and discovers that someone has backed into his Mercedes while it's been in the car park. He finds a note under the windscreen. It says, 'Sorry about wrecking your car. The policeman watching me from over there thinks I'm leaving you my details. But I'm not.'

⊙ The team boss asked his driver why there were so many dinks on the driver's side of the racing car. He said the brakes must be bad on that side.

A speeding motorist was caught by radar from a police helicopter. An officer pulled him over and began to issue a traffic ticket. 'How did you know I was speeding?' the frustrated driver asked.

The police officer pointed sombrely towards the sky.

'You mean,' asked the motorist, 'that even He is against me?'

A traffic cop flagged down a racing driver and said, 'I'm arresting you for going through three red lights.'

'Yeah, well, I'm colour blind,' said the motorist.

'In addition to that, you were exceeding the speed limit,' said the policeman.

'So what?' said the motorist.

'And on top of all that you were going the wrong way down a one-way street,' added the officer.

'I always did have a lousy sense of direction,' said the motorist with a smile.

At that point, his wife leaned forward from the back seat and said, 'Don't pay any attention to him, officer. He always talks like this when he's had a few drinks.'

⊙ An elderly racing driver decided to end it all: 'James, I'm now ninety and rather bored with life, so I want to commit suicide. Kindly drive over the next cliff.'

I once drove in a race to the south of France in six days. It took me four days to get there and two days to fold up the road maps.

The DVLA recently revealed a programme they had funded with carmakers for the past five years. Carmakers were installing black boxes in four-wheel drives in an effort to determine, in fatal accidents, the circumstances in the last fifteen seconds before the crash.

There were three bees, a squirrel and a man in a car. They were driving along a country lane and the car broke down.

The first bee said, 'Don't worry, I'll give us a few extra miles by peeing in the tank.'

It worked for a couple of miles, that is until they broke down again. And so the second bee decided to do the same as the first bee, but this lasted another couple of miles until they broke down again, so the third bee did exactly the same. Then finally the car broke down for a fourth time.

The squirrel said, 'I'll pee in the tank.'

The man replied, 'Sorry, mate, this car only runs on BP!'

Ten things not to say if you're pulled over:

- I can't reach my licence unless you hold my beer.

- Sorry, officer, I didn't realize my radar detector wasn't plugged in.

- Aren't you the guy from the Village People?

- You must've been doin' about 125 mph to keep up with me! Good job!

- Excuse me, is stick 'em up hyphenated?

- I thought you had to be in relatively good physical condition to be a police officer?

- I was going to be a cop, but I decided to finish school instead.

- You're not gonna check the boot are you?

- Is it true that people become cops because they are too dumb to work at McDonald's?

- Well, when I reached down to pick up my bag of crack, my gun fell out of my lap and got lodged between the brake pedal and the accelerator, forcing me to speed out of control.

☺ You never really learn to swear until you learn to drive.

A blonde rally driver walked into a petrol station and told the manager, 'I locked my keys in my car and I was wondering if you had a coat hanger I could stick through the window and unlock the door.'

'Why, sure,' said the manager, 'we have something that works especially for that.'

A couple of minutes later, the manager walked outside to see how the blonde was doing. He heard another voice.

'No, no, a little to the left,' said the blonde navigator inside the car.

Junior had just received his brand new driver's licence. The family goes out to the driveway and climbs in the car, where he is going to take them for a ride for the first time. Dad immediately heads for the back seat, directly behind the new driver.

'I'll bet you're back there to get a change of scenery after all those months of sitting in the front passenger seat teaching me how to drive,' says the beaming boy to his dad.

'Nope,' comes Dad's reply, 'I'm gonna sit here and kick the back of your seat as you drive, just like you've been doing to me all these years.'

⊙ They were surprised to find that the last words of 75% of drivers in fatal crashes were, 'Help!' Only in the countryside were things different, where the remaining 25% of final words were, 'Hey, hold my beer and watch this!'

A tourist is visiting New York City when his car breaks down. He jumps out and starts fiddling under the bonnet. About five minutes later, he hears some thumping sounds and looks around to see someone taking stuff out of his trunk. He runs around and yells, 'Hey, bud, this is my car!'

'OK,' the man says. 'You take the front and I'll take the back.'

A man was speeding down the highway, feeling secure in a group of cars all travelling at the same speed. However, as they passed a speed trap, he got nailed with an infrared speed detector and was pulled over.

The officer handed him the ticket, received his signature and was about to walk away when the man asked, 'Officer, I know I was speeding, but I don't think it's fair – there were plenty of other cars around me who were going just as fast, so why did I get the ticket?'

'Ever go fishing?' the policeman suddenly asked the man.

'Um, yeah ...' the startled man replied.

The officer grinned and added, 'Did you ever catch all the fish?'

(!) I bought a second-hand car. It only had one previous owner. A little old lady who only used it on a Sunday – when she took it drag racing.

One day, a racing driver was on his way home from work when the most remarkable thing happened. Traffic was heavy as usual, and as he sat there at a red light, out of nowhere a bird slammed into his windscreen. If that wasn't strange enough, the poor creature got its wing stuck under the windscreen wiper.

Just then the light turned green and there the guy was with a bird stuck on his windscreen. Without any other apparent options, he turned on the windscreen wipers to try to get rid of the bird. It actually worked. On the upswing, the bird flew off, and it slammed right onto the windscreen of the car behind him. Unfortunately, the car behind him was a police car.

Immediately the lights went on and he was forced to pull over. The officer walked up and told him that he saw what had happened at the light. Trying to plead his case fell on deaf ears. The officer simply stated, 'I am going to have to book you for flipping me the bird.'

(!) My wife wanted a foreign convertible, so I bought her a rickshaw.

A lawyer opened the door of his BMW, when suddenly a car came along and hit the door, ripping it off completely. When the police arrived at the scene, the lawyer was complaining bitterly about the damage to his precious BMW. 'Officer, look what they've done to my Beemer!' he whined. 'You lawyers are so materialistic, you make me sick!' said the officer. 'You're so worried about your stupid BMW, that you didn't even notice that your left arm was ripped off!' 'Oh NO!' replied the lawyer, finally noticing the bloody left shoulder where his arm once was. 'Where's my Rolex?'

How many car salesmen does it take to change a light bulb? I'm going to work this out on my calculator, and I think you'll be pleasantly surprised.

A traffic policeman stops a woman and asks to see her driving licence.
'Lady, it says here that you should be wearing glasses when driving.'
'Well,' replies the woman, 'I have contacts.'
'Lady, I don't care who you know, you're still going to get a ticket.'

Wife: 'There's trouble with the car. It has water in the carburettor.'
Husband: 'Water in the carburettor? That's ridiculous.'
Wife: 'I tell you the car has water in the carburettor.'
Husband: 'You don't even know what a carburettor is. Where's the car?'
Wife: 'In the swimming pool.'

A couple of young speeders are pulled over by a highways officer. The officer walks up, asks for the driver's licence and registration, and when he doesn't get it quickly enough, whacks the driver in the head. 'That's for not having your driver's licence ready,' he snaps. 'I ain't got all day.' After he issues the driver a ticket, the patrolman walks around to the other side of the car and whacks the passenger in the head. 'Owwww!' hollers the passenger. 'What'd you do that for?' 'That's to make your dream come true,' replied the cop. 'I know that when you'd got half a mile down the road, you were gonna say to your friend here, "Wish he'd tried that with me!"'

Some signs you're at an F1 fan's funeral:

- Casket features an exact replica of the Ferrari paint scheme.

- Heart-stirring eulogy delivered by Martin Brundle.

- 'Amazing Grace' is performed by a revving engine carried in especially for the ceremony.

- Only the first twenty cars are allowed in the procession.

- Hearse referred to as the pace car.

- Procession weaves back and forth to keep heat in the tyres.

- Cars caught speeding leaving the church have to go to the rear of the procession.

You know you're obsessed with motorsport when:

- You think the primary purpose of wings is to PREVENT flight.

- You take your helmet along when you go to buy new glasses or check out cars.

- You feel compelled on a road trip to beat your previous best time.

- When something falls off your car, you wonder how much weight you just saved.

- When you hear the phrase 'overcooked it', instead of food you think 'at the track'.

- You change engine oil every other week.

- You sometimes hear little noises from your passengers when you get on the throttle right after turning into a corner

- Your racing budget is one of the big three: mortgage, car payments, food for the children.

- Your email address refers to your race car rather than to you.

- You bought a racing car before buying a house.

- You bought a racing car before buying furniture for the new house.

- You're looking for a towing vehicle and still haven't bought furniture!

- You measure all family acquisitions in terms of the number of racing tyres that could have been purchased.

- Your garage holds more cars than your house has bedrooms.

- You have enough spare parts to build another car.

- You have car parts on your desk at work.

- Your Christmas list begins with another set of track ends and piston rods and your 'significant other' knows what they are.

- You have a separate drawer for 'garage clothes'.

- People know you by your class letter, car number and car colour.

- You talk to other cars on the road, calling them by the manufacturer's name.

- Your friends don't recognize you without a helmet and driver's suit.

- Your family remembers your hair colour as 'grease'.

- You plan your wedding around the racing schedule.

- You remember the dates and details of every race you've ever been in, but can't remember your phone number.

- Your family brings the couch into the garage so they can spend some time with you.

- You complain when cars in front of you on motorway exit ramps don't stay on the line, causing your exit speed to drop.

- A neighbour asks if you have any oil, to which you ask, 'Synthetic or organic?' and they reply, 'Vegetable or olive.'

- You refer to the corner down the street from your house as 'Turn One'.

- You enjoy driving in the rain on the way to work or school.

- You can't stand anyone telling others how to drive. Of course, you are the best.

- You will gladly pay up to £50 for a gallon of engine oil.

- You think that traction control and ABS are for those who can't drive.

- You save broken car parts as 'mementos'.

- You've found your lawnmower runs pretty well on nitrous oxide.

- The local tyre shop won't honour the tread life warranty on any car you have been within fifty yards of ...

- The shop manager at your local car dealer mutters 'dear Lord' under his breath after he sees the size of your exhaust pipe.

- The local police have a picture of your car taped to their dashboard.

- You spend more time polishing your exhaust tip every day than you do bathing.

- You would choose a roll bar over air conditioning if it were an option.

- You enjoy driving through wet, empty car parks and using the handbrake to kick the back end out.

- White smoke coming out from under your tyres is a common sight.

- You spend more on insurance premiums than on food.

- You own five cars and only one of them is street legal.

- You've embarrassed your significant other at least once by insisting on wearing your full face helmet while driving to the shops

- You regularly test your engine on that straight that's a little too long for second but not worth going into third for.

- You've started looking for sponsors for your daily commute.

A policeman stopped a motorist one evening and asked him, 'Excuse me sir, but do you realize you are driving without a rear light?' The driver jumped out, ran to the rear of his car and gave a huge groan. His distress seemed so obvious that the policeman was sympathetic. 'Now, you don't have to take it so hard,' he said. 'It isn't all that serious.'

'Isn't it?' cried the motorist. 'What's happened to my caravan?'

There are five blokes touring Europe in an Audi Quattro and they get to the Spanish border. 'Passports please,' asks the attendant. So they hand them over. After a few minutes examining the passports the attendant says, 'There are five of you in this four-person car.' 'There's allowed to be,' argues the driver 'it's a five-person car, it says here in the manual.' 'No,' argues the attendant, 'Quattro means four.' After more arguing the driver asks to see the border controller. 'Oh, he's busy at the moment,' replies the attendant, 'over there with those two guys in that Fiat Uno!'

Netball

Why does an attacker carrying a feather on her head? She's a wing attacker!

Why do Russians play the game with no ball? Because it is n(y)et ball.

$!$ Why was Cinderella such a bad netball player?
Because she had a pumpkin for a coach.

If netball was easy they would call it football.

$!$ Why do men prefer basketball to netball?
Because they like to dribble before they shoot.

Olympics

At the Olympic Games, a girl bumps into a man carrying an eight-foot-long metal stick.

'Excuse me,' says the girl to the man. 'Are you a pole vaulter?'

'No,' says the man, 'I'm German, but how did you know my name is Walter?'

Boris Johnson is opening the London Olympic Games and has to read a speech.

'Oh,' he says. 'Oh, oh, oh … '

An aide nudges him, 'Mr Johnson, stop,' he says. 'You're reading the Olympic symbol!'

Did you know that Liverpool had put a bid in for the Olympics? Here is a section of their bid that was leaked from the IOC:

- OPENING CEREMONY: The Olympic flame will be ignited by a petrol bomb thrown into the arena by a native of the Toxteth area of the city, wearing the traditional costume of a shell suit.

- THE EVENTS: In previous Olympics Liverpool's competitors have not been particularly successful. In order to redress the balance some of the events have been altered slightly to the advantage of the local athletes.

- 100 METRES SPRINT: Competitors will have to hold a video recorder and a microwave oven (one under each arm) and on the sound of a starting pistol a police dog will be released ten metres behind the athletes.

- 110 METRES HURDLES: As above but with added obstacles, i.e. car bonnets, hedges, gardens, fences, walls, etc.

- HAMMER: The competitors will be allowed to make a choice of hammer, (claw, sledge, etc). The winner will be the one who can cause the most grievous bodily harm to members of the public within their allotted time.

- WEIGHTLIFTING: From a standing position, competitors will have various electronic goods placed in their arms. In order to complete a lift these must then be taken through the shop door and placed in a mate's van.

- FENCING: Entrants will be asked to dispose of as much stolen jewellery as possible within five minutes.

- SHOOTING: A series of targets will be set up to establish the competitor's ability over a range of disciplines. The targets to be as follows: 1 – A Moving Police Van, 2 – A Post Office Clerk, 3 – A Bank Teller or Securicor Driver 4 – Any target to be followed by the ritual cry of 'I thought he was a Bizzy' or 'He pulled a knife on me'.

- BOXING: Entry to be restricted to husband and wife teams and will take place on every Friday and Saturday night of the games. The husband will be given fifteen pints of Stella and the wife will be told not to make him any tea when he gets home. The bout will then commence.

- CYCLING TIME TRIALS: Competitors will be asked to break into the Liverpool University bike shed and take an expensive mountain bike owned by some mummy's boy from the south on his first trip away from home against the clock.

- CYCLING PURSUIT: As above; however, this time the break, in must occur at Liverpool Police Station and must be witnessed by an officer.

- TIME TRIAL: The competitor who can waste most of the court's valuable time before being found guilty will be adjudged the winner.

- MODERN PENTATHLON: Amended to include mugging, breaking and entering, flashing, joyriding and arson.

- THE MARATHON: A safe route has yet to be decided, but the competitors will be issued with sharp sticks and bags with which to pick up dog mess, crisp packets and used hypodermic syringes on their way round.

- MEN'S 50km WALK: Why does the Mersey run through Liverpool? Because if it walked it would get mugged. Therefore for safety reasons this event has been cancelled.

- RELAY: Each of four competitors to remove an appliance of their choice from a house in Cheshire and get it back to Liverpool using at least four different stolen cars.

- ARCHERY: Each competitor will be given three needles, the winner will be the person who gets nearest to three different main veins in their own body.

- DISCUS: Will be decided by which contestant can get a hubcap off a car and throw it to his mate the fastest. In addition the following 'exhibition events' designed at promoting the local culture will be introduced.

- GRAFFITI: To be decided on who can spray the most obscenities on a neighbour's wall in five minutes. N. B. In order not to disadvantage local competitors marks will not be deducted for misspelling.

- BASEBALL: Each competitor to be given a stainless-steel baseball bat. Last person standing wins.

- CLOSING CEREMONY: In an attempt to capture the timeless beauty of Liverpool, competitors from every nation will be chased across Stanley Park by knife-wielding locals.

They will then scatter to the four corners of the city to find their car aerial ripped off, driver side window broken and stereo liberated, with no sign of the lad who charged 50p 'to look after their motor'.

Their assailants will return to the park providing a riot of colour and sound as their shell suits converge. The Olympic flame (if still in place) will be extinguished by eight Scallies forming a circle and urinating on it.

The closing speech will consist of the words, 'Everyone in Liverpool's a natural comedian you know.' No one will laugh. Each visitor will be hugged on exiting the stadium and will return home to find their wallet missing.

Redneck Olympics

- Doves released during opening ceremonies are promptly shot by the crowd and sold as concession snacks.

- In an amazing coincidence, every proposed Olympic venue turns out to be owned by the Governor.

- Instead of shooting at boring targets, archers take aim at muskrats and out-of-towners.

- Urine drug test transformed into 'Distance Competition'.

- Olympic Village replaced with Olympic Trailer Park.

- Awards of gold, silver and bronze medals replaced by award of gold, silver, and bronze teeth.

- Opening ceremony is a tape of 'Sweet Home Alabama' and a trunk full of bottle rockets.

- Hometown favourites falter in gymnastics competitions due to all them extra toes.

- Billy Bob-sledding.

- Ballroom dancing will be replaced with a hoe-down and participants must be from the same family.

- The pistol in the hundred-yard dash will be loaded with real bullets, 'Jist so's we can git a wurld recurd out of dem runners.'

- Beach volleyball will be replaced with Swingball (ball will be punctured by dog teeth prior to the start of the event).

- The equestrian event will be replaced with pit-bull fighting.

Parachuting

A plane was once flying over an island when the passengers heard the pilot's voice: 'Ladies and gentlemen, if you look on the right side of the plane, you'll see an engine on fire. If you look on the left side, you'll see a wing on fire. And if you look down, you'll see me and my co-pilot in parachutes, waving at you. This is a recording.'

⊙ What do you call an all-blonde skydiving team? A new version of the Lawn Darts game.

There are five people on a plane that's crashing. There is the pilot, Bill Gates, David Beckham, Lewis Hamilton and a big, fat lady and four parachutes. The pilot jumps out and yells, 'God bless me!' Bill Gates jumps out and yells, 'God bless me and my bank account!' David Beckham jumps out and yells, 'God bless me and my team!' Lewis Hamilton jumps out and yells, 'God bless me and Formula 1!'

The big, fat lady jumps out without a parachute and yells, 'God bless me and the people I land on!'

⊙ What kind of crazy bird yells 'Polly wants a cracker!' when he jumps from an aeroplane? A parrot trooper.

A bunch of new recruits are making their first parachute jump. The sergeant gives instructions: 'After you jump out of the plane, count slowly to ten. Your parachute will automatically open. If it doesn't, pull the emergency cord. When you get to the drop zone, there'll be trucks waiting to take you back to the base. Move out!'

Mr Maxwell, the founder/president of Maxwell House, was recently killed in an unfortunate accident. Mr Maxwell was an avid skydiver and during a recent jump his parachute failed to open and he was killed on impact. His friends remember the fact that he was an INCREDIBLY pleasant, nice man before his fatal jump. And so on his tombstone they inscribed: 'Mr Maxwell, good to the last drop.'

☉ For sale: parachute. Only used once, never opened, small stain ...

A man is having his first skydiving lesson. 'If our chute doesn't open, and the reserve doesn't open, how long do we have until we hit the ground?' he asks. The jumpmaster looked at him, 'Oh,' he answered. 'The rest of your life.'

A blind man was describing his favourite sport – parachuting. When asked how this was accomplished, he said that things were all done for him: 'I am placed in the door and told when to jump. My hand is placed on my release ring for me, and out I go.' 'But how do you know when you are going to land?' he was asked. 'I have a very keen sense of smell and I can smell the trees and grass when I am 300 feet from the ground,' he answered. 'But how do you know when to lift your legs for the final arrival on the ground?' he was again asked. He quickly answered, 'Oh, the dog's leash goes slack!'

☉ Why do birds sing? They don't have to pack when they've landed.

One sunny day a man decided to go jump from an airplane. When he jumped there was good and bad news ...
Good news: He had a parachute. Bad news: It didn't work.
Good news: There was a haystack down below. Bad news: There was a pitchfork in the haystack.
Good news: He missed the pitchfork. Bad news: He missed the haystack.

On the first day of training of parachute jumping, a blonde listened intently to the instructor. He told them to start preparing for landing when they are at 300 feet.

The blonde asked, 'How am I supposed to know when I'm at 300 feet?'

'That's a good question. When you get to 300 feet, you can recognise the faces of people on the ground.'

After pondering his answer, she asked, 'What happens if there's no one there I know?'

⊙ Yo Mama's so enormous that when she went to the dry cleaners to hand in her underwear, they put up a sign 'NO PARACHUTES ALLOWED.'

Two friends, a blonde and a brunette, are parachuting. The blonde pulls her cord and the chute works perfectly. The brunette pulls her cord and nothing happens. She continues falling straight down. As the brunette passes her friend, the blonde gets angry, unbuckles her harness and yells, 'Oh, so you want to race, huh?'

⊙ As scared as they are, they all make it out the door. The last recruit jumps out and slowly counts to ten – nothing. He frantically fumbles around and finds the emergency handle. He jerks on the cord, and it comes off in his hand. Raising his head to the heavens, he screams, 'I bet the trucks aren't waiting either!!'

The Malfunctioning Aeroplane

You are one of two people on a malfunctioning aeroplane with only one parachute. How would you react? Here are the likely responses from major groups of people:

- Pessimist: you refuse the parachute because you might die on the jump anyway.

- Optimist: you refuse the parachute because people have survived crashes just like this before and someone else will have a chance that way.

- Procrastinator: you play a game of Monopoly for the parachute.

- Bureaucrat: you conduct a feasibility study on parachute use in multi-engine aircraft under code red conditions.

- Lawyer: you charge one parachute for helping to sue the airline.

- Doctor: you say you need to run more tests, then take the parachute in order to make your next appointment.

- Engineer: you make another parachute out of aisle curtains and dental floss.

- Philosopher: you ask how they know the parachute actually exists.

- Environmentalist: you refuse to use the parachute unless it is biodegradable.

Polo

I have been playing the game, but where is the mint, do we get it at the end of the game?

At the end of a game, a player gave an interview: 'I am great a polo player,' he boasted. 'I have won the championship with a great shot, and have covered every blade of grass.' 'Yes,' replies the interviewer, 'but what is more impressive is that you are a horse!'

😀 I am not saying that polo is a sport mainly played by the upper class, but the horses don't say, 'Neigh, neigh,' they say, 'Ya, ya, ya.'

I am not saying that polo is a sport mainly done by the upper classes, but the horses don't live in a stable, they live in stately stable.

I'm not saying that polo is a sport mainly done by the upper classes, but the crowd doesn't do a Mexican wave, it does a royal one.

😀 I tried to bribe the other polo team's horse but when I asked if it would take the bribe all it said was 'neigh'.

Yo momma is so fat the horse on her polo shirt is real.

Rugby

Rugby league is a game of inches, and that's how some teams move the ball.

☺ If you see a full-back with chalk on his back, he's had a bad day.

Did you hear about the second row who was so strong he could throw horseshoes while they're still on the horse?

I thought one of the props had a tattoo on his leg but it turned out to be a government meat inspection stamp.

☺ The hooker was so huge instead of a number he should have a licence plate.

Some chickens were in a barnyard when a rugby ball flew over the fence. A rooster walked by and said, 'I'm not complaining, girls, but look at the work they're doing next door!'

I gave up my hope of being a star fly half the first day of practice. One prop grabbed my left leg, another grabbed my right leg, and the hooker looked at me and said, 'Make a wish!'

The English pack are so huge that it takes just four of them to make a dozen.

The kicker missed his attempt at a conversion. He was so angry he went to kick himself and missed again.

! Everyone knew the prop was on steroids. His IQ and neck size were the same number.

Old scrum-halves never die. They just pass away.

We have so many players on the injured list the team bus can park in a handicapped space.

! This team employs their famous 'Doughnut Defence', the one with the big hole in the middle.

The only way they can gain any yards is to run their game tapes backward.

Why didn't the bicycle play rugby? It was two tyred.

A rugby coach was asked his secret of evaluating his new recruits. 'Well,' he said, 'I take 'em out in the woods and make 'em run. The ones that run round the trees, I make into backs. The ones that run straight into the trees, I turn into props.'

! What has six arms and an IQ of sixty? A front row.

After spending all day watching rugby, Jimmy fell asleep in front of the TV and spent the whole night in the chair. In the morning, his wife woke him up. 'Get up dear,' she said, 'it's twenty to seven.' He awoke with a start and said, 'In who's favour?'

The Seven Dwarfs were marching through the forest one day when they fell in a deep, dark ravine. Snow White, who was following along, peered over the edge of the steep chasm and called out to the fallen dwarfs. From the depths of the dark hole a voice returned, 'Saracens are Heineken Cup contenders.' Snow White thought to herself, 'Thank the Lord ... at least Dopey's survived!'

Rugby player: 'Doctor, doctor, every morning when I get up and look in the mirror I feel like throwing up. What's wrong with me?'
Doctor: 'I don't know, but your eyesight is perfect.'

Why do rugby players like smart women? Opposites attract.

☉ How do you kill a rugby fan when he's been drinking? Slam the toilet lid on his head.

Two rugby fans are arguing about how to pronounce the team name Wigan. The first fan says, 'I say it's Vigan,' but the other fan says, 'No, it's not, it's Wigan. I bet you five pounds I'm right. 'OK,' says the first fan, 'you're on. I'll ask that man walking up the street. So he stops the man walking up the street and says, 'Excuse me, my friend and I are having an argument. Do you say Wigan or Vigan?' 'It's Vigan.' 'Ta, mate,' says the first fan as he collects his five pounds. 'You're velcome,' says the man walking up the street.

Why did the rugby manager take all the pencils off his players? To stop them drawing.

Teacher: 'I thought you told me you wouldn't be in school yesterday because you had to see your doctor?' Pupil: 'That's right.'
Teacher: 'Then how come I saw you at the rugby match with a tall man in a suit?'
Pupil: 'That was my doctor.'

☉ Why was the car not allowed to play rugby?
It only had one boot.

A man went to the doctor one day and said: 'I've just been playing rugby and when I got back I found that when I touched my legs, my arms, my head, my tummy and everywhere else, it really hurt.' So the doctor said: 'You've broken your finger.'

A rugby player was in a restaurant: 'Waiter, this vinegar is rather lumpy.'
Waiter: 'That's because they're pickled onions, sir.'
A second rugby player at a Chinese restaurant: 'Waiter, these noodles are a bit crunchy.'
Waiter: 'That's because they're the chopsticks, sir.'

What's a bee's favourite sport? Rugbee.

☺ Why did the rugby player go to see the vet?
His calves were hurting.

Third rugby player in a restaurant: 'Waiter, I say, there are two ears in my soup.'
Waiter: 'Eh?'

Husband: 'Hey, Helen, do you have anything you want to say before the rugby season starts?'

☺ Our flanker knows how to do everything with a ball except autograph it.

A father and his son, Bobby, arrive at the local rugby match and Dad can't find the tickets. Dad said to Bobby, 'Nip home and see if I left the tickets there.' Bobby replied, 'No probs, Dad.' Half an hour later Bobby returns to his dad who is patiently waiting outside the stadium and says, 'Yep, they're on the kitchen table where you left them.'

A scrum-half joined a big northern club and found himself dwarfed by the big 200-pounders. Nobody seemed to pay any attention to him and he began to wonder whether he was being deliberately snubbed. He approached the captain and told him of his troubles. The captain patted him on the shoulder and said, 'Don't worry about it, son. They're not giving you the cold shoulder. They just haven't seen you yet.'

☺ Why do people tend to hate rugby players on sight?
Because it saves time.

A rugby player was hurt very badly during a scrum and he had both of his ears ripped off. Since he was permanently disfigured, he decided to give up playing rugby for good. His club and insurance company ensured that a large sum of money went his way. One day, he decided to invest his money in a small but growing sportswear business. He bought the company outright but after signing on the dotted line, realized that he knew nothing about business. He decided to employ someone to run the shop. The next day he set up three interviews. The first guy was great. He knew everything he needed to and was very enthusiastic. At the end of the interview, the former rugby player asked him, 'Do you notice anything different about me?' And the man replied, 'Why, yes, I couldn't help noticing you have no ears.' The rugby player got angry and threw him out. The second interview was with a woman, and she was even better than the first guy. He asked her the same question, 'Do you notice anything different about me?' She replied: 'Well, you have no ears.' He got upset again and showed her the door. The third and last interview was with the best of the three. He was a very young man fresh out of college. He was smart and handsome and seemed to know all about the sportswear business. The rugby player was anxious, but went ahead and asked him the same question: 'Do you notice anything different about me?' To his surprise the young man answered: 'Yes, you wear contact lenses.' The former rugby player was shocked, and said, 'What an incredibly observant young man you are. How in the world did you know that?' The young man fell off his chair laughing hysterically and replied, 'Well, it's pretty hard to wear glasses with no flipping ears.'

☺ Why don't rugby players have mid-life crises?
They stay stuck in adolescence.

I was in the cemetery the other day, and I saw four rugby players carrying a coffin. A couple of hours later I saw the same four men with the same coffin. I thought to myself, 'They've lost the plot.'

A man was dancing with a rather snooty partner who was getting increasingly annoyed at his clumsiness. After stepping on her toes for the third time, he apologized, 'Do forgive me. I'm just a little stiff from rugby.' 'I don't care where you come from,' she replied. 'This is the last time I'm dancing with you!'

The manager of a lowly Yorkshire pit village rugby club took his team on an African safari holiday, and while there, he came across a native athlete who could run, kick, pass and juggle a coconut like a born rugby player. Excitedly, the manager called a meeting of all the players and introduced the young athlete to them. 'This fellow's brilliant' he said, 'and I've persuaded him to join the team, on six months' trial. His name is Ugo Ettoo. Now then,' he continued, holding up a rugby ball, 'this – ball, BALL!' Then, pointing at the goalposts, he said, 'That – goal – GOAL! That – goal line – GOAL LINE! You put BALL over GOAL LINE: or kick BALL over CROSSBAR.' 'You don't need to explain the game in those simple and rather patronizing terms, old boy,' said Ugo. 'I played for Harrow when at school there, and later for Cambridge University.' 'I'm not talking to you,' said the manager. 'I'm talking to the rest of the team!'

⊙ A front-row forward was driving to Manchester for an important match. On the way, he picked up a girl hitchhiker, and halfway there, he put his hand on her knee. 'You can go further if you want,' she said softly. So he went on to Aberdeen.

A rugby player ran into an old mate in the pub and they stayed drinking until quite late. 'You'd better come and spend the night at my house,' said one. 'You'll have to sleep with my brother-in-law, and I must warn you he snores! I hope he won't keep you awake.' The next morning, when his mate came down to breakfast, he asked, 'How did you sleep?' 'Fine,' said his friend. 'I slept like a log all night.' 'Didn't my brother-in-law's snoring keep you awake?' 'No,' came the reply. 'Just before we put out the light, I kissed him on the cheek and said, "Sleep tight, honey-bun!" He never closed his eyes all night.'

First girl: 'I hear you're going out with a rugby player. Is he any good in bed?'
Second girl: 'No, not much. I got him to take some rhino-horn pills.'
First girl: 'What for?'
Second girl: 'They're supposed to be an aphrodisiac.'
First girl: 'Did they do any good?'
Second girl: 'Yes but the trouble is that now every time he sees a Land Rover, he charges at it.'

! A reporter visited an International full-back in hospital the day after a big match. 'I understand you were the victim of a late tackle,' he said. 'You could call it a late tackle, I suppose,' said the full-back. 'He knocked me down in the bar after the game!'

The coach burst into the changing room as the second half of the game was about to begin. 'All right!' he roared. 'All of you lazy, no-good, thick-headed scumbags out on that field now!' All the players jumped to their feet and rushed out onto the field except for the little scrum-half sitting in the corner. 'Well!' roared the coach. 'Well!' said the little scrum-half. 'There certainly were a lot of them, weren't there!'

! What do you get when you put the girlfriends of a dozen St Helens fans in one room? A full set of teeth!

A man meets an Aussie friend and sees that his friend's car is a total write-off and covered with leaves, grass, branches, dirt and blood. He asks his friend, 'What's happened to your car?'

'Well,' the friend responds, 'I ran over Jonny Wilkinson.'

'OK,' says the man, 'that explains the blood ... But what about the leaves, the grass, the branches and the dirt?'

'Well, he tried to escape through the park.'

The wife of a second-row rugby player was suing for divorce on the grounds that he was too uncultured and slobbish to live with. 'Whenever we go into a restaurant,' she explained to the judge, 'he always drinks his coffee with his pinkie sticking out.' 'Well, that sounds harmless,' said the judge. 'Lots of people drink their coffee with their little finger sticking out.' 'Who said anything about his little finger?' she replied.

Wales v England at Cardiff. A small group of Wales supporters, unable to get tickets, gather outside the stadium shouting up at the England supporters for updates on the state of play. There is a massive roar from the sell-out crowd. The Welsh supporters outside shout up, 'What's happening, what's happening?' The English shout back, 'All the Welsh team have been carried off injured, the only man they have left on the field is Shane Williams!' Ten minutes pass, then there is another massive roar from the crowd. The Welsh boys shout up again, 'What's happening? Shane scored, has he?'

☉ What do you call an Englishman with the Triple Crown in his hands? The engraver!

Two men are talking about their boss's upcoming wedding. One bloke says, 'It's ridiculous, he's rich, but he's ninety-five years old, and she's just twenty-four! What kind of a wedding is that?'
    The other says, 'Well, we have a name for it in my family.'
    'What do you call it?'
    'We call it a rugby wedding.'
    The first asks, 'What's a rugby wedding?'
    The other says, 'She's waiting for him to kick off!'

☉ Did you hear about the new code to help hookers? Clubs will write on their shorts: This End Up. On their boots they put, T. G. I. F. 'Toes go in first.'

A rugby player's wife gets onto a bus with her baby.

The bus driver says, 'That's the ugliest baby that I've ever seen. Ugh!'

The woman goes to the rear of the bus and sits down, fuming. She says to a man next to her, 'The driver just insulted me!'

The man says, 'There's no call for that. You go right up there and tell him off. Go ahead, I'll hold your monkey for you.'

☺ If you see a Wasps fan on a bike, why should you not swerve to hit him? It could be your bike!

After having their eleventh child, a St Helens player decided that was enough.

He went to his doctor and told him that he and his wife didn't want to have any more children. The doctor told him there was a procedure called a vasectomy that would fix the problem but it was expensive.

A less costly alternative was to go home, get a firework, light it, put it in a beer can, then hold the can up to his ear and count to ten.

The rugby player said to the doctor, 'I may not be the smartest guy in the world, but I don't see how putting a firework in a beer can next to my ear is going to help me.'

'Trust me, it will do the job,' said the doctor.

So the man went home, lit a banger and put it in a beer can. He held the can up to his ear and began to count: '1, 2, 3, 4, 5,' at which point he paused, placed the beer can between his legs so he could continue counting on his other hand ...

The Saracens squad got together at training after their latest defeat.

'Right lads,' shouted the coach, 'we're going to try a new defence drill today to get to the bottom of these sloppy tries we keep letting in. Right, everyone in your places!'

So with that they all ran and stood behind the posts.

Rugby dictionary

Foul play: what the other side do. If your side do it, it's called 'using your initiative'.

Ruck: informal, impromptu get-together for forwards and a few close friends.

Mark: if you can cleanly catch a ball kicked several hundred feet in the air within your own 22-metre line and call 'mark' while the entire other side is pounding towards you intent on doing you damage, you can have a free kick. You deserve it.

Offside: a natural break in the play called by the referee every 35 seconds to let everyone get their breath back.

Calcutta Cup: historically the game between the two strongest international representative teams, England and Scotland (circa 1871–1899). The title is now given to an annual fixture involving one of rugby's strongest nations helping to bring on a developing nation (England vs Scotland circa 2002).

Conversion: the situation when a Welshmen remembers that he's Welsh after he has been ignored by the All Blacks/Australian/South African/English selectors.

Free kick: the punishment for lying on the wrong side of a ruck or maul.

Grubber: mistimed drop kick from anywhere on the field.

Offside (as in offside line): an imaginary line passing through a ball without puncturing it.

Ruck: accidental stepping on an opponent lying in an offside position.

Sidestep: a manoeuvre perfected by South African rugby administrators to avoid choosing black players.

Try: the verb used to describe what Wales do every year in the Six Nations, often with little or no success.

Up-and-under: (an integral calculus term in rugby competitions) the inversion of global geographics – the southern hemisphere teams are usually 'up', while the northern hemisphere teams are usually 'under'.

Wing (1): northern hemisphere – extra defender.

Wing (2): southern hemisphere – top try scorer.

International call-up: the invitation to Twickenham that rugby league players receive along with their first pay packet.

Prop: front row position that has finally solved the mystery of who did actually eat all of the pies.

London Irish: as their name suggests, a group of South Africans that play rugby in Reading.

Rugby league: version of rugby commonly played in the north of England. The teams consist of thirteen players on each side. This is largely due to the number of wingers moving to rugby union, resulting in a player shortage in the super league.

☺ It was a really tough game. The full-back started praying. A distant voice came back saying: 'Please don't include me in this.'

Travelling in a train were a Wallaby, an All Black, a spectacular-looking blonde and an older lady. After several minutes of the trip, the train happens to pass through a dark tunnel, and the unmistakable sound of a slap is heard. When they leave the tunnel, the Wallaby has a big red slap mark on his cheek.

The blonde thought, 'That horrible Wallaby wanted to touch me and by mistake, he must have put his hand on the lady, who in turn must have slapped his face.' The older lady thought, 'This dirty Wallaby laid his hands on the blonde and she smacked him.

'The Wallaby thought, 'That bloody All Black put his hand on that blonde and by mistake she slapped me.'

The All Black thought, 'I hope there's another tunnel soon so I can smack that stupid Wallaby again!'

☺ Wife to friend, watching the Challenge Cup: 'The most exciting bit of the season was when Fred sat on the cheese dip.'

The club president, coach, a prop and a winger are taking a flight to the Heinken Cup finals when the engines cut out. The pilot enters the passenger compartment and says, 'We're going down. There's only four parachutes! Since I'm the pilot I'm taking one,' and then jumps from the plane. The coach says, 'Without me the team won't have a chance, so I'm taking one,' and he jumps out. The winger says, 'I'm the fastest and smartest man on the pitch and without me the team can't win a game, so I'm taking one,' and he jumps out of the plane. The club president looks at the prop and says, 'You take the last parachute. The team needs you more than it needs me.' The prop responds, 'We both can take a parachute. The smartest man on the pitch just jumped out of the plane with my kit bag on his back.'

In 1983 three kids were playing in the street in Cardiff when they were hit by a train. They all go to heaven and God says to them, 'You weren't supposed to die, you were all supposed to live out your lives. This was not your time. To make it up to you, I'll let you choose what you want to do with your life. Take a running jump off that cloud over there, and as you're flying back down to Earth, shout out what you want to do. And so it shall be.' The first kid takes a running leap and shouts 'lawyer!' and so, twenty years later, he is a very successful lawyer, making lots of money, with an upcoming appointment to the bench. The second kid takes his turn and shouts 'brain surgeon!' and so, twenty years later, he is the most admired man in his field of medicine and making a ton of money saving lives. The third kid goes to take his turn, and as he runs he trips over his own feet and stumbles off the cloud muttering 'stupid clumsy idiot'. Twenty years later, he's playing second row for Wales.

☺ I would have played rugby, but I have an intestinal problem – no guts.

The Welsh coach has a busy day and tells the team just to practise passing round some plastic cones for training. After eighty minutes he sees them trudging back looking depressed.

'How did the session go, lads,' he asks.

'The cones won 18–12,' replies Shane Williams.

☺ The hooker wore number 53. Unfortunately, that was his IQ score.

Three rugby players are sitting in the maternity ward of a hospital waiting for the imminent birth of their respective children. One is a Welshman, one English, and the other a West Indian.

They are all very nervous and pacing the floor – as you do in these situations. All of a sudden the doctor bursts through the double doors, saying, 'Gentlemen, you won't believe this but your wives have all had their babies within five minutes of each other.' The men are beside themselves with happiness and joy. 'And,' said the doctor, 'they have all had little boys.' The fathers are ecstatic and congratulate each other over and over. 'However, we do have one slight problem,' the doctor said. 'In all the confusion we may have mixed the babies up getting them to the nursery and would be grateful if you could join us there to try and help identify them.'

With that the Welshman raced past the doctor and bolted to the nursery. Once inside he picked up a black infant with dreadlocks saying, 'There's no doubt about it, this boy is mine!' The doctor looked bewildered and said, 'Well, sir, of all the babies I would have thought that maybe this child could be of West Indian descent.'

'Maybe,' said the Welshman, 'but one of the other two is English and I'm not taking the risk.'

☺ What do you do for a drowning New Zealand rugby player? Nothing. You could drag him to the top, but he'll choke anyway.

☺ What have the All Blacks got in common with a two-pin plug? Both are useless in Wales.

① What do you call fifteen men sitting around the TV watching the Rugby World Cup final? The All Blacks.

Four surgeons are taking a coffee break. The first one says, 'Accountants are the best to operate on because when you open them up everything inside them is numbered.'

The second surgeon says, 'Nah, librarians are the best; everything inside them is in alphabetical order.'

The third surgeon says, 'Try electricians. Everything inside them is colour-coded.'

The fourth one says, 'I prefer New Zealand Rugby players. They're heartless, spineless, gutless and their heads and bums are interchangeable.'

① Our local club has lots of veterans on this year's squad. Unfortunately they're all from World War II.

The Welsh team is playing England and just before kick-off Shane Howarth slips, pulls a muscle and can't play. The coach is desperate as there aren't any other full-backs in Wales and is forced to play a goose (it's OK, it's got Welsh grand-parents).

Rather surprisingly the goose has a brilliant first half. One minute it's clearing off its own line and making cover tackles, the next it's joined the line linking up perfectly with the backs. At half time the coach is very pleased and everyone runs back onto the pitch for the second half.

On the way the ref starts chatting with the goose. 'Great first half, goose, you must be really fit.' 'Thanks,' replies the goose, 'I try to keep myself fit but it's difficult finding the time so I try to do an hour in the gym each morning before work.' 'What do you do then?' asked the ref. 'I'm a chartered accountant,' replies the goose. At which point the ref immediately brandishes the red card and sends the goose off. The bemused team-mates gather round the ref and start complaining.

'Sorry lads,' says the ref, 'I had no choice. Professional fowl.'

Albert Einstein arrives at a party and introduces himself to the first person he sees and asks, 'What is your IQ?' to which the man answers, '241.' 'That's wonderful!' says Albert. 'We will talk about the grand unification theory and the mysteries of the universe. We will have much to discuss!'

Next Albert introduces himself to a woman and asks, 'What is your IQ?' to which the lady answers, '144.' 'That is great!' responds Albert. 'We can discuss politics and current affairs. We will have much to discuss!'

Albert goes to another person and asks, 'What is your IQ?' to which the man answers, '51.' Albert responds, 'So, what do you reckon happened to the Welsh?'

☺ Old rugby players never die, they simply have their balls taken away.

Did you hear the Post Office has just recalled their latest batch of stamps?

They had photos of the Scottish rugby team on them and people couldn't figure out which side to spit on.

An Englishman wanted to become an Irishman to secure his international place, so he visited a doctor to find out how to go about this. 'Well,' said the doctor, 'this is a very delicate operation and there is a lot that can go wrong. I will have to remove half your brain.' 'That's OK,' said the Englishman. 'I've always wanted to be Irish and I'm prepared to take the risk.' The operation went ahead but the Englishman woke to find a look of horror on the face of the doctor. 'I'm so terribly sorry!!' the doctor said. 'Instead of removing half the brain, I've taken the whole brain out!' The patient replied, 'No worries, mate!!'

Scuba diving

⊙ Classified Ad: Seeking Diver
Young attractive male seeks female dive buddy for shared recreation and friendship, must have boat. Please send photo of boat.

SCUBA instructors always stress that you should never go diving alone. If you have equipment problems, your buddy can help you. If you run out of air, your buddy can help you. If you meet an aggressive shark, your odds are 50-50 instead of 100%.

A diver was shipwrecked onto a lonely and tropical shore. As he stood up he noticed his hands were purple, he looked at his feet and they were purple, worriedly he unzipped his wetsuit and his chest and stomach were purple. With his head in his hands he cried, 'Oh my God! I've been marooned!'

A dive boat runs into a terrible storm. Rain and wind and huge waves pound the boat. The divers are quiet but really scared. They are sure the boat is going to sink and they are all going to die. At the height of the storm, a young woman jumps up and exclaims: 'I can't take this any more! I can't just sit here and drown like an animal. If I am going to die, let me die feeling like a woman. Is there anyone here man enough to make me feel like a woman?' One of the dive masters stands up – a tall, handsome, muscular man – he smiles and starts to walk up to her. As he approaches her, he takes off his shirt. She sees his huge muscles – already, she is glad for her decision. He stands in front of her, muscles bulging, shirt in hand and says to her: 'Here, iron this!'

One day, a diver was enjoying the aquatic world twenty feet below sea level. He noticed a man at the same depth he was, with no scuba gear on whatsoever. The diver went down another ten feet, but the man joined him a minute later. The diver went below fifteen more feet and a minute later, the same man joined him. This confused the diver, so he took out a waterproof chalkboard, and wrote, 'How the heck are you able to stay under this deep without equipment?' The man took the board and chalk, erased what the diver had written, and wrote, 'I'm drowning, you moron!'

⊙ How many people does it take to circumcise a whale? Four skin divers.

Skating

Torvill and Dean do it on thin ice.

☺ Have you heard about the new Tonya Harding ice-skating doll? Assault and battery sold separately.

How is music like ice skating? If you don't C sharp you'll B flat.

☺ Seen on a poster shortly after Tonya Harding came tenth in the first half of the women's figure-skating competition: 'Tonya Harding: Nine clubbings away from Gold!'

Tonya Harding went to the zoo. She was later questioned by police about a crane seen standing on one leg.

☺ Did you hear that Tonya Harding just got a new endorsement? 'Lucky Strike' cigarettes.

A new drink has been invented in honour of Lorena Bobbitt and Tonya Harding: A club soda with a slice.

☺ Did you here why Tanya divorced her ex-husband? He kept hitting on other skaters.

A young lady entered a crowded bus with a pair of skates slung over her arm. An elderly gentleman arose to give her his seat. 'Thank you very much, sir,' she said, 'but I've been skating all afternoon, and I'm tired of sitting down.'

It is the Olympic men's figure skating. Out comes the Russian competitor, he skates around to some classical music in a slightly dull costume, performs some excellent leaps but without any great artistic feel for the music.

The judges' scores read: Britain 5.8: Russia 5.9: United States 5.5: Ireland 6.0.

Next comes the American competitor in a sparkling stars and stripes costume, skating to some rock and roll music. He gets the crowd clapping, but is not technically as good as the Russian. He slightly misses landing a triple salchow and loses the centre during a spin. But, artistically, it is a more satisfying performance.

The judges' scores read: Britain 5.8: Russia 5.5: United States 5.9: Ireland 6.0.

Finally out comes the Irish competitor wearing a tatty old donkey jacket, with his skates tied over his wellies. He reaches the ice, trips straight away and bangs his nose, which starts bleeding. He tries to get up, staggers a few paces then slips again. He spends his entire 'routine' getting up then falling over again. Finally he crawls off the ice a tattered and bleeding mess.

The judges' scores read: Britain 0.0: Russia 0.0: United States 0.0: Ireland 6.0.

The other three judges turn to the Irish judge and demand in unison, 'How the hell can you give that mess 6.0?!'

To which the Irish judge replies, 'You've gotta remember, it's damn slippery out there!'

① Why can't you tell a joke at ice skating?
Because the ice might crack up.

Old skaters never die, they just lose their ice sight.

Skiing

The skier's paradox: by the time you learn to stand up, you can't sit down

Did you hear about the Irish skier who got nasty frostbite on his legs because he couldn't work out how to get his ski pants over his skis?

☺ Skiing can be a time-consuming sport. I spent one day skiing and seven in the hospital.

Skiing: A winter sport that people learn in several sittings.

All things are possible with the exception of skiing through a revolving door.

☺ Did you hear about the businessman charged with operating a monopoly? Three ski lodges and a hospital.

Sign at the foot of a ski slope: Laws of Gravity Strictly Enforced.

Old skiers never die ...they just go over the hill.

☺ Ski jumping is where you race down a steep hill and fly three hundred feet through the air. There's just got to be a better way to meet nurses.

Two dyslexic skiers about to make their first ever descent are stood at the top of a slope. One says to the other, 'I can't remember, should we zig zag or zag zig down the slope?' The other says, 'I can't remember either – let's ask that bloke over there with the sledge.' They shuffle over and ask the bloke with the sledge, 'When you ski down do you zig zag or zag zig?' The man looks at them blankly and says, 'Don't ask me, I'm a toboggonist.'

The first skiier replies, 'Oh really, can I have twenty Rothmans, please?'

☺ Old toboggannists never die, they are simply deluged.

A man decided to take a week off from the pressures of the office and went skiing. Alas, no sooner did he reach the slopes than he heard an ominous rumbling: moments later a sheet of snow came crashing towards him. Fortunately, he was able to jump into a cave just before the avalanche hit. Just as fortunately, he had matches with him and was able to light a fire. Hours later, when everyone but him had returned, a rescue team was sent to search. After several hours they saw smoke curling from the cave and went to investigate. Poking his head into the entrance, one of the rescuers yelled, 'Mr Smith, are you there? It's the Red Cross.'

An angry reply came back: 'Get lost. I gave at the office!'

☺ I got a useful pamphlet with my new skis. It tells you how to convert them into a pair of splints.

On the first day of her holiday, a woman fell and broke her leg. As the doctor examined her, she moaned, 'Why couldn't this have happened on my last day of skiing?'

He looked up and replied, 'This IS your last day of skiing!'

Ski instructors

How many ski instructors does it take to put in a light bulb? Eleven. One to put the bulb in and ten to analyse each turn.

(!) Where does an instructor keep his money?

In a snow bank!

What do ski instructors and snowboard instructors have in common? They both can't snowboard.

(!) How do you get the ski instructor off your front porch? Pay for the pizza.

'Mum, Mum, I want to be a ski instructor when I grow up!'
'Now, Billy, you can't do both!'

(!) What do you call a successful ski instructor?
A guy whose girlfriend has two jobs.

Two men were walking down the street. One was destitute and the other was also a ski instructor.

(!) Skiers do it with their legs together.

(!) Skiers do it on the piste.

(!) Skiers go down faster.

What would a ski instructor do if he won the Lottery? Keep working until the money ran out!

☺ Old ski-jumpers never die, they simply lose their inclination.

Prepare for the ski season by:

- Visit your local butcher and pay thirty pounds to sit in the walk-in freezer for half an hour. Afterwards, burn two fifty-pound notes to warm up.

- Soak your gloves and store them in the freezer after every use.

- Fasten a small, wide rubber band around the top half of your head before you go to bed each night.

- If you wear glasses, begin wearing them with glue smeared on the lenses.

- Throw away a fifty-pound note now.

- Find the nearest ice rink and walk across the ice twenty times in your ski boots carrying two pairs of skis, accessory bag and poles. Pretend you are looking for your bus stop. Sporadically drop things.

- Place a small but angular pebble in your shoes, line them with crushed ice, and then tighten a C-clamp around your toes.

- Buy a new pair of gloves and immediately throw one away.

- Secure one of your ankles to a bed post and ask a friend to run into you at high speed.

- Fill a blender with ice, hit the button and let the spray blast your face. Leave the ice on your face until it melts. Let it drip into your clothes.

- Drink two pints of water. Dress up in as many clothes as you can and then proceed to take them off because you have to go to the toilet.

- Slam your thumb in a car door. Don't go to see a doctor.

Snooker and pool

Snooker players do it bending over a table.

'Doctor, doctor I feel like a snooker ball!'
'Get to the end of the cue!'

⊙ What do a snooker table and a coat have in common? They both have pockets.

Why did the snooker player go to the toilet? To pot the brown.

Two drunks went into a pub and found the snooker table set up for a game. 'Can we have a game?' they asked the barman. 'Sure, it's free,' came the reply. After an hour neither of them had potted a ball. 'Let's speed things up,' said the first drunk. 'How?' asked the other. 'We'll take the balls out of the frame!'

'The formalities are now over and it's down to business, Steve Davis is now adjusting his socks!'

⊙ What did the cue ball say when it was hit by surprise? I'm stunned!

Why would snooker players make good gardeners? Because they know everything about pots and plants.

Why do actors like snooker halls so much? Because it's where they get their best cues.

Why can't DJs play pool? Because they always scratch!

A guy walks into a bar with his pet monkey. He orders a drink and while he's drinking, the monkey starts jumping all over the place. The monkey grabs some olives off the bar and eats them, then grabs some sliced limes and eats them, then jumps up on the pool table, grabs the cue ball, sticks it in his mouth and swallows it whole. The bartender screams at the guy, 'Did you see what your monkey just did?' The guy says, 'No, what?' 'He just ate the cue ball off my pool table whole!' says the bartender. 'Yeah, that doesn't surprise me,' replies the patron. 'He eats everything in sight, the little jerk. I'll pay for the cue ball and stuff.' He finishes his drink, pays his bill, and leaves. Two weeks later he's in the bar again, and he has his monkey with him. He orders a drink and the monkey starts running around the bar again. While the man is drinking, the monkey finds a maraschino cherry on the bar. He grabs it, sticks it up his bum, pulls it out, and eats it. The bartender is disgusted. 'Did you see what your monkey did now?' 'Now what?' asks the patron. 'Well, he stuck a maraschino cherry up his butt, then pulled it out and ate it!' says the barkeeper. 'Yeah, that doesn't surprise me,' replies the owner. 'He still eats everything in sight, but ever since he ate that cue ball he measures everything first!'

☉ What do you call a gorilla playing snooker?
Hairy Potter!

Did you hear about the underwater snooker player? He was a pool shark!

☉ Old snooker players never die, they simply go to pot.

Did you hear about the snooker player who went to the doctor because he didn't feel well. 'What do you eat?' asked the doctor. 'For breakfast I have a couple of red snooker balls, and at lunchtime I grab a black, a pink and two yellows. I have a brown with my tea in the afternoon, then a blue and another pink.' 'I know why you're not feeling well,' said the doctor, 'you're not getting enough greens!'

Snowboarding

What is the difference between a snowboarding beginner and a snowboard instructor? About an hour and a half.

① What do you call a snowboarder who breaks up with his girlfriend? Homeless.

What are the usual last words of a snowboarder? 'Dude, watch this!'

Why are most snowboard jokes one-liners? So the skiers can understand them.

What do you say to a snowboarder in a three-piece suit? 'Will the defendant please rise.'

① What's the difference between a snowboarder and a bond? Eventually a bond will mature and make money.

What's the difference between an onion and a snowboard? You don't cry when you cut a snowboard in half.

How many snowboarders does it take to change a light bulb? Three – one to hold it, one to video-tape it and the other to say 'AWESOME, DUDE!'

① How does a snowboard instructor meet his pupil group? He rides into them!

Sport – general

Nothing is ever so bad that it can't be made worse by firing the coach.

☹ A free agent is a contradiction in terms.

Whoever thought up 'It's only a game' probably just lost one.

It is always unlucky to be behind at the end of a game.

☹ The trouble with being a good sport is that you have to lose to prove it.

It doesn't matter whether you win or lose until you lose.

☹ In sports teamwork is essential. It enables you to blame someone else.

Old archers never die, they simply bow out.

Old croquet players never die, they simply peg out.

Old shot-putters never die, they just get weak.

Sporting life – gambling

A man rushes into his house and yells to his wife, 'Mary, pack up your things! I just won the pools!' 'Mary replies, 'Should I pack for warm weather or cold?' The man responds, 'I don't care. Just get out!'

Two dog owners were bragging about the intelligence of their pets.

'The brightest dog I ever had,' said one, 'was a Great Dane that could play cards. He was a whiz at poker, but I had him put to sleep.'

'You had him put to sleep, a bright dog like that? A dog like that would be worth a million.'

'Had to,' the man replied. 'Caught him using marked cards!'

☉ Why do the people who run the Football Pools always have chequebooks four feet wide?

A blackjack dealer and a player with a thirteen count in his hand are arguing about whether or not it's appropriate to tip the dealer.

The player says, 'When I get bad cards, it's not the dealer's fault. Accordingly, when I get good cards, the dealer has nothing to do with it. Why should I tip him?'

The dealer says, 'When you eat out, do you tip the waiter?'

'Yes,' the player says.

'Well, that's because the waiter serves you food. I serve you cards, so you should tip me.'

'OK,' the player says, 'but the waiter gives me what I ask for!'

⊙ There are two secrets to success at poker. Rule number one: never tell your secrets.

A man walks into a bar and notices a poker game at the far table. Upon taking a closer look he sees a dog sitting at the table. This piques his curiosity, so he walks closer and sees cards and chips in front of the dog.

The next hand is dealt and cards are dealt to the dog just like everybody else. The dog acts in turn with all of the other players: calling, raising, discarding, and doing everything that the human players are doing.

Oddly, none of the other players seems to pay any attention to the fact that they are playing with a dog. They treat him just like any other player.

Finally, the man can no longer contain his curiosity, so between hands he says quietly to one of the human players, 'I can't believe that dog is playing poker! He must be the smartest dog in the world!'

The player smiles and says, 'He's not that smart. Every time he gets a good hand he wags his tail.'

A guy named Joe finds himself in dire trouble. His business has gone bust and he's in serious financial trouble. He's so desperate he decides to ask God for help. He begins to pray. 'God, please help me. I've lost my business and if I don't get some money, I'm going to lose my house as well. Please let me win the lottery.'

Lottery night comes and somebody else wins it.

Joe again prays, 'God, please let me win the lottery! I've lost my business, my house and I'm going to lose my car as well.'

Lotto night comes and Joe still has no luck.

Once again, he prays, 'My God, why have you forsaken me? I've lost my business, my house and my car. My wife and children are starving. I don't often ask you for help and I have always been a good servant to you. PLEASE just let me win the lottery this one time so I can get my life back in order.'

Suddenly there is a blinding flash of light as the heavens open and Joe is confronted by the voice of God Himself: 'Joe, meet me halfway on this. Buy a ticket.'

A man walks along a lonely beach. Suddenly he hears a deep voice: DIG! He looks around: nobody's there. I am having hallucinations, he thinks. Then he hears the voice again: I SAID, DIG!

So he starts to dig in the sand with his bare hands, and after some inches, he finds a small chest with a rusty lock. The deep voice says: OPEN!

OK, the man thinks, let's open the thing. He finds a rock with which to destroy the lock, and when the chest is finally open, he sees a lot of gold coins. The deep voice says: TO THE CASINO!

Well, the casino is only a few miles away, so the man takes the chest and walks to the casino. The deep voice says: ROULETTE!

So he changes all the gold into a huge pile of roulette tokens and goes to one of the tables, where the players gaze at him with disbelief. The deep voice says: TWENTY-SEVEN!

He takes the whole pile and drops it at the twenty-seven. The table nearly bursts. Everybody is quiet when the croupier throws the ball.

The ball stays at the twenty-six.

The deep voice says: BLAST!

☺ Did you hear about the new three-million-euro Irish lottery? The winner gets three euro a year for a million years.

Some people just seem to have a lot of luck. A friend of mine is one of those card players who can almost always draw whatever he needs to win a hand in poker, but loses big time at the races. I asked him about this once and he replied, 'Well … they won't let me shuffle the horses.'

A man comes home from his weekly poker game late. His annoying wife is waiting for him. 'Where have you been?'

'Sorry, but I lost you in a poker game. You'll have to leave.'

'How did you manage that, you fool?' 'It wasn't easy. I had to fold a royal flush.'

(!) What did the giraffe say to the leopard at the poker table? I thought you were a cheetah.

A doctor answers his phone and hears the familiar voice of a colleague on the other end of the line. 'We need a fourth for poker,' said the friend.

'I'll be right over,' whispered the doctor. As he was putting on his coat, his wife asked, 'Is it serious?' 'Oh yes, quite serious,' said the doctor gravely. 'In fact, there are three doctors there already!'

A rabbi, a minister, and a priest are playing poker when the police raid the game. Addressing the priest, the lead officer asks: 'Father Murphy, were you gambling?' Turning his eyes to heaven, the priest whispers, 'Lord, forgive me for what I am about to do.' To the police officer, he then says, 'No, officer, I was not gambling.' The officer then asks the minister: 'Pastor Johnson, were you gambling?' Again, after an appeal to heaven, the minister replies, 'No, officer, I was not gambling.' Turning to the rabbi, the officer again asks: 'Rabbi Goldstein, were you gambling?' Shrugging his shoulders, the rabbi replies: 'With whom?'

(!) I was playing poker with tarot cards the other night. I got a full house and four people died.

A regular Friday night poker game was still going strong well after midnight when one of the players returned from the bathroom with an urgent report. 'Keith, listen,' he told the host, 'Frank's in the kitchen making love to your wife.' 'OK, that's it, gents,' Keith says. 'This is positively the last deal.'

(!) Some cowboys were playing poker in an Old West saloon. One of them laid down the winning hand, and another jumped up, yelling, 'He's cheatin! He ain't playin the cards I dealt him!'

The regular Friday night poker game was going on when John lost five hundred pounds on a single hand, had a heart attack, and died. 'Who's going to tell his wife?' They drew cards, and Bill drew the low card. He knocked on John's door and told his wife, 'John lost five hundred pounds at poker tonight.'

She turns red and yells, 'Tell that idiot to DROP DEAD!'

Bill walks away sheepishly and says, 'I'll tell him.'

Chuck Norris owns the greatest poker face of all time. It helped him win the 1983 world series of poker despite him holding just a joker, a two of clubs, a seven of spades, a scratchcard from the garage and a Monopoly 'get out of jail free' card.

☺ Never do card tricks for the group you play poker with.

Dear Steve,

I have been unable to sleep since I broke off our engagement. Won't you forgive and forget? Your absence is breaking my heart. I was a fool – nobody can take your place. I love you.

All my love, Christine. xxxxoooxxxx

P.S. Congratulations on winning this week's pools.

A man was down on his luck in Las Vegas. He had gambled away all his money and had to borrow a dime from another gambler just to use the men's room. The stall happened to be open, so he used the dime in a slot machine and hit the jackpot. He took his winnings and went to the blackjack table and turned his small winnings into ten million dollars. Wealthy beyond his wildest dreams, he went on the lecture circuit, where he told his incredible story. He told his audiences that he was eternally grateful to his benefactor, and if he ever found the man he would share his fortune with him. After months of lectures, a man in the audience jumped up and said, 'I'm that man. I was the one who gave you the dime.' 'You're not the one I'm looking for. I'm looking for the guy who left the door open!'

A tramp asks a man for five pounds. The man says, 'Will you buy booze?' The tramp says, 'No.' The man says, 'Will you gamble it away?' The tramp says, 'No.' So the man says, 'Will you come home with me so my wife can see what happens to a man who doesn't drink or gamble?'

After examining a three-thousand-year-old mummy an archaeologist announces that it's the body of a man who died of a heart attack. 'How can you tell?' asks one of his students. 'I examined a piece of parchment found in the mummy's hand,' replies the archaeologist. 'It was a betting slip that said, "Five thousand on Goliath."'

For months a little boy has been pestering his father to take him to the zoo. Eventually Dad gives in and off they go. When they get back the boy's mother asks him if he had a good time. 'It was great,' replies the boy. 'And Daddy had fun too, especially when one of the animals came home at thirty to one.'

☺ Old card players never die, they simply shuffle off.

Two casino workers are waiting for someone to try their luck at the craps table. An attractive woman comes in and puts down a twenty-thousand-dollar bet on a single roll of the dice. 'I hope you don't mind,' says the woman. 'But I feel much luckier when I'm bottomless.' With this she strips naked from the waist down and rolls the dice, yelling, 'Momma needs a new pair of pants!' The dice fall and the lady jumps up and down shouting, 'Yes! I win! I win!' She then picks up her winnings and leaves. The casino workers look at each other. One says, 'So what did she roll anyway?' The other replies, 'I don't know. I thought you were watching the dice!'

☺ Old on-course bookmakers never die, they simply go off the rails.

Squash

A squash racket is like a toothbrush – once you give it to somebody you don't want it back.

☺ What game do monsters like to play when they are all on a bus? Squash.

Who invented squash? An Englishman with too many sisters.

What game does an elephant like most? Squash.

☺ Squash players do it against the wall.

Surfing

The best day working is not as good as the worst day surfing.

☺ Golf: that is what people do who don't know how to surf.

A woman was surfing one day when she happened to find a bottle floating in the ocean and when she picked it up, a great genie appeared. 'This is terrific,' the woman said. 'Does this mean that I get three wishes granted?' she enquired. 'Yes,' replied the genie. 'But be careful, for whatever you wish, your husband will get ten times greater.' So, the woman thought and she finally said, 'Make me the best surfer at my break.' The genie told her, 'You will be the best female surfer at your break, but your husband will be ten times better.' 'OK,' she said. 'Give me a million dollars.' The genie replied, 'It is granted, but your husband now has ten million dollars.' The genie said, 'You have only one wish left, so use it wisely.' And the woman replied, 'Give me a slight heart attack.'

☺ It's the most fun I've ever had with my shorts on.

While surfing off the Florida coast, a tourist snapped his board. He could swim, but his fear of alligators kept him clinging to the broken board. Spotting an old beachcomber standing on the shore, the tourist shouted, 'Are there any gators around here?!' 'Naw,' the man hollered back, 'they ain't been around for years!' Feeling safe, the tourist started swimming leisurely towards the shore. About halfway there he asked the guy, 'How'd you get rid of the gators?' 'We didn't do nothin',' the beachcomber said. 'Wow,' said the tourist. The beachcomber added, 'The sharks got 'em.'

☺ Give a man a surfboard, and you've distracted him for a day. Teach a man to surf, and you can't get him to work.

The best thing about surfing is that even though you're scared enough to wet your pants, nobody notices.

☺ Windsurfers do it standing up.

Swimming

What kind of stroke can you use on toast?
BUTTER-fly!

① Why can male elephants swim whenever they want?
They always have trunks with them!

What is a polar bear's favourite stroke?
Blubber-fly!

① Why did the girl have problems swimming?
She didn't have boy-ancy!

Why wasn't Susan afraid when she saw a shark while she was swimming in the water?
Because it was a man-eating shark!

Why do you keep doing the backstroke?
I've just had lunch and don't want to swim on a full stomach.

① Did you hear about the slow swimmer?
He could only do the crawl.

What do you call a swimming team made up of girls named Jennifer?
Hydrogens.

Where do ghosts like to go swimming?
Lake Eerie (also, the Dead Sea).

☺ What kind of swimmer makes a good gardener?
One with great seed times!

What do a dentist and a swimming coach have in common?
They both use drills!

Why was the swimmer at the meet so cold?
She couldn't find her heat!

Why did the vegetarians stop swimming?
They didn't like meets!

☺ What kind of exercises are best for a swimmer?
Pool-ups!

Why was Cinderella able to swim so fast?
Because the Prince found her glass flippers!

Have you heard what my blonde neighbour wrote on the bottom of her swimming pool? No smoking.

There was a competition to swim from one island to another doing only the breaststroke and the three women who entered the race were a brunette, a redhead and a blonde. After approximately fourteen hours, the brunette staggered up on the shore and was declared the fastest breaststroker. About forty minutes later, the redhead crawled up on the shore and was declared the second place finisher. Nearly four hours after that, the blonde finally came ashore and promptly collapsed in front of the worried onlookers. When the reporters asked why it took her so long to complete the race, she replied, 'I don't want to sound like I'm a bad loser, but I think those two other girls were using their arms.'

⊙ What kind of dive are army men best at?

Cannon-ball!

A millionaire throws a massive party for his fiftieth birthday. During the party, he's a bit bored and decides to stir things up a bit. He grabs the mic and announces to his guests that down in the garden of his mansion he has a swimming pool with two great white sharks in it. He offers anything he owns to anyone who will swim across that pool.

The party continues for some time with no one accepting his offer, until suddenly there's a loud splash. All the party guests run to the pool to see what has happened, and in the pool a man is frantically swimming as hard as he can. Fins come out of the water and jaws are snapping and the guy just keeps on going. The sharks are gaining, but the guy manages to reach the end and he leaps out of the pool, exhausted.

The millionaire grabs the mic and says, 'I am a man of his word, anything of mine I will give – for you are the bravest man I have ever seen. So, what will it be?' the millionaire asks. The guy grabs the mic and says, 'Why don't we start with the name of the person that pushed me in!'

⊙ Swimming pool sign: 'Welcome to our _OOL, Notice there is no 'P' in it. We'd like to keep it that way.'

⊙ Swimming pool sign: 'We don't swim in your toilet so don't wee in our pool.'

Little Johnny was at the public swimming pool when he was approached by the lifeguard.

'Listen, young man,' the lifeguard said, 'you are not allowed to pee in the pool. I'm going to have to report you.'

'But sir, everyone pees in the pool,' replied Little Johnny.

'Perhaps,' said the lifeguard, 'but not from the diving board!'

⊙ Did you hear about the Irish man who tried to drown his fish?

An eighty-year-old man goes to the doctor for a check-up. The doctor is amazed at what good shape the guy is in and asks, 'How do you stay in such great physical condition?' 'I'm a swimmer,' says the old guy, 'and that's why I'm in such good shape. I'm up well before daylight and go swimming.' 'Well,' says the doctor, 'I'm sure that helps, but there's got to be more to it. How old was your dad when he died?' 'Who said my dad's dead?'

The doctor is amazed. 'You mean you're eighty years old and your dad's still alive. How old is he?' 'He's a hundred years old,' says the old swimmer. 'In fact he swam with me this morning, and that's why he's still alive ... he's a swimmer too.' 'Well,' the doctor says, 'that's great, but I'm sure there's more to it than that. How about your dad's dad? How old was he when he died?' 'Who said my grandpa's dead?' Stunned, the doctor asks, 'You mean you're eighty years old and your grandfather's still living! Incredible, how old is he?' 'He's a hundred and eighteen years old,' says the old man. The doctor is getting frustrated at this point. 'So, I guess he went swimming with you this morning too?' 'No. Grandpa couldn't go this morning because he's getting married today.' At this point the doctor is close to losing it. 'Getting married! Why would a one-hundred-and-eighteen-year-old guy want to get married?' 'Who said he wanted to?'

⊙ A judge once said, 'I'm surprised the man had beaten the shark in a race so he will receive a gold med – Hey! Where's his head?'

One day a man had brought his dog to play ping-pong with his friends. 'Why'd you bring your dog with you?' a friend asked. 'I am going to teach him dog paddle!' replied the man.

In which direction does a chicken swim? Cluck-wise!

When during a competition could you act crazy and not get disqualified? When you're swimming freestyle!

Why did the musician go to the pool? He needed to write some notes about the water.

Why did the swimmer fly out of the water? He was doing the butter-fly!

☺ Why did the teacher jump into the water?
She wanted to test the water!

Why did the swimmer go back in time? Because he was doing the backstroke!

What race is never run? A swimming race.

How do elephants dive into swimming pools? Head first!

What barks and kills swimmers? Jaws.

☺ How did a person survive a 500-mile drop from the sky into the water? He used a glider.

There's a redhead, a brunette, and a blonde, all stranded on an island.
   The first day they look north for land, and they don't see anything.
   The second day, they look to the south for land, but don't see anything.
   The third day, they look east for land, but again, don't see a thing.
   Then, finally the fourth day, they see land to the west.
   First the redhead tries to swim across to land, but drowns quarter of the way there.
   Then, the brunette tries, but only gets halfway, then drowns.
   Finally the blonde tries. She swims three-quarters of the way, gets tired, and swims back to the island.

An old farmer in Kansas had owned a large farm with a nice pond in the back. It was fixed up nice: picnic tables, horseshoe courts, and some apple and peach trees.

One evening the old farmer decided to go down to the pond, as he hadn't been there for a while, and look it over. He grabbed a five-gallon bucket to bring back some fruit. As he neared the pond, he heard voices shouting and laughing with glee. As he came closer he saw it was a bunch of young women skinny-dipping in his pond.

He made some noise so the women would know he was there and they all went to the deep end of the pond. One of the women shouted to him, 'We're not coming out until you leave!'

The old man frowned, 'I didn't come down here to watch you swim naked or make you get out of the pond naked.' Holding up the bucket he said, 'I'm here to feed the alligator.'

⚐ Backstrokers do it without getting their face wet.

⚐ Divers do it deeper than anyone else.

⚐ Swimmers do it with the breaststroke.

Tennis

Tennis players start with love.

An English tourist and his wife are driving through Texas on holiday when they see a horseman riding along the road. They stop to ask if he is a real cowboy. 'Yes,' the man answers, 'Sure am, pardner.'

'We recognize your hat, shirt, leather vest and Levi's as authentic Western wear,' the man says, 'but why are you wearing tennis shoes?'

'Because if I wore boots people would think I was a truck driver,' he replies.

☺ Anyone who can leap a three-foot net after a match should take up track and field.

What do you get if you cross a skunk and a pair of tennis rackets? Ping Pong!

What do you serve but not eat? A tennis ball.

☺ What's a tennis player's favourite city? Volley wood!

Looking around at all the tennis coaches milling around in the lobby of a posh hotel during a big reception, one of the coaches, who had a pretty high opinion of his own superiority, turned to his neighbour, a sports editor, and said, 'How many really great coaches do you think there are in this room?' 'One less than you think,' replied the editor.

☺ The Bible records the first tennis match in history when Moses served in Pharaoh's court.

A tennis player went to the doctor because he heard music whenever he played. The physician cured him by removing his headband.

I used to play tennis professionally. In fact, I made quite a name for myself. I remember the day I returned from a match in Australia. When I got off the plane at Heathrow, there was a crowd of several hundred, cheering and applauding. If you don't believe me, ask Andy Murray. He was standing right beside me.

After a two-year study, the National Science Foundation announced the following results on recreational preferences:

1. The sport of choice for unemployed or incarcerated people is: basketball.

2. The sport of choice for maintenance-level employees is: football.

3. The sport of choice for blue-collar workers is: rugby.

4. The sport of choice for supervisors is: cricket.

5. The sport of choice for middle management is: tennis.

6. The sport of choice for corporate officers is: golf.

Conclusion: The higher you rise in the corporate structure, the smaller your balls become.

⊙ Why are fish never good tennis players? They don't like getting close to the net.

How many tennis players does it take to screw in a light bulb? What do you mean it was out, it was in!

Age has no bearing on your tennis game. It just keeps you from winning.

⊙ What is the definition of endless love?
Ray Charles and Stevie Wonder playing tennis.

! Why is a tennis game a noisy game?
Because each player raises a racket.

! To err is human. To put the blame on someone else is doubles.

We have five hundred players in our tennis club. Well, actually there are fifty. The other four hundred and fifty are waiting for a court.

! You know you play too much tennis when instead of fighting someone who stole your girlfriend, you challenge him to a five-set match.

My brother went to the doctor. He said, 'Doctor, I am obsessed with the idea that I am John McEnroe playing at Wimbledon.'

The doctor said, 'Way out, man.'

My brother said, 'You can't be serious...!'

! What do you call a tennis player with two brain cells? Pregnant.

There was this group of people on a tour bus. The guide on the bus asked if someone on the bus could tell the rest a joke, whereupon a man got up and said that he could tell a tennis player joke. Suddenly, a bloke in the back of the bus said, 'No, don't do that. I'm a tennis player.' The guide looked at him and said, 'That's OK. We'll explain it to you afterwards.'

! You should never marry a tennis player, because to them love means nothing.

⊙ What do you see when you look into a tennis player's eyes? The back of his head.

A badminton player, a squash player and a tennis player decided to stay at a country inn, but when they arrived there, the innkeeper told them he only had two beds free and one of them would have to sleep in the barn.

'That's OK,' said the badminton player, 'I'll sleep in the barn.' So off he went.

A few moments later there was a knock at the inn door. The innkeeper opened the door to see the badminton player, who explained that he was unable to sleep in the barn as there was a pig in there, and he could not sleep with a pig.

'That's OK,' said the squash player, 'I'll sleep there.'

So off he went. A few moments later there was a knock at the inn door. The innkeeper opened the door to see the squash player there, who explained that he was unable to sleep in the barn as there was a cow in there, and he could not sleep with a cow.

'That's OK,' said the tennis player, 'I'll sleep there.' So off he went. A few moments later there was a knock at the inn door. The innkeeper opened the door to see a cow and a pig stood there ...

⊙ Old tennis players never die, they are simply put out to grass.

A badminton player runs into the toilet absolutely desperate to relieve himself. He runs up to the urinal and after some fumbling pulls out a very impressive twelve-inch penis and begins urinating. In relief he cries out, 'Just made it!'

A tennis player who was standing at the next urinal turns to him and says 'Really? can you make me one too?'

Volleyball

What does a carpenter have in common with a volleyball player? They both like to hammer spikes.

What can you serve but never eat? A volleyball.

⊕ Why do volleyball players want to join the armed forces? For the chance to gain some experience in the service.

What do you do when you play a volleyball team of Satanists? You beat the hell out of them.

⊕ How many middle-hitters does it take to screw in a light bulb? Just one, but first the setter has to put it perfectly into their hand.

Latest news reports advise that a cell of four terrorists has been operating, hiding and playing volleyball in various tournaments across Europe.

⊕ How do hens encourage their volleyball teams?
                                    They egg them on!

Where do religious school children practise sports? In the prayground!

Interpol advised earlier today that three of the four terrorists have been caught and detained for questioning. The Commissioner stated that the terrorists, Bin Spikin, Bin Diggin and Bin Servin have been arrested on immigration issues.

The police advise further that they can find no one fitting the description of the fourth cell member, Bin Drinkin, in Europe. Police fear that anyone who looks and acts like he's Bin Drinkin will blend in well within the European community.

Be advised, undercover investigators from Interpol may attempt to trick you into implicating yourself as a cell member by asking seemingly simple questions like, 'So, you Bin Drinkin?' Always answer, 'No, of course not!'

☺ Don't trust a volleyball player with your drink – they might spike it.

Waterskiing

Why don't the Amish waterski? The horses would drown.

☺ Did you hear about the blonde who got a pair of waterskis? She's still looking for a lake with a slope!

Why can you not teach blondes to waterski? When they get wet, they roll over on their backs!

☺ A small girl watching a waterskier said to her father, 'That man is so silly. He'll never catch that boat!'

Wrestling

Three men, a Scot, an Englishman and a sumo wrestler, were going to commit suicide by jumping off the top of a building. The Scot jumped off and shouted, 'God save Scotland!' The Englishman jumped off and shouted, 'God save England!' The sumo wrestler jumped off and shouted, 'God save the person who I land on!'

☺ Hulk Hogan is reportedly working on his first book. Hopefully he'll be finished reading it soon.

☺ In the past six months, four sumo wrestlers have been suspended for allegedly smoking marijuana. No wonder sumo wrestlers are so heavy – they always have the munchies.

Two wrestlers are in critical condition when both fell through a window while wrestling each other in a hotel room during a drunken party. They failed to call 999 right away because they thought that although they recieved head injuries, They'd just walk this one off.

☺ Friends report that reality star and wrestler Hulk Hogan has been quarrelling nearly non-stop with his wife. Luckily no one has been hurt as all of their fights are heavily choreographed and planned out in advance.

You know you watch too much wrestling when:

- You begin to shake someone's hand in public, but then hesitate to look for the crowd's response.

- You'll only come out of your room to music.

- You get fired from work then show up the next day wearing a mask.

☺ What's a wrestler's favourite drink? Fruit punch.

Yoga

What did the yogi say to the sandwich vendor at the ball game? 'Make me one with everything!'

After the man received his sandwich, he gave the vendor twenty pounds. The vendor just smiled. The man, infuriated, demanded, 'Where is my change?'

The vendor replied, 'O, one with everything, change comes from within.'

☺ What did the yogi tell the door-to-door salesperson who came to his home selling vacuum cleaners? Too many attachments!

☺ What did the sign in the window of the yoga master searching for a new disciple say? Enquire within!

☺ Why did the yogi refuse anaesthesia when having his wisdom teeth removed?
He wanted to transcend-dental-medication!

A group of bats, hanging from the ceiling of a cave, discover a single bat standing upright underneath on the floor of the cave. Surprised by this unusual behaviour, they ask him: 'What's wrong with you? What are you doing down there?' He shouts back: 'Yoga!'

☺ Yoga police: 'You have the right to remain silent!'

Two old friends were meeting. 'How are you and your family?' asks one. 'Oh, we're all fine,' the other answers. 'We're all healthy and have work to earn our keep. But how about your son? Is he still unemployed?' 'Not at all,' the first one answers, 'he's doing meditation now.' 'Meditation? What's this? What is he doing?' 'I don't know exactly,' the first one answers, 'but I'm sure it's better than just sitting down and doing nothing!'

① Don't just do something – sit there!

Knock, knock.
Who's there?
Yoga.
Yoga who?
Yoga to try this, it feels amazing.

① On the anniversary of his birth, devotees of a certain yogi asked what gifts they might bring. The yogi replied, 'I wish no gifts, only presence.'

A young woman who was worried about her habit of biting her fingernails down to the quick was advised by a friend to take up yoga. She did, and soon her fingernails were growing normally. Her friend asked her if yoga had totally cured her nervousness. 'No,' she replied, 'but now I can reach my toenails so I bite them instead.'

① Time is the best teacher, although it kills the students.

① My karma ran over my dogma.

⊕ What do yoga meditation and an apple peeler have in common? They both take you to the core.

How many yoga monks does it take to change a light bulb? Three. One to *change* the light bulb. One to *not* change the light bulb. One to *neither* change nor not change the light bulb.

In yoga, it's just one thing after another – breathe, breathe, breathe.

⊕ How many yogis does it take to change a light bulb? Into what?

Change is inevitable, except from vending machines.

Three yogis are doing meditation in a remote cave. One day a sound is heard from outside the cave. After about six months, one of the yogis says, 'Did you hear that goat?' Once again, there was silence. About a year later, one of the other yogis says, 'That wasn't a goat; it was a mule.' Again, there was silence. About two years later the third yogi says, 'If you two don't stop arguing, I'm leaving.'

⊕ Have you heard of the cow who attained Nirvana? It was dyslexic and kept on repeating; 'OOOOMMM!'

Four monks were meditating in a monastery. All of a sudden the prayer flag on the roof started flapping. The younger monk came out of his meditation and said: 'Flag is flapping.'
   A more experienced monk said: 'Wind is flapping.'
   A third monk who had been there for more than twenty years said: 'Mind is flapping.'
   The fourth monk who was the eldest said, visibly annoyed: 'Mouths are flapping!'

An aspiring Yogi wanted to find a guru. He went to an Ashram and his teacher told him: 'You can stay here but we have one important rule – all students observe a vow of silence. You will be allowed to speak in twelve years.' After practising for twelve long years the day came when the student could say his one thing or ask his one question.

He said: 'The bed is too hard.'

He kept going for another twelve years of hard and austere discipline and got the opportunity to speak again. He said: 'The food is not good.'

Twelve more years of hard work and he got to speak again. Here are his words after thirty-six years of practise: 'I quit.'

His guru quickly answered: 'Good, all you have been doing anyway is complaining.'

Blessed are the flexible, for they shall not be bent out of shape.